Introducing Microsoft Quantum Computing for Developers

Using the Quantum Development Kit and Q#

Johnny Hooyberghs

Apress®

Introducing Microsoft Quantum Computing for Developers: Using the Quantum Development Kit and Q#

Johnny Hooyberghs
Willebroek, Belgium

ISBN-13 (pbk): 978-1-4842-7245-9
https://doi.org/10.1007/978-1-4842-7246-6

ISBN-13 (electronic): 978-1-4842-7246-6

Managing Director, Apress Media LLC: Welmoed Spahr
Acquisitions Editor: Joan Murray
Development Editor: Laura Berendson
Coordinating Editor: Jill Balzano

Cover designed by eStudioCalamar

Cover image designed by Freepik (www.freepik.com)

Distributed to the book trade worldwide by Springer Science+Business Media LLC, 1 New York Plaza, Suite 4600, New York, NY 10004. Phone 1-800-SPRINGER, fax (201) 348-4505, e-mail orders-ny@springer-sbm.com, or visit www.springeronline.com. Apress Media, LLC is a California LLC and the sole member (owner) is Springer Science + Business Media Finance Inc (SSBM Finance Inc). SSBM Finance Inc is a **Delaware** corporation.

For information on translations, please e-mail booktranslations@springernature.com; for reprint, paperback, or audio rights, please e-mail bookpermissions@springernature.com.

Apress titles may be purchased in bulk for academic, corporate, or promotional use. eBook versions and licenses are also available for most titles. For more information, reference our Print and eBook Bulk Sales web page at http://www.apress.com/bulk-sales.

Any source code or other supplementary material referenced by the author in this book is available to readers on GitHub via the book's product page, located at www.apress.com/9781484272459. For more detailed information, please visit http://www.apress.com/source-code.

Printed on acid-free paper

Dedicated to my wife, Marijke,
my parents, Chantal and Albert, and science!

Table of Contents

About the Author xi

About the Technical Reviewer xiii

Acknowledgments xv

Introduction xvii

Part I: Introduction to Quantum Computing 1

Chapter 1: What, Why, and How? 3

Why? 3

    Why Do We Need Quantum Computers? 7

What? 8

    What Is Quantum Mechanics? 8

    What Is Quantum Computing? 21

How? 22

The Last Word 24

Chapter 2: The Qubit and Quantum State 27

Storing Data 27

What Is the Quantum State of a Qubit? 29

    The State of a Single Qubit 29

    The State of Multiple Qubits 39

Physical Implementation 44

The Last Word 45

Solutions to Exercises 46

Chapter 3: Quantum Gates and Circuits..**49**

    Quantum Gates 49

        Reversible Gates...50

        Single-Qubit Gates...50

        Multiple Qubit Gates 58

    Quantum Circuits 60

        Entanglement 61

        Teleportation 63

    Exercises...64

    The Last Word 65

    Solutions to Exercises..66

Part II: The Microsoft Quantum Development Kit and Q# 69

Chapter 4: Develop with the Microsoft Quantum Development Kit.......................71

    Quantum Development Kit 71

    Installing the Quantum Development Kit...72

        Prepare Your .NET Environment..72

        Prepare for Command-Line Development 76

        Prepare for Visual Studio Code Development 78

        Prepare for Microsoft Visual Studio Development...............88

        Prepare for Python Development...96

    The Last Word 100

Chapter 5: Your First Quantum Program **101**

    A True Random Number Generator 101

        Generating a Random Bit..103

        Generating a Random Number 113

    The Last Word 120

Chapter 6: Q# Language Overview and the Quantum Simulator...........121

Q# Project Structure..121

Q# Application Structure...123

    Comments 123

    Namespaces...125

    Variable Declarations and Assignments 128

    Scopes..129

    Quantum Data Types...131

    Types 135

    Arrays 135

    User-Defined Types..136

    Operators..139

    Statements 143

    Callables 151

The Last Word 167

Chapter 7: Testing and Debugging Your Quantum Programs...............169

Simulators...169

    The Full-State Simulator..169

    The Resources Estimator...172

    The Toffoli Simulator..175

Testing Your Quantum Programs...178

    Testing Qubit in the $|0\rangle$ State 181

    Testing Qubit in the $|1\rangle$ State..182

    Testing Qubit in the Superposition State 183

Debugging Your Quantum Programs 184

    DumpMachine 193

    DumpRegister...196

The Last Word 202

Part III: Quantum Algorithms 203

Chapter 8: Deutsch's Algorithm 205

The Deutsch Oracle 205

A Quantum Oracle 207

Back to the Deutsch Oracle 208

    Constant-0 208

    Constant-1 211

    Identity 214

    Negation 217

Deutsch's Algorithm in Q# 220

    A Classical Version 220

    The Quantum Version 225

The Last Word 231

Chapter 9: Deutsch-Jozsa Algorithm 233

The Deutsch-Jozsa Oracle 233

The Classical Deutsch-Jozsa Algorithm in Q# 234

    Constant-0 234

    Constant-1 235

    Modulo 2 236

    Odd Number of Ones 237

    The Full Implementation in Q# 239

Back to the Quantum World 245

    Constant-0 247

    Constant-1 250

    Modulo 2 253

    Odd Number of Ones 258

    The Full Quantum Implementation in Q# 263

The Last Word 269

Chapter 10: The CHSH Game 271

Measuring Qubits 271

Computational Basis 271

Sign Basis 273

Measuring in Any Basis 275

The CHSH Game 276

Playing the Classic CHSH Game 276

Implementing the Classic CHSH Game 279

Playing the quantum CHSH game 284

Implementing the Quantum CHSH Game 294

The Last Word 303

Part IV: What to Do Next? 305

Chapter 11: Azure Quantum 307

Quantum Computing 308

Azure Quantum 308

Quantum Workspace 311

Providers and Targets 312

Jobs 317

The Last Word 339

Chapter 12: What's Next? 341

Quantum Supremacy 341

Quantum Error Correction 342

Quantum Intermediate Representation 342

Additional Resources 345

Part V: Appendixes 355

Appendix I: Trigonometry 357

Right-Angled Triangle... 357

Degrees and Radians.. 359

Trigonometric Ratios... 360

The Unit Circle... 361

Common Trigonometric Values.. 364

The Last Word.. 366

Solutions to Exercises... 366

Appendix II: Complex Numbers 369

Complex Numbers.. 369

Visualizing a Complex Number.. 371

Calculating with Complex Numbers.. 372

Adding Complex Numbers.. 372

Subtracting Complex Numbers... 373

Multiplying Complex Numbers... 374

Complex Conjugates.. 374

Dividing Complex Numbers.. 375

Absolute Value or Modulus for Complex Numbers 376

The Last Word.. 378

Solutions to Exercises... 378

Appendix III: Linear Algebra 383

Vectors and Vector Spaces.. 383

Matrices... 385

Matrix Operations... 386

Transformation Matrix... 389

The Last Word.. 390

Solutions to Exercises... 390

Index.. 395

About the Author

Johnny Hooyberghs is a software engineer and consultant for Involved, a Belgium-based company centered on the design, development, and delivery of custom-made software, where his expertise has been on .NET architecture, backend development, and training. Since 2020, Johnny is a Microsoft Most Valuable Professional (MVP) in the category of Developer Technologies. He has been passionate about .NET from its first release and possesses a deep knowledge of C#, .NET, .NET Core, ASP.NET, Entity Framework, Azure, and ALM using the Microsoft Stack. He enjoys the occasional web development using JavaScript. For more than a decade, he has allocated a portion of his free time to teaching .NET and C# at the adult education institute CVO Antwerpen. When he is not working or teaching, he can be found gaming, scuba diving, learning to play the piano, traveling the world, and visiting as many theme parks as possible.

About the Technical Reviewer

Bart J. F. De Smet is a principal software development engineer at Microsoft with a passion for language-related innovation and core framework development. He is a highly regarded speaker at many global tech conferences and online venues. He was actively involved in the design and implementation of Reactive Extensions (Rx) for .NET and prior to that in an extended "LINQ to Anything" mission. His main interests include programming languages, runtimes, functional programming, and all sorts of theoretical foundations. Before joining Microsoft, Bart was a Microsoft MVP for C# four years in a row, while completing his Master of Civil Engineering and Computer Science studies at Ghent University, Belgium.

Acknowledgments

First and foremost, my wife Marijke Derieuw deserves my special thanks for supporting me throughout the late evening writing sessions. The time I spent at my home office, behind my computer, was time not spent with her. I love you, and you deserve an infinite amount of snuggles for the rest of your life!

Secondly, I would like to thank my parents, Chantal Vaesen and Albert Hooyberghs, for allowing me to grow up with enough freedom to be passionate about the things I do, to be interested in too many things for me to handle in a lifetime, and to be an all-round happy fellow. You will always be my loveliest mama en papa.

I really want to thank my best friend Tom Vergult for proofreading my manuscript and providing me with loads of useful comments and insights. Your help this past year was extremely consistent, and I'll never forget that. I would also like to thank my technical reviewer, Bart De Smet. You pushed me into the world of quantum computing thanks to your presentation at Techorama Belgium, and you gave me many great points on how to improve my book.

I want to mention my ex-colleagues Johan Vanhove, Geert Wyffels, Peter De Cuyper, and Jan Rauter for believing in me, supporting me, and allowing me the freedom to become a great software developer (Yes, I just called myself a great software developer! There, I did it again). I learned a whole lot from you guys, and I am sure you will always stay a source of inspiration to me.

I also want to thank Michael Richardson. Thank you for inviting me to the Momentum Developer Conference, my first US conference as a speaker, to talk about quantum computing and Microsoft Q#. Also, thank you for being such an amazing host: I remember Cincinnati, Cincinnati Chili, and ice cream.

Finally, I would like to thank the team at Apress, Jill Balzano, Joan Murray, and Jonathan Gennick specifically, for allowing me the opportunity to write my first book with them and for their patience and understanding during the entire process.

Introduction

I have always been interested in new and shiny things, more specifically, things that I do not understand and want to understand. When I heard about the existence of quantum computing, I wanted to learn how something deterministic like a computer could work in the world of quantum magic. Hmmm, this makes me think of that famous quote from one of my favorite science-fiction authors, Arthur C. Clarke:

Any sufficiently advanced technology is indistinguishable from magic.

I was first introduced to quantum computing many years ago by Bart De Smet. He was doing a presentation on Microsoft Q# at Techorama Belgium, and I was sold immediately. I wanted to learn more about it, bought several books, and started playing around with it. How cool it is to be able to live through a period where something completely new is being worked on!

After a few years, I started telling other people about the wonders of quantum and quantum computing. In 2019, I started doing public presentations for international software developer conferences, and in 2020, I decided to start to write this introductory book.

About This Book

This book is an introduction in quantum computing, specifically targeting software developers who are familiar with the Microsoft ecosystem. My goal is not to convert you to the best quantum theorists out there. My goal is to provide an easy-to-understand introductory book that opens the path to further learning without throwing too much math and abstract science at your head.

This book has the right amount of theory, combined with some "getting-your-hands-dirty" content and exercises. You will learn by reading, exploring, and experimenting. Don't stop with the examples and exercises in this book. Make changes and try new things. Learning to write software is easy! You can't hurt anyone if you make a mistake, yet...

Chapter Overview

This book is divided into 5 parts with a total of 12 chapters and 3 appendixes. The following list will give you a quick preview of each chapter:

Part 1. The first part of this book talks mostly about the theoretical side of quantum computing. There are no programming skills required just yet.

Chapter 1. What, Why, and How? This chapter describes the basics of quantum physics, how this relates to quantum computers, and why we need quantum computers.

Chapter 2. The Qubit and Quantum State. This chapter describes the most important part of a quantum computer: the qubit and its quantum state.

Chapter 3. Quantum Gates and Circuits. This chapter describes how to manipulate the quantum state by applying gates and combining multiple gates into quantum circuits.

Part 2. The second part of this book talks about the Microsoft Quantum Development Kit and the Q# programming language.

Chapter 4. Develop with the Microsoft Quantum Development Kit. This chapter describes what the Microsoft Quantum Development Kit is, how to install it on your PC, and how to use it.

Chapter 5. Your First Quantum Program. This chapter guides you toward building your first quantum program using Q#: a quantum random number generator.

Chapter 6. Q# Language Overview and the Quantum Simulator. This chapter describes many of the Q# language features in much detail. How should you write code, what statements and expressions can you use and build, and how should you use quantum operations?

Chapter 7. Testing and Debugging Your Quantum Programs. This chapter describes how to test and debug your quantum programs using Q# and Visual Studio Code or Microsoft Visual Studio. Testing and debugging in the quantum simulator can help you explore and learn more quickly.

Part 3. The third part of this book talks about some existing quantum algorithms and implements them using Q#. These algorithms are still easy enough to understand for every beginner. This makes sure that this book is perfect for people without any advanced physics or mathematics background.

Chapter 8. Deutsch's Algorithm. This chapter describes and implements the famous algorithm from David Deutsch. The comparison is made between the classical version and the quantum version and shows you how the quantum version provides the most optimal solution.

Chapter 9. Deutsch-Jozsa Algorithm. This chapter describes and implements an improved algorithm by David Deutsch and Richard Jozsa. Again, a comparison is made between the classical version and the quantum version to help you ease into the thought process.

Chapter 10. The CHSH Game. This chapter describes the CHSH game: A hypothetical game that can be played, or rather won, with greater success in the world of quantum thanks to entanglement. You will build a classical version and a quantum version of this game and see the improved winning chances for the quantum version.

Part 4. The fourth part of this book concludes the introduction of quantum computing with a sneak preview of the world of quantum cloud thanks to Microsoft Azure Quantum.

Chapter 11. Azure Quantum. This chapter describes the Azure Quantum preview and how to run your quantum programs, written in Q#, on actual physical quantum hardware thanks to the power of the cloud.

Chapter 12. What's Next? This chapter quickly touches a few additional concepts from quantum computing and leaves you with a bunch of Internet links to broaden your horizon.

Part 5. The fifth and final part of this book contains a few appendixes for your reference. To understand some of the mathematics used throughout this book, you will need to refresh your knowledge. These appendixes can help you do just that.

Appendix I. Trigonometry. This appendix helps you with some trigonometry basics like triangles, degrees vs. radians, and trigonometric ratios.

Appendix II. Complex Numbers. This appendix helps you with complex numbers and how to perform calculations with them.

Appendix III. Linear Algebra. This appendix helps you with concepts from linear algebra like calculating with matrices and vector spaces.

Code Samples

All the code samples in this book are also available through the Apress website and on my personal GitHub. I will keep these samples up to date and fix future issues if there are any.

Feedback

Writing this book, my first ever, was a challenge that I will never forget. I hope that you will enjoy reading it as much as I enjoyed writing it. Sometimes, you will experience joy if you learn something new just like I experienced joy when I finished another chapter. Sometimes, you will get frustrated by a hard topic and you will need to read it again, just like I got frustrated while trying to explain something but couldn't find the right words or drawings for it.

If you enjoyed this book, please let me know and make my day! If you hated it, also let me know and help me improve it by telling me what I can do better or different.

PART I

Introduction to Quantum Computing

CHAPTER 1

What, Why, and How?

You have probably heard of quantum computing or quantum in general; otherwise, you would not have bought this book. Quantum is a concept from the world of physics, where it goes by the name quantum mechanics. Its development started in the beginning of the 20th century by well-known physicists like Max Planck, Niels Bohr, Werner Heisenberg, Albert Einstein, Erwin Schrödinger, Richard Feynman, and many others. Quantum mechanics studies the behavior and properties of nature on an atomic scale. Thanks to the discoveries in the field of quantum mechanics, we can leverage these discoveries and create a new tenor in computer science.

However, before I start to dig deeper and explain what quantum mechanics and quantum computing are all about, let me first take the time to tell you why quantum and, more specifically, quantum computing could be beneficial to us.

Take your time and try to not get overwhelmed by the details. The goal is to teach you about quantum computing, the Microsoft Quantum Development Kit, and the Q# language and not 100 years of detailed quantum mechanics and math. Just remember the famous words from Richard Feynman, an American theoretical physicist specializing in quantum mechanics:

I think I can safely say that nobody understands quantum mechanics.

Why?

Let's start the why of quantum computing with a personal story from when I was about 14 years old. I have been interested in computers and especially programming since my early teens. During a practical class in school - it was about mechanical drawings using AutoCAD if I remember correctly – I was done with my exercises. At that time, without smartphones, tablets, or even cheap portable computers, if I had some spare time, I would doodle some code on a personal notebook so I could try it out later on my

© Johnny Hooyberghs 2022
J. Hooyberghs, *Introducing Microsoft Quantum Computing for Developers*,
https://doi.org/10.1007/978-1-4842-7246-6_1

parents' computer when I got home. The teacher had noticed this and proposed me with a challenge: He told me about the game of chess and that there is one piece called a knight. The knight is represented by a horse, and it can move or jump to a square that is two squares away horizontally and one square vertically, or two squares vertically and one square horizontally. See Figure 1-1 for a graphical representation of this move.

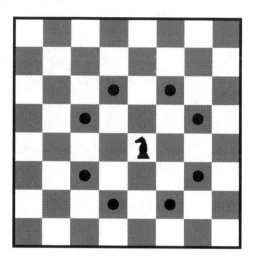

Figure 1-1. *The eight possible destinations for a knight's move*

The teacher continued his story by telling me that it is possible for the knight to start at a random position on an eight-by-eight chessboard and jump from one square to another, visiting all of the squares on the board without jumping on a square more than once. He challenged me: "Write a computer algorithm that tries this and present me with a solution when it is found!" I was very excited about this challenge, started to doodle some code in my notebook, and could not wait until I got home to start running my algorithms! Figure 1-2 shows you a possible solution out of many for this challenge.

Figure 1-2. *A possible solution for the knight's tour challenge on a regular chessboard*

It was not until I was many years older that I learned that this challenge is a popular mathematical problem called "A Knight's Tour." The description of the problem is exactly as the teacher described it to me. The catch is that while writing a computer algorithm to try to solve this problem by brute force is not that hard, actually finding a computer that is fast enough to execute it to completion is a lot harder. At the time, when PCs were not that powerful - I think I was using a PC with an Intel 80486 CPU - I let my algorithm run for a couple of hours and never got a successful result from it. Even if I let it run through the night, I still would not get a result. Because of this, I thought I made an error and, for a reason I cannot remember, probably computer games, I abandoned the challenge.

Because I am writing this book, I tried to rewrite this algorithm again. Based on the order of steps you let the algorithm decide on, it can reach a successful conclusion very quickly or very slowly. On my first try, I started on the most top-left square and tried to jump until I got to the finish. Finding a single path to visit all the 64 squares took about 10 minutes on my modern 3Ghz Intel Core i7 CPU. There are some variations on how to travel the path. If you would jump to the next square, where the number of options for the next step are high, it will take significantly more time to find a valid path. If you would jump to the next square, where the number of options for the next step are lowest, it will take significantly less time to find a valid path. Back when I was a teenager, I must have made the wrong choices making the algorithm run even slower on my already slow CPU.

The reason that I'm telling this story is that the Knight's Tour problem seems to be very easy to solve if you think about it. The challenge only uses an eight-by-eight board, which totals 64 squares. It is hard to acknowledge that a modern CPU would take minutes or hours to solve a single path and even longer than a lifetime to find all possible paths. Sometimes, a seemingly simple algorithm can get into so many iterations that finding a solution takes too long for a classical computer to handle. These kinds of problems are exponential in nature, and the larger the dataset, the exponentially longer it takes to solve it.

Note   Throughout this book, I will talk about quantum computers vs. classical computers. A classical computer is the computer architecture we use today in many devices like your desktop computer, laptop, and smartphone.

Another fun story is about folding a standard piece of paper. A standard piece of paper is about 0.1mm thick. If you were to fold that piece of paper 42 times, the accumulated thickness would reach from the earth to the moon. A quick Internet search tells me that the distance from the earth to the moon is something like 384,400km or 384,400,000,000mm. Thinking about such a huge number is hard; imagining that folding a piece of paper 42 times would reach this distance is crazy. However, the calculation is pretty simple. Search your home for a calculator, use an application on your PC or smartphone, or just use Google and double 0.1mm 42 times.

$$0.1*2*2*2*2*2*2*2*2*2*2*2*2*2*2*2*2*2*2*2*2*2$$
$$*2*2*2*2*2*2*2*2*2*2*2*2*2*2*2*2*2*2*2*2$$

or

$$0.1mm * 2^{42} = 439,804,651,110mm$$

The result of this expression should return the number 439,804,651,110 which is a bit more than the 384,400,000,000 needed to reach the moon. This means we will not only reach the moon; we will pass it. If we would only fold the paper 41 times, we would reach only 219,902,325,555, which is half of the previous number for obvious reasons, and we would not reach the moon.

Of course, it is not physically possible to fold a piece of paper 42 times. If we could, putting the first human on the moon would have been achieved much earlier in history!

The last story I want to share also uses the chessboard as the culprit and is about a legend of the Indian inventor of chess. This inventor would have asked for wheat in exchange for his invention, but he wanted a specific amount of wheat grains. He told his emperor to only put a single grain of wheat on the first chessboard square but then double it on the next square. The emperor should repeat this process, doubling the number of wheat grains for each square until all the 64 squares were filled. Little did the emperor know that this was an exponential problem and the number of necessary wheat grains would grow very big, very quickly. If you do the calculation, which is very much like the paper-folding story, how many grains of wheat would be on the last square?

$$1\ grain * 2^{63} = 9,223,372,036,854,775,808\ grains$$

This number only represents the number of grains on the last square. To get the total sum, you should add all the values for all squares together.

$$1 + 2 + 4 + 8 + 16 + \ldots + 9,223,372,036,854,775,808 = 18,446,744,073,709,551,615$$

If this story has any truth to it, I think the emperor would still be collecting wheat today to pay off his debt to the inventor.

Why Do We Need Quantum Computers?

If we look at a classical computer, the power it harnesses does not scale exponentially. A modern CPU is made from billions of little transistors, the fundamental building block of a classical computer. If you would want to double the power of a CPU, you need to roughly double the number of transistors. For years, we have been doing this, and just like the prediction of Gordon Moore, we are still able to achieve this doubling process every two years. This prediction of doubling the number of transistors in an integrated circuit is called Moore's law. Doubling the number of transistors is getting harder and harder. In order to keep integrated circuits and CPUs small, we have to make the transistors smaller. Because there is a limit to this, we are actually combining multiple CPUs or cores inside a single CPU to keep up with Moore's law.

If you look at the physical world we live in, a lot of day-to-day problems are exponential in nature. Solving these kinds of problems is very hard for a classical computer because it does not scale exponentially. Adding a single variable to a problem could mean that we need to double the computing power. Adding 4 variables would then mean we need 16 times the processing power. The traveling salesman problem is a very popular problem that is exponential in nature. If a salesman needs to find the fastest route between a number of cities, the problem becomes exponentially more complex if there is only one city added to the list of cities to visit.

In the world of quantum mechanics, we could have access to objects with properties that are able to scale exponentially. Thanks to the concept of superposition, some properties can hold multiple values at the same time, which in turn help us to store more complex state inside these objects.

What?

In order to understand quantum computing, you have to understand some of the laws and concepts of quantum mechanics. In the next few paragraphs, I will explain some of these concepts so that you will be prepared to work with them for the remainder of this book.

Note This book is not a deep-dive into physics or quantum mechanics; it is an introduction into quantum computing. My goal is to make you understand quantum computing without scaring you away with advanced physics and mathematics.

What Is Quantum Mechanics?

Quantum mechanics, also known as quantum physics, is a theory that describes properties of nature on a very small scale. Just like Einstein's theory of relativity, which is mostly applicable on a very large scale where objects travel at a speed close to the speed of lights or with large gravitational fields, quantum mechanics is only applicable on an atomic scale. Unfortunately, the human species have not yet developed a unified theory that is applicable to nature as a whole, so today, we need to use different areas of physics to be able to work with everything around us. This means we use basic physics to calculate effects based on day-to-day properties, we use Einstein's theory of relativity to calculate effects on space scale, and we use quantum mechanics to calculate effects on a molecular, atomic, and subatomic scale.

Both Einstein's theory of relativity and quantum mechanics are considered hard to understand for most people who are not familiar with advanced physics and mathematics. The main reason for this is because these theories seem to describe weird behavior and people do not react well to weirdness when they are confronted with it for the first time. The world of quantum mechanics is fundamentally different from the world you and I live in; thus, the rules and effects are different from what we would expect. Because quantum computing is based entirely on quantum mechanics, we need to understand a couple of these weird quantum concepts, and we must accept the rules that are widely accepted by the physics community.

The Double Slit Experiment

Very early in the 19th century, about a century before quantum mechanics were even something to discuss, the double slit experiment was first performed by the scientist Thomas Young. The point of the experiment was to prove that light acted as a wave. It was then believed that light was either a wave or a beam of particles, but nobody could be sure because it was not yet experimentally proven.

The double slit experiment includes a light source that shines through a solid board with two equally sized openings or slits and observes the illumination of a solid back plate that absorbs the incoming light. The experiment continues to state that if light is indeed a wave, it should show the same pattern as other well-known waves, like waves in water, would do. In the following paragraphs, I will describe the experiment step by step, but for simplicity, I will use waves of water. Since you are hopefully more familiar with a wave pool, it will be easier to grasp the importance of the double slit experiment.

Imagine you have a square pool filled with water and you drop a marble in the center of it. You will notice a circular pattern of waves moving to the outside of the pool. The pattern will look like the schematic in Figure 1-3.

Figure 1-3. *The wave pattern traveling in a circular path after a marble was dropped in the center of a square pool*

The wave will start at the center of the pool and will travel to the edges. The further the wave travels, the lower it gets. This happens because the total energy making the wave travel outward needs to be divided among a greater circumference. The moment the wave reaches the edge of the pool, the height of the water impacting the edge will be based on the distance the wave needed to travel. This means that the height of the water impacting the edges will be lower in the corners than elsewhere because the corners will be the furthest from the center of the pool.

If you would hit one side of the square pool with equal force spread across the entire width, the wave will not be circular, but it will travel to the other side of the pool in a straight line. The pattern will look like the schematic in Figure 1-4.

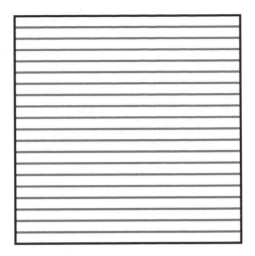

Figure 1-4. *The wave pattern traveling in a straight line after one of the sides of a square pool was hit*

You can represent the wave in both examples as a sine wave like in Figure 1-5. The wave will travel the surface of the water, pushing the water up. Just before and after that wave, you will notice a dip because water cannot be created out of thin air.

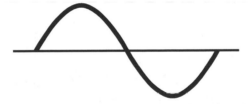

Figure 1-5. *A sine wave representing the wave in our pool of water*

Now, to really start on the double slit experiment, if you put a divider halfway the square pool and create two gaps or slits, the wave will hit the divider for most of it, but where there are slits, the wave will continue to travel forward. Because the wave does not span the entire width of the pool, it will actually spread out in a circular way, just like when we drop a marble in the center of the pool.

Because there are two slits, two separate circular waves will form, and eventually, they will meet each other. If two waves meet each other, they will interfere, just like in Figure 1-6.

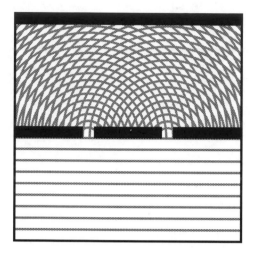

Figure 1-6. *The wave pattern after the wave passes through two slits*

If two waves meet, they will react based on their respective height. If the two waves are at their maximum height, the result will be an even higher wave. If the two waves are at their minimum height, the result will be an even deeper dip. If a wave at its maximum height meets another wave at its minimum height, they will be smoothed out or even cancel each other out if their amplitudes are exactly equal. These kinds of interferences with waves are called constructive and destructive interferences, where constructive interference will create the higher wave and deeper dip and destructive interference will smooth out the wave. In Figure 1-7, you can see these two kinds of interference based on the sine wave from Figure 1-5. Two sine waves that are in phase will create a sine wave with greater amplitude. Two sine waves that are out of phase by 180 degrees will cancel each other out.

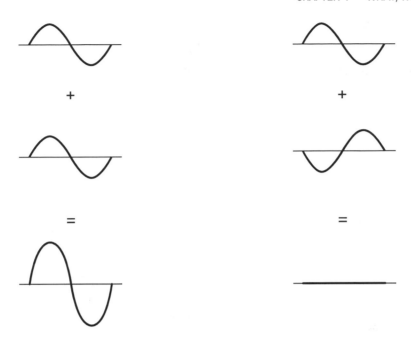

Figure 1-7. *Constructive interference and destructive interference for sine waves*

Finally, when the waves in our pool of water reach the edge furthest from the initial pushed edge, they will create a pattern. At some places, the waves will be high or the dips will be deep. At other places, the waves will have been smoothed out. This pattern is called an interference pattern.

The double slit experiment, executed by Thomas Young with light, created this exact interference pattern as shown in Figure 1-8 and proved that light was indeed a wave.

Figure 1-8. *The resulting interference pattern for the double slit experiment with light*

This kind of interference pattern is found everywhere in nature. They can occur with sound waves, light, water waves, and radio waves. If you have a laser pointer and an empty writeable compact disc at home, you can even try to create an interference pattern with light yourself. First, peel off the aluminum protective layer from the disc; this will help you to be able to shine the laser light through the plastic disc instead of reflecting it. Because a compact disc is filled with microscopic holes, it is very much like the double slit experiment. If you shine your laser pointer through this disc in the dark, you should be able to see the interference pattern on a wall if you fiddle a bit with the direction of the laser light and the angle of the disc. You can find many video's on YouTube on how to perform this experiment at home.

The Double Slit Experiment, More Than a Century Later

More than a century later, in the 1970s, the double slit experiment was repeated with electrons instead of a light source. We learnt in school that matter is made up of molecules, which in turn are made up of atoms. Each atom has a core called the nucleus and contains protons and neutrons. Protons have a positive charge and neutrons have no charge. In order to create the necessary equilibrium, there are a number of electrons that orbit the nucleus which have a negative charge. Electrons are physical objects, and therefore, we can create a device that is able to shoot them through a slit, onto a surface behind the barrier containing that slit.

If we just use a barrier with a single slit, we can see some of the electrons hitting the barrier, not making it through the slit, and we can see some of the electrons hitting the surface behind the barrier, thus making it through the slit. If we continue to shoot many more electrons, we will see a vertical bar on the surface behind the barrier, created from the impact of all the electrons hitting it. Figure 1-9 shows a graphical representation of this behavior.

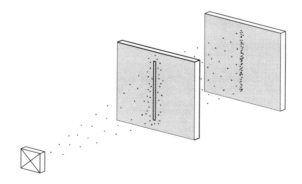

Figure 1-9. *An electron gun shooting electrons through a single slit barrier onto a surface*

If we change to a barrier with two slits, just like the experiment from Thomas Young, and we start shooting electrons through, you would expect to get two vertical lines on the surface behind the barrier, in line with the slits. However, it seems that the same interference pattern from before is emerging. You can see this behavior in Figure 1-10.

How can this be possible? Electrons should not behave as if they are a wave. Maybe they are bouncing off of each other and flying all over the place, still creating this interference pattern.

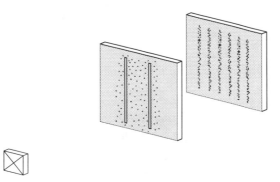

Figure 1-10. *An electron gun shooting electrons through a double slit barrier onto a surface, showing an interference pattern*

If we shoot the electrons one by one, and take a long break in between the shots, they can't interfere with each other, and we should expect to see the two vertical lines. Now, things become interesting. Even if we shoot the electrons one by one, wait long enough so that they cannot interfere with each other, and keep doing this for long enough, still, the same interference pattern emerges. What is going on? The scientists performing this experiment were puzzled and tried to add different kinds of sensors to the slits. If they put a measurement device on one of the two slits to take a peek at what is happening with the electrons, the whole experiment seems to take notice. In 50% of the cases, the measurement device would bleep because an electron was detected to pass through the observed slit. In the other 50% of the cases, the measurement device would remain silent because it couldn't detect an electron because the electron chose to pass through the second, unobserved slit.

After continuing this experiment and shooting enough electrons through the slits, there was no interference pattern showing up. It seems that the electrons were hitting the back surface right behind the two slits, creating two distinct zones, just like in Figure 1-11.

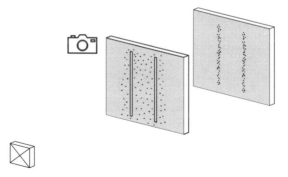

Figure 1-11. *An electron gun shooting electrons through a double slit barrier onto a surface, while being observed by a measurement device, collapses the wave function and does not show an interference pattern*

Based on this experiment, you could say that the electrons lose their connection with our reality the moment we shoot them from our electron gun. The electron now becomes a wave of probabilities or a wave function, as they call it in quantum mechanics. This wave function describes the probabilities of the electron's whereabouts the moment it comes into contact with our reality. That's why if we put a detecting mechanism on one of the slits, the wave function collapses into a particle passing through that slit or not passing through that slit. The electron, therefore, continues to be a single electron and can't interfere with itself, not creating the interference pattern. If there is no detecting mechanism on one of the slits, the wave function continues to exist and will pass through the two slits at the same time, interfering with itself. The moment the electron should hit the surface behind the barrier, the wave function collapses and decides, with a probability based on its amplitudes, where the electron should actually hit, thus creating the famous interference pattern if performed many times. This means that the interference pattern is based on the probability of the particle hitting that exact spot and not by the particle interfering with itself. In the center of the back surface, in between the two slits, the probability is highest. The more you move to the left or right, the lower the probabilities get. This is because the distance the wave needs to travel gets larger, and the amplitude gets lower.

Changing the state of a system by the act of the observation itself, like observing the double slit experiment using a detecting mechanism, is called the observer effect. Classical mechanics also knows about the observer effect, for example, checking the tire pressure is difficult without spilling some air and thus changing the pressure of the measured system. For quantum mechanics, the observer effect is a lot more unusual. Observing, or measuring, a quantum system will collapse the probabilistic nature of a wave function and is one of the key concepts of quantum mechanics.

Welcome to the weird world of quantum mechanics! We know that it exists, we know what to expect based on past experiments, but we don't always have answers to why. There is still a lot of discussion and speculation on how it exactly works. There are many theories like, for example, the many-worlds theory. The many-worlds theory states that for each chance or choice, there is an alternate world where that choice was made. I know it is hard to believe; even Albert Einstein was skeptical about all of this and told Niels Bohr, one of his colleagues:

God does not play dice!

Superposition

Some objects like electrons have properties that can be in a state of superposition where the state can be multiple values at the same time. An example that is used for electrons specifically is their spin. You don't really need to know anything about the spin of an electron, except that it can have exactly two discrete values, spin-up and spin-down, or it can be in a superposition of both. Figure 1-12 shows you a schematic graphical representation of this spin property. In the leftmost image, the electron is in a spin-up state. In the center image, the electron is in a spin-down state. In the rightmost image, the electron is in a superposition state of spin-up and spin-down.

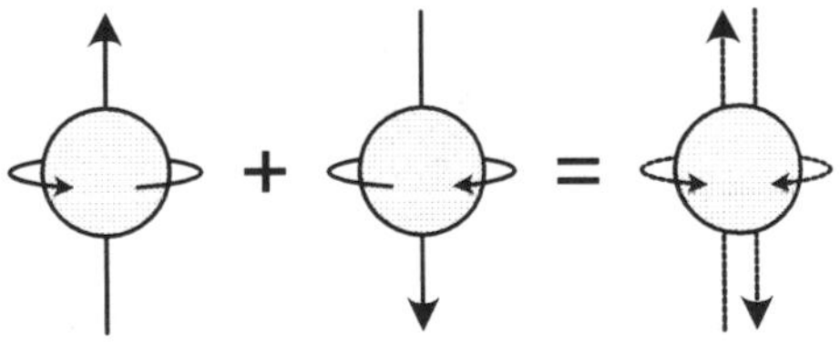

Figure 1-12. *The spin of an electron, both spin-up and spin-down combined results in a superposed spin*

A popular thought experiment based on the concept of superposition is that of Schrödinger's cat. This experiment was not an actual experiment; that's why it's called a thought experiment. Schrödinger just wanted to have his fellow scientists talk about how the quantum mechanical laws influence our day-to-day life.

Something macroscopic like a cat cannot manifest quantum phenomenon. A cat itself cannot be in a superposed state of being dead and alive at the same time. The reason for this is that a cat is built from a whole lot of quantum particles like molecules, atoms, and electrons. The probability of a lot of these quantum particles being in superposition is quite high, but the probability of all of these quantum particles being in the exact superposed state where the cat as a whole is either dead or alive is extremely low.

Figure 1-13. *On the left, the cat is alive because the radioactive material is not emitting radioactivity. On the right, the cat is dead because the the vial of poison is broken by the hammer, controlled by the radioactive material*

Schrödinger's thought experiment visits the idea of putting the cat in a very special quantum box that is closed, uncoupling it from our reality. Figure 1-13 shows a graphical representation of this box and the uncertainty whether the cat is dead or alive. Everyone agreed that the cat itself could not be in this state of superposition, but what if something else was put in the same box? What if a radioactive substance was also put in the same box and there was a 50% chance of that radioactive substance actually decaying and emitting some radioactivity? Based on this radioactivity, a Geiger counter would toggle a relay that, in turn, would open a tube of some highly toxic substance that would cause the cat to die immediately. In this case, the chances of the cat dying would be tightly linked to the superposition of the decaying atom. As long as we don't observe what is happening in the box, we would not know the state of the radioactive atom, and it would be in a superposition of decayed and emitting radioactivity and not decaying and not emitting radioactivity. As a result of this, the cat would be dead and alive at the same time.

Superposition is still subject to a lot of debate in the scientific world. Based on Schrödinger's thought experiment, where does a quantum system stop to exist as a superposition of states and collapses to one of the other? There are also many different interpretations as to what actually happens. Two well-known interpretations out of many are the Copenhagen interpretation and the many-worlds interpretation.

The Copenhagen interpretation is the interpretation that I'm referring to in most of this book. It talks about things like the quantum wave function, superposition, and collapsing quantum systems. It states that the system stops being in superposition when an observation is being made. In the case of Schrodinger's cat, an observation is made when the Geiger counter measures radioactivity, and therefore, the superposition collapses at that point in time.

The many-worlds interpretation denies the existence of the wave function, because it is not observable and states that reality branches into two new realities that cannot interact with each other: one reality where the cat ends up dead and the other reality where the cat is still alive. You as a person, looking inside of the box afterward, will also exist in these two new realities or worlds at the same time. One instance of you is looking at the dead cat, and the other instance of you is looking at a confused, but very much alive, cat.

Entanglement

Another concept from quantum mechanics is entanglement. Two quantum particles can be in a state of entanglement, which means that they can share a property which is in opposite state. If we revisit the spin of an electron, two electrons can be entangled causing their spins to be correlated. Figure 1-14 shows a visual representation of two entangled electron spins that are in superposition. Both electrons are in a superposition of spin-up and spin-down, but their spins are correlated. Just to be absolutely clear, Figure 1-14 is not what that actually looks like. It is just a visual representation to help us understand.

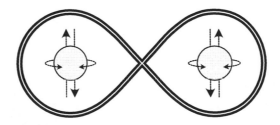

Figure 1-14. *Two entangled electrons in superposition*

If one of these electrons is observed and the spin property is measured, the spin of the other entangled electron will always be the opposite. There is a 50% chance of the spin to be spin-up, making the spin of the other electron to be spin-down, just like in Figure 1-15.

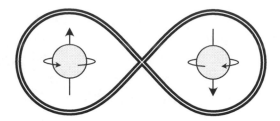

Figure 1-15. *The spin of two entangled electrons after measurement will always be each other's opposites*

An additional fact about entanglement is that this behavior of collapsing after measurement is not limited by locality. If two electrons are entangled and one is in possession of a person called Alice that lives in the United States and the other entangled electron is sent to a person called Bob in Australia, the same thing still happens. From the moment that either Alice or Bob observes the spin of their electron, the other will have its superposition collapsed and will show the opposite spin.

It has been proven by scientists many times that there is no communication between the entangled particles and that they did not agree to a specific configuration beforehand. The collapsing superposition happens instantaneously, and the resulting spins are completely random but always correlated. There were many scientists discussing about this in the early 20th century because there should be some kind of communication in order to make this kind of behavior possible. Today, scientists have come to terms with this behavior but can't exactly explain how it is physically possible. It somehow seems that both entangled particles are somehow a single quantum entity, not limited by their physical location. Some scientists even believe that the two entangled particles are somehow connected through something like a wormhole and can, therefore, communicate with each other without being limited by the laws of relativity. Albert Einstein was one of those scientists that famously stated that quantum mechanics allows two particles to affect each other's behavior instantly across vast distances, which he later called "spooky action at a distance."

The extremes of physics are very much real! Many modern technologies would never have been discovered without our ever-increasing knowledge of the universe. GPS wouldn't work without taking relativity into account, and flash memory is based on the effects of quantum tunneling. These are just two out of many examples of modern technologies developed using the laws of physics. Even though quantum mechanics seems very spooky, experimental science has proven on many occasions that quantum mechanics are a real thing, just like many concepts from classical mechanics.

What Is Quantum Computing?

In the early 20th century, scientific interest in quantum mechanics was purely theoretical. Scientists just wanted to know what the physical world was like on a microscopic level, and they invented all kinds of mathematical models to back their experimental results.

In the late 20th century, however, some scientists believed that quantum properties could help us create dramatically more performant computing algorithms. If a computer is able to maintain a value in memory that can be in a state of superposition and, even better, if we could manipulate that state without collapsing its superposition, we could leverage the idea of probability and actually visit multiple solutions for a problem at the same time. The range of possibilities would become even greater if we could achieve quantum entanglement.

Quantum computing starts from the same basic concept as classical computing and identifies a basic building block for storing a single binary value or a bit. The difference between a quantum computer and a classical computer lies in the fact that a quantum computer will extend the concept of a bit, which can hold the value zero or one, to something that can still hold the value zero or one but also a superposition of zero and one. This extended bit for quantum computers is called a quantum bit or qubit.

In Figure 1-16, you can see a classical bit on the left-hand side and a quantum bit or qubit on the right-hand side. The classical bit is in state zero, and the qubit is in a superposition of states zero and one. Think about the state of a qubit as a vector pointing toward zero/up or one/down on a state-circle. If the vector points somewhere in the middle between up and down, that qubit would be in a state of superposition.

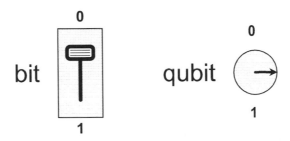

Figure 1-16. *A classical bit in state zero vs. a quantum bit in a state of superposition*

Thanks to our knowledge of quantum mechanics, we have access to physical objects that have properties that can be in a state of superposition. The spin of an electron, for example, can be in two different states, but it can also be in a superposition of these states and, therefore, be considered to be in the two states at the same time. If we can find such a physical object and leverage these quantum properties, we can use it as a basic building block, instead of a transistor in classical computers. This way, we could unlock a new range of possibilities when we write algorithms.

Thanks to these very specific properties, quantum computers are going to be very useful for simulating quantum systems. This will be useful for things like biological and chemical studies, working on drug development, artificial intelligence, machine learning, and cryptography. This class of problems and their algorithmic solutions are exponential in nature and can quickly become too complex to be solved by classical computers.

How?

Different companies and universities worldwide are working on building a physical quantum computer. The theoretical implementation already exists for many decades, but applying it to a physical machine proves to be extremely difficult.

Quantum effects manifest themselves all the time in our day-to-day life. Properties of quantum objects jump into superposition and return back to what we think is normal in a constant stream of what seems to be chaos. If we are to build a physical quantum computer, we need to make sure that quantum objects don't act like that, or at least be more stable and trustworthy. We need to be able to control them. We need to be able to put them into superposition when we need to, and we need to be able to decide when the superposition should collapse. Quantum objects are being bombarded with other microscopic particles continuously, and we need to prevent that from happening.

We know that air is full of particles. If we isolate a number of quantum objects in a vacuum, we can already rule out interference from other air particles. We also know that temperature has an impact on the movement of particles. If a physical body is hot, its atoms are moving very frantically. If it is cold, the atoms are moving much slower. By cooling down the core of our quantum computer to absolute zero, which is zero Kelvin, as close as possible, we make sure that the isolated quantum objects don't interfere with each other.

Even if we manage to minimize the external interference, qubits will always remain noisy. It is not possible to rule out every kind of interaction. If we talk about quantum computers and qubits in theory, we are talking about logical qubits. If your algorithm needs five qubits, it actually needs five logical qubits. When building quantum computers, every single logical qubit is actually backed by a multitude of physical qubits. The number of physical qubits needed to support a single logical qubit can range from a few hundred to a few thousand, depending on the stability needed and the physical implementation of the qubits. Figure 1-17 shows you a diagram where five noisy physical qubits make up a single stable logical qubit. The vector within each qubit represents the qubit state, where the physical qubits have a noisy state and the logical qubit has a well-defined state. The physical qubits are used as a means to do error correction and make the logical qubit more trustworthy.

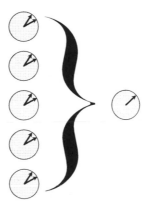

Figure 1-17. *A collection of noisy physical qubits make up a single logical qubit*

Today, a number of companies have implemented working quantum computers, but these quantum computers only have a limited capacity. All companies talk about the number of qubits their quantum computers have available, and it seems they are in a race to build the quantum computer with the highest number of available qubits. When talking about qubits, some will talk about physical qubits and some will talk about logical qubits. In an effort to be transparent about the actual power of their quantum computers, some companies will even talk about quantum volume instead of the number of qubits.

Since quantum computing is still very much in an experimental phase, a lot of different architectural approaches are being investigated. The nitty-gritty details of these architectures are outside the focus of this book, so I'll just name a number of them. This book is specifically targeted to Microsoft Q#, which is a quantum programming language used for universal quantum computers. Universal quantum computers are very difficult to implement but should be able to simulate any quantum system known in our universe. Microsoft is not only investing in quantum software development but is also working on physical quantum hardware, based on topological qubits. Google and IBM are other well-known companies that are working on universal quantum computers that use superconducting qubits. Other companies are working on quantum computers that are perfect for very specific use-cases. These quantum computers are called nonuniversal quantum computers. D-Wave is a company that is working on nonuniversal quantum computers using quantum annealing.

Quantum supremacy is also a term that is used very often lately. The real challenge is actually building a quantum computer that can solve a very specific problem significantly faster than any classical supercomputer. Different companies are in a race to build a quantum computer that can perform such a task. The quantum computers that are available today are able to perform quantum operations but have a capacity that can still be simulated by classical supercomputers. From the moment a quantum computer has the power to perform quantum operations that no classical supercomputer can simulate, quantum supremacy is reached!

It is a fact that quantum computing is still in its early days. Today, we are not sure if quantum computers will ever be able to allocate a large-enough number of stable logical qubits to actually be worthwhile. In the world of science, you should, however, never lose faith. Maybe someone reaches a breakthrough in the next couple of years; maybe it takes another 50 years. We'll see what happens, but we can always learn.

The Last Word

In this first chapter, I tried to explain why quantum computing matters by talking about the complexity of algorithms and how they are influencing the time it takes to come to a solution for a specific amount of data or variables. I talked about what quantum actually means in terms of the physics involved but also in terms of computer science. Finally, I explained where quantum computing is today and what we can expect in the future.

The rest of this book will use quantum phenomenon like superposition and entanglement to teach you about the specific power and possibilities of quantum computing algorithms by looking at the math and logic behind them.

In the next chapter specifically, I will dig deeper into what a logical qubit actually is. I will talk in more detail about the state of a qubit and the different ways we can represent that state. There will be a lot of schematics but also a lot of math. You should not be scared, however. I am not a math wizard myself, and this book will limit itself to high-school-level math as a requirement for you to understand the state of a qubit.

## CHAPTER 2

The Qubit and Quantum State

Now that you have a basic idea on what quantum computing is all about, let's dive a little deeper into the logical qubit, its implementation, and the actual quantum state it should represent.

Tip This chapter will throw some mathematics at you. Expect scary stuff like linear algebra, trigonometry, and complex numbers. If you'd like an optional refresher on these subjects, go ahead and read Appendixes I, II, and III at the end of this book.

Storing Data

You most likely know that the way to represent a basic value for a classical computer is by using the bit. A bit can hold the value zero or one, which is not very exciting in itself, but when you start to combine multiple bits together, you can represent all the data you can imagine. To represent data, there are a large range of conventions and formats to choose from. You can even invent your own standard to describe the data you need to represent using bits.

Numbers, for example, are represented with bits by converting our decimal numbering system from base-10 to binary or base-2. Decimal, or base-10, describes numbers using digits which range from zero to nine. In binary, we only have the digits zero and one to our disposal.

© Johnny Hooyberghs 2022
J. Hooyberghs, *Introducing Microsoft Quantum Computing for Developers*,
https://doi.org/10.1007/978-1-4842-7246-6_2

The decimal, or base-10, based number 123 is composed of the following components:

$$123 = 1 \times \mathbf{100} + 2 \times \mathbf{10} + 3 \times \mathbf{1} = 123$$

The binary, or base-2, based number 1111011 is composed of the following components:

$$1111011 = 1 \times \mathbf{64} + 1 \times \mathbf{32} + 1 \times \mathbf{16} + 1 \times \mathbf{8} + 0 \times \mathbf{4} + 1 \times \mathbf{2} + 1 \times \mathbf{1} = 123$$

Because base-2 takes a lot of space when writing down large numbers, computer programs sometimes use a hexadecimal, or base-16, notation to visualize numbers. A hexadecimal, or base-16, notation needs 16 unique digits, and so it is decided to use the numbers 0 through 9 and the letters A through F. The following is a base-16 notation for the same number as before:

$$7B = 7 \times \mathbf{16} + 11 \times \mathbf{1} = 123$$

Text is represented using bits by assigning each known character in any language in the world to a specific binary code, based on a code table like the American Standard Code for Information Interchange (ASCII) or the Unicode Transformation Format (UTF).

The Latin letter Q is represented by the following binary number in the ASCII encoding:

$$Q = 1010001$$

The Greek letter lambda is represented by the following binary number in the UTF-8 encoding:

$$\Lambda = 1100111010011011$$

Audio, pictures, and movies are represented with bits by taking many samples and encoding all the sample information into a standardized format by using a codec. Pictures will be rasterized into a grid of pixels, and each pixel will be encoded with a specific color. For audio, a common sample size is 44,100 samples per second, and the amplitude of the soundwave is measured and stored for each of these samples. For video, a common sample size is 24 still images or frames per second. These images can be stored using a similar technique as pictures, and displaying the images in rapid succession will make them look like a moving image. Classical computers and their central processing units (CPUs) can perform basic operations with arrays of bits and can move them from one memory location to another.

Qubits, which are the basic building blocks for quantum computers, are more interesting when it comes to holding a value. Where a bit can only hold the values zero or one, a qubit can also hold a superposition of zero and one in addition to the discrete values zero or one. So, for storing the distinct zero and one values, there is no difference between a bit and a qubit. Quantum computers are still using the binary system, and we don't need to change the way we think about holding binary data. Things become more complicated when we are talking about the superposition of the states zero and one, and this chapter discusses just that!

What Is the Quantum State of a Qubit?

Finding a real-life object with a binary property that can hold a value equivalent to zero and one should be easy enough. Just think about a light switch that can be in two positions, on or off, and you have a perfectly valid storage mechanism for a bit. Combine many light switches, and you can store all kinds of data. Collect around 100 billion light switches and a lot of free time and you should be able to store a high-definition movie. Finding a real-life object with a property that can be in a state of superposition is more challenging. The quantum state of a logical qubit is exactly this: a property that can be in a superposition state and, therefore, hold the complex superposition state that has been described in the theory of quantum computing.

The State of a Single Qubit

You are probably used to thinking about bits. Thinking about bits should be fairly easy because they can only represent the values zero and one. Performing operations on a single bit is also very easy to do from the top of your head. If you, for example, want to negate the value of a bit, you just flip it from zero to one or from one to zero. Easy enough!

For qubits and their quantum state, just like the classical bit, the state zero and one for a qubit are easy to comprehend, work with, and represent. Things become more difficult if you want to think about superposition and how this state of superposition affects the qubit or operations performed on this qubit.

Because a state of superposition for a qubit is a probability wave describing the chances of the qubit collapsing to the state zero or one after measurement, the state is nothing more than a mathematical model that can accurately predict this outcome.

The Mathematical Representation

Thanks to linear algebra, the state of a qubit can be represented by a matrix. This state holds two values organized in a column matrix. The following two matrices hold the distinct zero and one states:

$$\begin{pmatrix} 1 \\ 0 \end{pmatrix} \qquad \begin{pmatrix} 0 \\ 1 \end{pmatrix}$$

On the left-hand side, you can see a column matrix with two values, one on the top and zero on the bottom. On the right-hand side, you can see a column matrix with two values, zero on the top and one on the bottom. The matrix on the left-hand side represents the state zero, and the matrix on the right-hand side represents the state one.

A mnemonic I use to remember which matrix represents state zero and which represents state one goes as follows: If the number one is located in the first row of the column matrix, it represents the state zero because it is located at index zero of the array. If the number one is located in the second row of the column matrix, it represents the state one because it is located at index one of the array. Another way to remember these matrices is to think about the top value being the chance of this qubit being in zero state and the bottom value being the chance of this qubit being in the one state. The value 1 represents a 100% chance, and the value 0 represents a 0% chance.

Because writing down a matrix every time you want to represent the state of a qubit is quite cumbersome, and just talking about zero and one is confusing if you work with bits and qubits, there is a second option to represent the state of a qubit. This option is called the bra-ket or Dirac notation, named after the physicist Paul Dirac.

$$\begin{pmatrix} 1 \\ 0 \end{pmatrix} = |0\rangle \qquad \begin{pmatrix} 0 \\ 1 \end{pmatrix} = |1\rangle$$

Thanks to the Dirac notation, you can represent the state as if it were a simple zero or one but with some added characters to distinguish it from the classical bit state. The $|0\rangle$ state is pronounced as "ket 0" and the $|1\rangle$ state is pronounced as "ket 1."

If we talk about superposition, the mathematical representation of the quantum state becomes more interesting. We need to be able to represent the probability of the superposition collapsing to either $|0\rangle$ or $|1\rangle$. An arbitrary quantum state ψ equals some value α times the $|0\rangle$ state added with some value β times the $|1\rangle$ state. These α and β values can be noted inside the column matrix:

$$|\psi\rangle = \alpha\,|0\rangle + \beta\,|1\rangle = \begin{pmatrix} \alpha \\ \beta \end{pmatrix}$$

For the quantum state to be valid, it needs to be normalized, and the α and β values must fulfill the following constraint, where the absolute value of α squared added with the absolute value of β squared should always equal one. This makes sense: α and β are coefficients that represent the probabilities for collapsing to either $|0\rangle$ or $|1\rangle$. The sum of the squares constraints the total probability to equal 1 or 100%:

$$|\alpha|^2 + |\beta|^2 = 1$$

Using these mathematical concepts, the column matrices for states zero and one can be easily explained:

$$\begin{pmatrix} 1 \\ 0 \end{pmatrix} = 1|0\rangle + 0|1\rangle = |0\rangle \text{ where } |1|^2 + |0|^2 = 1$$

$$\begin{pmatrix} 0 \\ 1 \end{pmatrix} = 0|0\rangle + 1|1\rangle = |1\rangle \text{ where } |0|^2 + |1|^2 = 1$$

If you look at the quantum superposition state with an equal chance of collapsing to either zero or one, the matrix will look like this:

$$\begin{pmatrix} \dfrac{1}{\sqrt{2}} \\ \dfrac{1}{\sqrt{2}} \end{pmatrix} = \frac{1}{\sqrt{2}}|0\rangle + \frac{1}{\sqrt{2}}|1\rangle \text{ where } \left|\frac{1}{\sqrt{2}}\right|^2 + \left|\frac{1}{\sqrt{2}}\right|^2 = \frac{1}{2} + \frac{1}{2} = 1$$

To make things even more fun, the values for α and β are complex numbers. So, α and β are numbers in the format $a + bi$, where a is an imaginary number and b is a real number. The normalization formula $|\alpha|^2 + |\beta|^2 = 1$ expects the result to be one, which is a real number. This should not be an issue, because squaring the complex number i results in -1, eliminating the imaginary component of the complex number and only leaving the real component.

Tip   Multiple exercises can be found throughout this book. You can find possible
solutions and guidance at the end of each chapter.

EXERCISE 2-1

A qubit is in superposition and, after measurement, has a 25% chance of collapsing to $|0\rangle$ and
a 75% chance of collapsing to $|1\rangle$. Write down the mathematical representation of this qubit
state using the bra-ket (Dirac) notation and using a matrix:

$$\alpha\,|\,0\rangle + \beta\,|\,1\rangle$$

$$\begin{pmatrix} \alpha \\ \beta \end{pmatrix}$$

You don't have to think about complex numbers to complete this exercise. α and β can be real
numbers. Don't forget about the normalization formula $|\alpha|^2 + |\beta|^2 = 1$.

The Bloch Sphere

If you have a more graphical mind, the quantum state of a single qubit can also be
visualized as a vector in three-dimensional space using the Bloch sphere. The Bloch
sphere, named after the physicist Felix Bloch, is a geometrical representation of the
quantum state for a single qubit. Figure 2-1 displays the Bloch sphere with x-, y-, and
z-axes to help you imagine it as a three-dimensional sphere where the dotted lines
represent the invisible backside curve of the sphere.

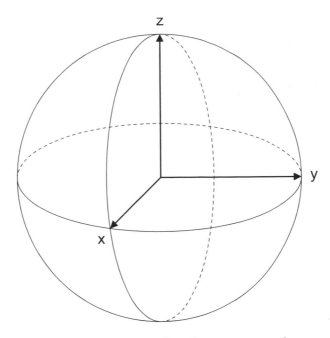

Figure 2-1. *The Bloch sphere, visualized with its x-, y-, and z-axes*

The north and south poles on the Bloch sphere usually represent the basis vector states $|0\rangle$ and $|1\rangle$. The vector describing the quantum state always originates in the center of the sphere and points to somewhere on the surface. Because of this, the length of the vector is always considered to be one, which corresponds to the constraint you learned previously:

$$|\alpha|^2 + |\beta|^2 = 1$$

Note   Unfortunately, the Bloch sphere can only be used to represent the quantum state of a single qubit and cannot be used to visualize the state of multiple qubits.

Figure 2-2 shows a quantum state $|\varphi\rangle$ visualized using the Bloch sphere. Notice the vector originating in the center of the sphere and pointing toward the surface, somewhere on the plane shared by the y- and z-axes.

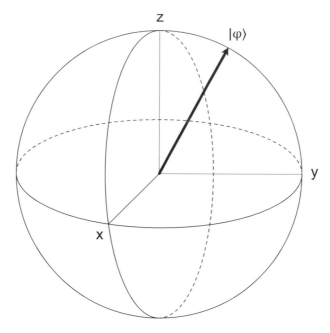

Figure 2-2. *A quantum state |φ⟩ represented on the Bloch sphere*

As I explained before, the states |0⟩ and |1⟩ are located on the z-axis. |0⟩ being on the northern side of the z axis and |1⟩ on the southern side of the z-axis. All other possible orientations for the quantum state vector are representing some kind of superposition. The orientation of the quantum state vector will, therefore, describe a linear combination between the states |0⟩ and |1⟩. This also means that measuring a qubit, will cause the quantum state vector to collapse to either its |0⟩ basis state or |1⟩ basis state with a probability based on its original orientation. Figure 2-3 shows the six straightforward quantum state vectors, aligned with the x-, y-, and z-axes.

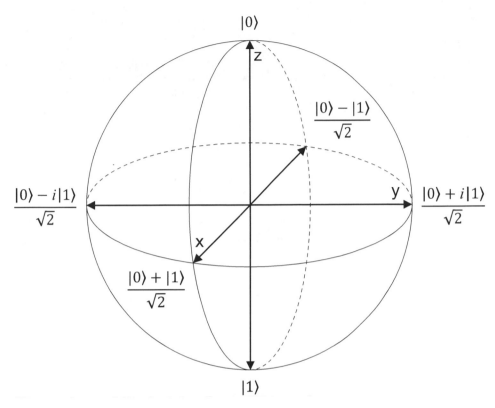

Figure 2-3. *The six most straightforward quantum state vectors, aligned with the x-, y-, and z-axes*

If you ignore the y-axis for simplicity and only look at the plane formed by the x-axis and z-axis, you are looking at the trigonometric unit circle. From this, you can calculate the state, based on the angle of the vector and vice versa.

Tip   If you need a refresh on trigonometry, look at Appendix I at the end of this book. It will quickly guide you through subjects like trigonometric ratios and the unit circle.

To calculate the coefficients α and β for a given state vector angle θ, you can use the formula

$$cos\left(\frac{\theta}{2}\right)|0\rangle + sin\left(\frac{\theta}{2}\right)|1\rangle \ \text{ where } cos^2 + sin^2 = 1$$

For the state $|0\rangle$ in Figure 2-4, where the vector is pointing up on the z-axis, the angle θ is zero radians or zero degrees:

$$\cos\left(\frac{\theta}{2}\right)|0\rangle + \sin\left(\frac{\theta}{2}\right)|1\rangle = \cos\left(\frac{0}{2}rad\right)|0\rangle + \sin\left(\frac{0}{2}rad\right)|1\rangle = 1|0\rangle + 0|1\rangle$$

$$\begin{pmatrix} \cos\left(\dfrac{\theta}{2}\right) \\ \sin\left(\dfrac{\theta}{2}\right) \end{pmatrix} = \begin{pmatrix} \cos\left(\dfrac{0}{2}rad\right) \\ \sin\left(\dfrac{0}{2}rad\right) \end{pmatrix} = \begin{pmatrix} 1 \\ 0 \end{pmatrix}$$

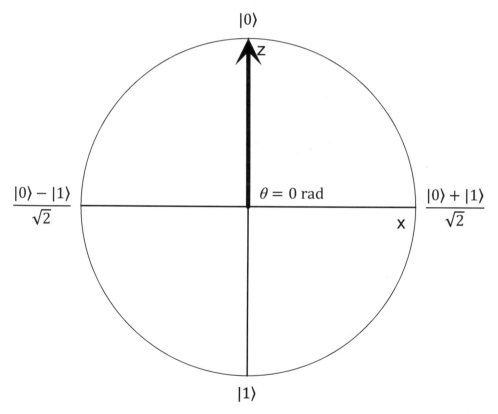

Figure 2-4. *The quantum state $|0\rangle$ with an angle θ of zero radians or zero degrees*

For the state $|1\rangle$ in Figure 2-5, where the vector is pointing down on the z-axis, the angle θ is π radians or 180 degrees:

$$cos\left(\frac{\theta}{2}\right)|0\rangle + sin\left(\frac{\theta}{2}\right)|1\rangle = cos\left(\frac{\pi}{2}rad\right)|0\rangle + sin\left(\frac{\pi}{2}rad\right)|1\rangle = 0|0\rangle + 1|1\rangle$$

$$\begin{pmatrix} cos\left(\dfrac{\theta}{2}\right) \\ sin\left(\dfrac{\theta}{2}\right) \end{pmatrix} = \begin{pmatrix} cos\left(\dfrac{\pi}{2}rad\right) \\ sin\left(\dfrac{\pi}{2}rad\right) \end{pmatrix} = \begin{pmatrix} 0 \\ 1 \end{pmatrix}$$

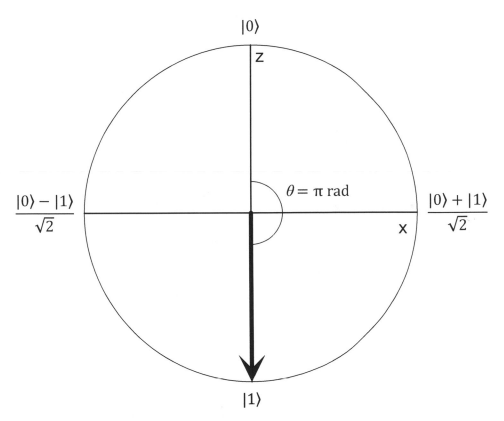

Figure 2-5. The quantum state $|1\rangle$ with an angle θ of π radians or 180 degrees

For the superposition state $\frac{1}{\sqrt{2}}|0\rangle + \frac{1}{\sqrt{2}}|1\rangle$ in Figure 2-6, the vector is pointing left on the x-axis and has an angle of π over two radians or 90 degrees:

$$cos\left(\frac{\theta}{2}\right)|0\rangle + sin\left(\frac{\theta}{2}\right)|1\rangle = cos\left(\frac{\pi\,rad}{4}\right)|0\rangle + sin\left(\frac{\pi\,rad}{4}\right)|1\rangle = \frac{1}{\sqrt{2}}|0\rangle + \frac{1}{\sqrt{2}}|1\rangle$$

$$\begin{pmatrix} cos\left(\frac{\theta}{2}\right) \\ sin\left(\frac{\theta}{2}\right) \end{pmatrix} = \begin{pmatrix} cos\left(\frac{\pi}{4}rad\right) \\ sin\left(\frac{\pi}{4}rad\right) \end{pmatrix} = \begin{pmatrix} \frac{1}{\sqrt{2}} \\ \frac{1}{\sqrt{2}} \end{pmatrix}$$

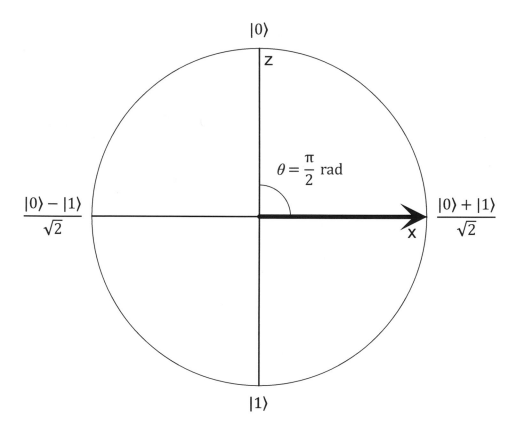

Figure 2-6. *The quantum state $\frac{1}{\sqrt{2}}|0\rangle + \frac{1}{\sqrt{2}}|1\rangle$ with an angle θ of $\frac{\pi}{2}$ radians or 90 degrees*

EXERCISE 2-2

Draw the state of the qubit from Exercise 2-1 on the Bloch sphere and include the angles. You only need to draw the z-axis and the x-axis.

You can use some of the formulas you've learned before to calculate angles.

The State of Multiple Qubits

The state of a single qubit is represented by a linear combination of the basis states $|0\rangle$ and $|1\rangle$; combining multiple qubits in a single system creates an exponentially more complex state. A two-qubit system has a linear combination of four basis states $|00\rangle, |01\rangle, |10\rangle$, and $|11\rangle$. A three-qubit system has a linear combination of eight basis states $|000\rangle, |001\rangle, |010\rangle, |011\rangle, |100\rangle, |101\rangle, |110\rangle$, and $|111\rangle$. You can probably guess that the number of basis states will keep doubling with each qubit that gets added to the system.

Unfortunately, we are not able to visualize the state of a multi-qubit system using the Bloch sphere, so we will need to fall back to the mathematical representation:

$$\alpha|000\rangle + \beta|001\rangle + \gamma|010\rangle + \delta|011\rangle + \varepsilon|100\rangle + \zeta|101\rangle + \eta|110\rangle + \theta|111\rangle$$

The Mathematical Representation

Thanks to linear algebra, you can write down these multi-qubit states using matrices or the bra-ket notation. Since the combined state of a two-qubit system should be able to describe the probabilities that the measured result can collapse to $|00\rangle, |01\rangle, |10\rangle$, or $|11\rangle$, we need to write it down as a linear combination of these four basis states:

$$|\psi\rangle = \alpha|00\rangle + \beta|01\rangle + \gamma|10\rangle + \delta|11\rangle = \begin{pmatrix} \alpha \\ \beta \\ \gamma \\ \delta \end{pmatrix}$$

The normalization formula you learned for a single-qubit system is still valid and constraints the α, β, γ, and δ values:

$$|\alpha|^2 + |\beta|^2 + |\gamma|^2 + |\delta|^2 = 1$$

If you write down the state of a single qubit as a column matrix and want to combine the state of two qubits, you should perform a tensor product.

Tip   If you need a refresh on linear algebra, look at Appendix III at the end of this book. It will quickly guide you through subjects like matrix multiplication and tensor products.

In the next example, two qubits in state $|0\rangle$ will have a combined state $|00\rangle$:

$$00 = \begin{pmatrix} 1 \\ 0 \end{pmatrix} \otimes \begin{pmatrix} 1 \\ 0 \end{pmatrix} = \begin{pmatrix} 1 \\ 0 \\ 0 \\ 0 \end{pmatrix}$$

For a two-qubit system, the other three basis states are calculated as follows:

$$|01\rangle = \begin{pmatrix} 1 \\ 0 \end{pmatrix} \otimes \begin{pmatrix} 0 \\ 1 \end{pmatrix} = \begin{pmatrix} 0 \\ 1 \\ 0 \\ 0 \end{pmatrix}, \quad |10\rangle = \begin{pmatrix} 0 \\ 1 \end{pmatrix} \otimes \begin{pmatrix} 1 \\ 0 \end{pmatrix} = \begin{pmatrix} 0 \\ 0 \\ 1 \\ 0 \end{pmatrix}, |11\rangle = \begin{pmatrix} 0 \\ 1 \end{pmatrix} \otimes \begin{pmatrix} 0 \\ 1 \end{pmatrix} = \begin{pmatrix} 0 \\ 0 \\ 0 \\ 1 \end{pmatrix}$$

If a two-qubit system is in superposition, and we need to think of the normalization formula, it is represented and calculated in the following way:

$$\frac{1}{2}|00\rangle + \frac{1}{2}|01\rangle + \frac{1}{2}|10\rangle + \frac{1}{2}|11\rangle = \begin{pmatrix} \frac{1}{2} \\ \frac{1}{2} \\ \frac{1}{2} \\ \frac{1}{2} \end{pmatrix}$$

where

$$\left|\frac{1}{2}\right|^2 + \left|\frac{1}{2}\right|^2 + \left|\frac{1}{2}\right|^2 + \left|\frac{1}{2}\right|^2 = \frac{1}{4} + \frac{1}{4} + \frac{1}{4} + \frac{1}{4} = 1$$

If you have a lot of time on your hands, you can continue this process and keep adding an extra qubit to the system. As a last example, a three-qubit system with its qubits all in state $|0\rangle$ will have a combined state $|000\rangle$:

$$|000\rangle = \begin{pmatrix} 1 \\ 0 \end{pmatrix} \otimes \begin{pmatrix} 1 \\ 0 \end{pmatrix} \otimes \begin{pmatrix} 1 \\ 0 \end{pmatrix} = \begin{pmatrix} 1 \\ 0 \\ 0 \\ 0 \end{pmatrix} \otimes \begin{pmatrix} 1 \\ 0 \end{pmatrix} = \begin{pmatrix} 1 \\ 0 \\ 0 \\ 0 \\ 0 \\ 0 \\ 0 \\ 0 \end{pmatrix}$$

The other seven basis states are calculated as follows:

$$|001\rangle = \begin{pmatrix} 1 \\ 0 \end{pmatrix} \otimes \begin{pmatrix} 1 \\ 0 \end{pmatrix} \otimes \begin{pmatrix} 0 \\ 1 \end{pmatrix} = \begin{pmatrix} 1 \\ 0 \\ 0 \\ 0 \end{pmatrix} \otimes \begin{pmatrix} 0 \\ 1 \end{pmatrix} = \begin{pmatrix} 0 \\ 1 \\ 0 \\ 0 \\ 0 \\ 0 \\ 0 \\ 0 \end{pmatrix}$$

$$|010\rangle = \begin{pmatrix} 1 \\ 0 \end{pmatrix} \otimes \begin{pmatrix} 0 \\ 1 \end{pmatrix} \otimes \begin{pmatrix} 1 \\ 0 \end{pmatrix} = \begin{pmatrix} 0 \\ 1 \\ 0 \\ 0 \end{pmatrix} \otimes \begin{pmatrix} 1 \\ 0 \end{pmatrix} = \begin{pmatrix} 0 \\ 0 \\ 1 \\ 0 \\ 0 \\ 0 \\ 0 \\ 0 \end{pmatrix}$$

41

$$|011\rangle = \begin{pmatrix} 1 \\ 0 \end{pmatrix} \otimes \begin{pmatrix} 0 \\ 1 \end{pmatrix} \otimes \begin{pmatrix} 0 \\ 1 \end{pmatrix} = \begin{pmatrix} 0 \\ 1 \\ 0 \\ 0 \end{pmatrix} \otimes \begin{pmatrix} 0 \\ 1 \end{pmatrix} = \begin{pmatrix} 0 \\ 0 \\ 0 \\ 1 \\ 0 \\ 0 \\ 0 \\ 0 \end{pmatrix}$$

$$|100\rangle = \begin{pmatrix} 0 \\ 1 \end{pmatrix} \otimes \begin{pmatrix} 1 \\ 0 \end{pmatrix} \otimes \begin{pmatrix} 1 \\ 0 \end{pmatrix} = \begin{pmatrix} 0 \\ 0 \\ 1 \\ 0 \end{pmatrix} \otimes \begin{pmatrix} 1 \\ 0 \end{pmatrix} = \begin{pmatrix} 0 \\ 0 \\ 0 \\ 0 \\ 1 \\ 0 \\ 0 \\ 0 \end{pmatrix}$$

$$|101\rangle = \begin{pmatrix} 0 \\ 1 \end{pmatrix} \otimes \begin{pmatrix} 1 \\ 0 \end{pmatrix} \otimes \begin{pmatrix} 0 \\ 1 \end{pmatrix} = \begin{pmatrix} 0 \\ 0 \\ 1 \\ 0 \end{pmatrix} \otimes \begin{pmatrix} 0 \\ 1 \end{pmatrix} = \begin{pmatrix} 0 \\ 0 \\ 0 \\ 0 \\ 0 \\ 1 \\ 0 \\ 0 \end{pmatrix}$$

$$|110\rangle = \begin{pmatrix} 0 \\ 1 \end{pmatrix} \otimes \begin{pmatrix} 0 \\ 1 \end{pmatrix} \otimes \begin{pmatrix} 1 \\ 0 \end{pmatrix} = \begin{pmatrix} 0 \\ 0 \\ 0 \\ 1 \end{pmatrix} \otimes \begin{pmatrix} 1 \\ 0 \end{pmatrix} = \begin{pmatrix} 0 \\ 0 \\ 0 \\ 0 \\ 0 \\ 0 \\ 1 \\ 0 \end{pmatrix}$$

$$|111\rangle = \begin{pmatrix} 0 \\ 1 \end{pmatrix} \otimes \begin{pmatrix} 0 \\ 1 \end{pmatrix} \otimes \begin{pmatrix} 0 \\ 1 \end{pmatrix} = \begin{pmatrix} 0 \\ 0 \\ 0 \\ 1 \end{pmatrix} \otimes \begin{pmatrix} 0 \\ 1 \end{pmatrix} = \begin{pmatrix} 0 \\ 0 \\ 0 \\ 0 \\ 0 \\ 0 \\ 0 \\ 1 \end{pmatrix}$$

A three-qubit system in superposition will look like

$$\frac{1}{4}\left(|000\rangle + |001\rangle + |010\rangle + |011\rangle + |100\rangle + |101\rangle + |110\rangle + |111\rangle\right) = \frac{1}{4}\begin{pmatrix} 1 \\ 1 \\ 1 \\ 1 \\ 1 \\ 1 \\ 1 \\ 1 \end{pmatrix}$$

EXERCISE 2-3

Two qubits are in superposition and, after measurement, have a one in three chance of collapsing to $|00\rangle$, a one in three chance of collapsing to $|01\rangle$, and a one in three chance of collapsing to $|10\rangle$. There is a 0% chance of collapsing to $|11\rangle$. Write down the mathematical representation of this qubit state using the bra-ket (Dirac) notation and using a matrix:

$$\alpha|00\rangle + \beta|01\rangle + \gamma|10\rangle + \delta|11\rangle$$

$$\begin{pmatrix} \alpha \\ \beta \\ \gamma \\ \delta \end{pmatrix}$$

You don't have to think about complex numbers to complete this exercise. α, β, γ, and δ can be real numbers. Don't forget about the normalization formula $|\alpha|^2 + |\beta|^2 + |^3|^2 + |\delta|^2 = 1$.

Physical Implementation

The transistor is a physical implementation for the classical bit. You need to find something that you can use to physically implement the theoretical state concept, described in this chapter, for a qubit. The physical implementation for qubits is a new topic, and a lot of research is still ongoing. We need to find a quantum mechanical system that is able to exist in a superposition of two distinguishable quantum states.

One example of such a quantum mechanical system is the spin of an electron, which was discussed in Chapter 1. It can be in a spin-up state, a spin-down state, or in a superposition of spin-up and spin-down, just like Figure 2-7.

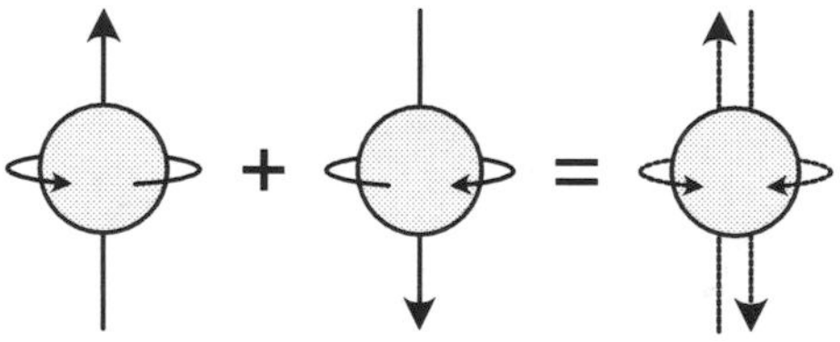

Figure 2-7. *The spin of an electron in a superposition of spin-up and spin-down*

Another example of a quantum mechanical system is the polarization of a photon, the elementary particle of light. A photon can be polarized in any orientation, but it is considered that any orientation that is not perfectly horizontal or vertical is a superposition of the horizontal and vertical polarization. If you take a horizontally polarized filter and send photons through it, the ones that are already polarized horizontally will pass. The ones that are already polarized vertically will be blocked. The ones that are polarized differently will have a chance of passing through based on the angle of polarization. So just like superposition, this chance is based on probabilities.

Figure 2-8 illustrates natural, randomly polarized light, passing through a vertically polarized filter. Because the light is randomly polarized, about 50% of the photons will be blocked, and about 50% of the photons will be able to pass through the filter.

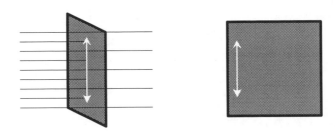

Figure 2-8. *Linear polarization with one vertically polorized filter*

Figure 2-9 illustrates natural, randomly polarized light, passing through two polarized filters. The first polarization filter is vertically polarized, and the second polarization filter is horizontally polarized. Because the light is randomly polarized, about 50% of the photons will be blocked by the first filter, and about 50% of the photons will be able to pass through the first filter.

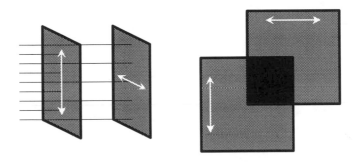

Figure 2-9. *Linear polarization with a vertically polorized filter and a horizontally polarized filter*

Because only the vertically polarized photons, or the ones that have taken a vertical polarization in line with their superposition state, will make it through the first filter, all will be blocked by the second filter. The second filter only allows horizontally polarized light, but all of the light has been vertically polarized.

The Last Word

In this chapter, you learned about the quantum state and its mathematical and visual representations. Thanks to the mathematics, you have the tools to work with quantum state vectors manually without the need for a computer. Thanks to the visual representation using the Bloch sphere, you have insight in how these quantum state vectors behave when they are in a superposition state.

In the next chapter, about quantum operations represented by gates and quantum algorithms represented by circuits, you will need to use the tools from this chapter to understand and reason about quantum state vectors.

Solutions to Exercises

EXERCISE 2-1

A qubit is in superposition and, after measurement, has a 25% chance of collapsing to $|0\rangle$ and a 75% chance of collapsing to $|1\rangle$. Write down the mathematical representation of this qubit state using the bra-ket (Dirac) notation and using a matrix.

Solution

$$\frac{1}{\sqrt{4}}|0\rangle + \frac{\sqrt{3}}{\sqrt{4}}|1\rangle \ \text{ or } \ \frac{1}{2}|0\rangle + \frac{\sqrt{3}}{2}|1\rangle \ \text{ or } \ \frac{1}{2}\left(|0\rangle + \sqrt{3}|1\rangle\right)$$

$$\begin{pmatrix} \dfrac{1}{\sqrt{4}} \\ \dfrac{\sqrt{3}}{\sqrt{4}} \end{pmatrix} \ \text{ or } \ \begin{pmatrix} \dfrac{1}{2} \\ \dfrac{\sqrt{3}}{2} \end{pmatrix} \ \text{ or } \ \frac{1}{2}\begin{pmatrix} 1 \\ \sqrt{3} \end{pmatrix}$$

EXERCISE 2-2

Draw the state of the qubit from Exercise 2-1 on the Bloch sphere and include the angles. You only need to draw the x-axis and the z-axis.

You can use some of the formulas you've learned before to calculate angles.

Solution

For the superposition state $\frac{1}{2}\left(|0\rangle + \sqrt{3}|1\rangle\right)$ the vector should be pointing to the left on the x-axis and a little more down towards the $|1\rangle$ on the z-axis because the chances of collapsing to $|1\rangle$ are higher. To get the numbers exactly right, the angle θ in Figure 2-10 should be $\frac{2\pi}{3}$ radians or 120 degrees.

$$cos\left(\frac{\theta}{2}\right)|0\rangle + sin\left(\frac{\theta}{2}\right)|1\rangle = cos\left(\frac{\pi}{3}\,rad\right)|0\rangle + sin\left(\frac{\pi}{3}\,rad\right)|1\rangle = \frac{1}{2}|0\rangle + \frac{\sqrt{3}}{2}|1\rangle$$

$$\begin{pmatrix} cos\left(\dfrac{\theta}{2}\right) \\ sin\left(\dfrac{\theta}{2}\right) \end{pmatrix} = \begin{pmatrix} cos\left(\dfrac{\pi}{3}\,rad\right) \\ sin\left(\dfrac{\pi}{3}\,rad\right) \end{pmatrix} = \begin{pmatrix} \dfrac{1}{2} \\ \dfrac{\sqrt{3}}{2} \end{pmatrix} = \frac{1}{2}\begin{pmatrix} 1 \\ \sqrt{3} \end{pmatrix}$$

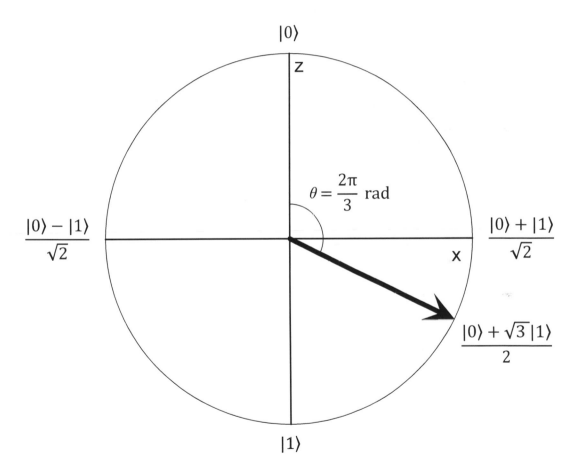

Figure 2-10. *With the angle θ at $\frac{2\pi}{3}$ radians or 120 degrees, the state vector will point exactly at the state $\frac{1}{2}|0\rangle + \frac{\sqrt{3}}{2}|1\rangle$*

EXERCISE 2-3

Two qubits are in superposition and, after measurement, have a one in three chance of collapsing to $|00\rangle$, a one in three chance of collapsing to $|01\rangle$, and a one in three chance of collapsing to $|10\rangle$. There is a 0% chance of collapsing to $|11\rangle$. Write down the mathematical representation of this qubit state using the bra-ket (Dirac) notation and using a matrix.

Solution

$$\frac{1}{\sqrt{3}}|00\rangle + \frac{1}{\sqrt{3}}|01\rangle + \frac{1}{\sqrt{3}}|10\rangle \ \text{ or } \ \frac{1}{\sqrt{3}}(|00\rangle + |01\rangle + |10\rangle)$$

$$\begin{pmatrix} \frac{1}{\sqrt{3}} \\ \frac{1}{\sqrt{3}} \\ \frac{1}{\sqrt{3}} \\ 0 \end{pmatrix} \ \text{ or } \ \frac{1}{\sqrt{3}}\begin{pmatrix} 1 \\ 1 \\ 1 \\ 0 \end{pmatrix}$$

## CHAPTER 3

Quantum Gates and Circuits

In the previous chapter, I discussed the state of a qubit and what putting that qubit in superposition does to its state. You learned about the complex nature of that state and how to represent it using some linear algebra and the Bloch sphere.

Storing a binary value inside a qubit or putting a qubit in superposition is not very useful in itself. Things become more useful if you can use multiple qubits together and perform operations on them in a specific order to create circuits.

This chapter will provide an overview of some of the most common quantum operations, which are also available in Q#, executed by putting the qubit through a quantum gate. If you start combining these quantum gates on your collection of qubits, you can create more complex circuits that form the basis of your quantum algorithms.

Quantum Gates

Classical bits can be operated on by using classical logic gates. You are probably familiar with some of these logical operations like NOT, AND, OR, and many more. In the classical world, combining these classical logic gates on a set of multiple bits can create circuits that form the base of an operation that can be executed on a CPU. Addition, for example, is using a combination of AND and XOR logic gates laid out in a circuit.

Quantum computers are using a similar concept and should be able to perform operations on qubits by applying the effects of gates, quantum gates in this case. Just like with classical bits, we distinguish gates that are applied on a single qubit and gates that are applied on multiple qubits.

© Johnny Hooyberghs 2022
J. Hooyberghs, *Introducing Microsoft Quantum Computing for Developers*,
https://doi.org/10.1007/978-1-4842-7246-6_3

Reversible Gates

Quantum computers are using quantum gates to manipulate the complex state of a qubit. These quantum gates are implemented as unitary operations because they are constrained by the unitarity property of quantum mechanics. If a quantum gate changes the state of a qubit, the sum of probabilities for all possible values should still be equal to 100%. Because of this, all quantum gates are reversible. No data is lost, and you should always be able to revert the state back to its original state.

Single-Qubit Gates

Most quantum gates are single-qubit gates, which means that they can only be applied to a single qubit. If you want to apply a single-qubit gate to multiple qubits, you need to put each qubit through its own copy of that gate.

A nice thing about single-qubit gates is that they can not only be represented by mathematical formulas but also by a rotation around the Bloch sphere. This rotation around the Bloch sphere helps us to better imagine the effect on the qubit state. Again, the Bloch sphere is very informative to visualize the state of a single qubit and some of the transformations caused by quantum gates. It is, however, limited because it cannot help us visualize multiple qubits or even entangled qubits. You, as a quantum computing beginner, should use the Bloch sphere as a learning tool, but as your knowledge and skill become more advanced, you should fall back on mathematics.

H-Gate or Hadamard Gate

A very fundamental but powerful quantum gate is the Hadamard gate, based on the Hadamard transform and named after the French mathematician Jacques Hadamard.

The Hadamard gate allows you to manipulate the state vector of a single qubit and put it in a superposition of the $|0\rangle$ and $|1\rangle$ states. In a graphical visualization for a circuit, which is shown in Figure 3-1, the Hadamard gate is often represented by a box with the capital letter H inside. Figure 3-1 also shows a wire, representing the lifetime of a qubit $|q\rangle$ in an arbitrary state.

Figure 3-1. *A wire representing a qubit $|q\rangle$ and the Hadamard gate applied to it*

If you visualize the Hadamard transformation on the Bloch sphere, think about a rotation of the state vector around a diagonal axis in between the x- and z-axes. Figure 3-2 illustrates this rotation of π radians or 180 degrees on the Bloch sphere.

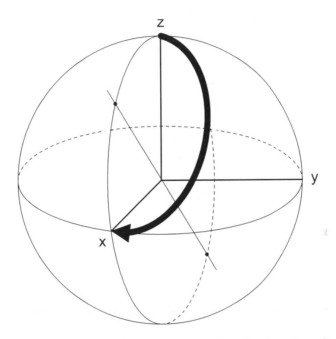

Figure 3-2. *The Hadamard transformation on the Bloch sphere, around a diagonal axis in between the x- and z-axes*

Imagine the two mathematical expressions from earlier. If the state of the qubit is $|0\rangle$ to begin with, it is oriented on the north pole of the z-axis. Applying the Hadamard gate to it will rotate it π radians or 180 degrees around the diagonal axis in between the x- and z-axes. The result is located on the x-axis closest to you and is a superposition state where the two components of the $\alpha|0\rangle + \beta|1\rangle$ linear combination are $\dfrac{1}{\sqrt{2}}$. This ends up with a 50% chance of collapsing to $|0\rangle$ and a 50% chance of collapsing to $|1\rangle$. If the state of the qubit is $|1\rangle$ to begin with, it is oriented on the south pole of the z-axis, and applying the Hadamard gate will rotate it around the same axis as before. But now, the resulting state will be positioned on the opposite side of the x-axis, and the second component in the $\alpha|0\rangle + \beta|1\rangle$ linear combination is now $-\dfrac{1}{\sqrt{2}}$. Thanks to the normalization formula $|\alpha|^2 + |\beta|^2 = 1$, the probabilities still equal to 50%. These two superposition states are often represented by $|+\rangle$ and $|-\rangle$.

To calculate with qubit states when the Hadamard gate is applied to them, the Hadamard gate is represented by the following unitary matrix:

$$\begin{pmatrix} \dfrac{1}{\sqrt{2}} & \dfrac{1}{\sqrt{2}} \\[2mm] \dfrac{1}{\sqrt{2}} & -\dfrac{1}{\sqrt{2}} \end{pmatrix}_H$$

If you use your knowledge from the previous chapter and calculate the Hadamard gate applied to both the $|0\rangle$ and $|1\rangle$ state, you will find the following result states:

$$|0\rangle \Rightarrow \begin{pmatrix} 1 \\ 0 \end{pmatrix} \begin{pmatrix} \dfrac{1}{\sqrt{2}} & \dfrac{1}{\sqrt{2}} \\[2mm] \dfrac{1}{\sqrt{2}} & -\dfrac{1}{\sqrt{2}} \end{pmatrix}_H = \begin{pmatrix} \dfrac{1}{\sqrt{2}} \\[2mm] \dfrac{1}{\sqrt{2}} \end{pmatrix} = \dfrac{|0\rangle + |1\rangle}{\sqrt{2}} = |+\rangle$$

$$|1\rangle \Rightarrow \begin{pmatrix} 0 \\ 1 \end{pmatrix} \begin{pmatrix} \dfrac{1}{\sqrt{2}} & \dfrac{1}{\sqrt{2}} \\[2mm] \dfrac{1}{\sqrt{2}} & -\dfrac{1}{\sqrt{2}} \end{pmatrix}_H = \begin{pmatrix} \dfrac{1}{\sqrt{2}} \\[2mm] -\dfrac{1}{\sqrt{2}} \end{pmatrix} = \dfrac{|0\rangle - |1\rangle}{\sqrt{2}} = |-\rangle$$

If you apply the Hadamard gate to a qubit that is already in superposition, it will revert it back to its original $|0\rangle$ or $|1\rangle$ state. This makes the reversible nature of the Hadamard gate very clear:

$$|+\rangle \Rightarrow \begin{pmatrix} \dfrac{1}{\sqrt{2}} \\[2mm] \dfrac{1}{\sqrt{2}} \end{pmatrix} \begin{pmatrix} \dfrac{1}{\sqrt{2}} & \dfrac{1}{\sqrt{2}} \\[2mm] \dfrac{1}{\sqrt{2}} & -\dfrac{1}{\sqrt{2}} \end{pmatrix}_H = \begin{pmatrix} 1 \\ 0 \end{pmatrix} = |0\rangle$$

X-Gate or Pauli X

Another fundamental quantum gate is the X-gate, which is also sometimes called the bitflip gate. The X-gate allows you to flip the $|0\rangle$ state to a $|1\rangle$ state and vice versa. Because of this, it is very similar to the classical NOT gate.

In a circuit, the X-gate is often visualized as a box with the capital letter X inside. Figure 3-3 shows a circuit where a qubit $|q\rangle$ has the X-gate applied to it.

Figure 3-3. *A wire representing a qubit |q⟩ and the X-gate applied to it*

If you visualize the X-gate on the Bloch sphere, you should think about a π radians or 180-degree rotation around the x-axis. Figure 3-4 shows this rotation if you start with a |0⟩ state making you end up with the |1⟩ state.

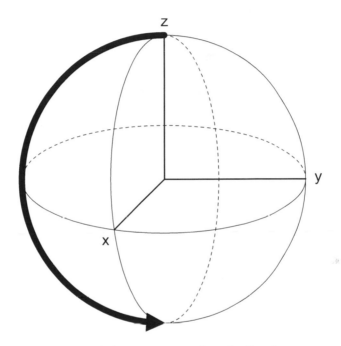

Figure 3-4. *A rotation around the x-axis on the Bloch sphere*

If you need to apply the X-gate in your calculations, it is represented by the following unitary matrix:

$$\begin{pmatrix} 0 & 1 \\ 1 & 0 \end{pmatrix}_X$$

If you apply the X-gate to the basis states $|0\rangle$ and $|1\rangle$, you basically flip their bit value:

$$|0\rangle \Rightarrow \begin{pmatrix} 1 \\ 0 \end{pmatrix}\begin{pmatrix} 0 & 1 \\ 1 & 0 \end{pmatrix}_X = \begin{pmatrix} 0 \\ 1 \end{pmatrix} = |1\rangle$$

$$|1\rangle \Rightarrow \begin{pmatrix} 0 \\ 1 \end{pmatrix}\begin{pmatrix} 0 & 1 \\ 1 & 0 \end{pmatrix}_X = \begin{pmatrix} 1 \\ 0 \end{pmatrix} = |0\rangle$$

If you apply the X-gate to a perfect 50%/50% superposition state, nothing changes because the 50% chance of collapsing to either $|0\rangle$ or $|1\rangle$ is flipped, which still results in a 50% chance of collapsing to either $|1\rangle$ or $|0\rangle$:

$$|+\rangle \Rightarrow \begin{pmatrix} \dfrac{1}{\sqrt{2}} \\ \dfrac{1}{\sqrt{2}} \end{pmatrix}\begin{pmatrix} 0 & 1 \\ 1 & 0 \end{pmatrix}_X = \begin{pmatrix} \dfrac{1}{\sqrt{2}} \\ \dfrac{1}{\sqrt{2}} \end{pmatrix} = \frac{|0\rangle + |1\rangle}{\sqrt{2}} = |+\rangle$$

If you apply the X-gate to another superposition state, it flips the probabilities:

$$\frac{1}{2}|0\rangle + \frac{\sqrt{3}}{2}|1\rangle \Rightarrow \begin{pmatrix} \dfrac{1}{2} \\ \dfrac{\sqrt{3}}{2} \end{pmatrix}\begin{pmatrix} 0 & 1 \\ 1 & 0 \end{pmatrix}_X = \begin{pmatrix} \dfrac{\sqrt{3}}{2} \\ \dfrac{1}{2} \end{pmatrix} = \frac{\sqrt{3}}{2}|0\rangle + \frac{1}{2}|1\rangle$$

Y-Gate or Pauli Y

Just like the X-gate, the Y-gate will rotate the state vector with an angle of π radians or 180 degrees, but this time, around the y-axis.

Very similarly to the H- and X-gate, the Y-gate is visualized in a circuit as a box with the capital letter Y inside. Figure 3-5 shows the Y-gate applied to a qubit $|q\rangle$.

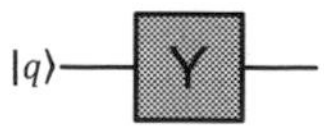

Figure 3-5. *A wire representing a qubit $|q\rangle$ and the Y-gate applied to it*

You can visualize the Y-gate on the Bloch sphere by thinking about a π radians or 180-degree rotation around the y-axis. Figure 3-6 shows this rotation if you start with a $|0\rangle$ state making you end up with the $|1\rangle$ state.

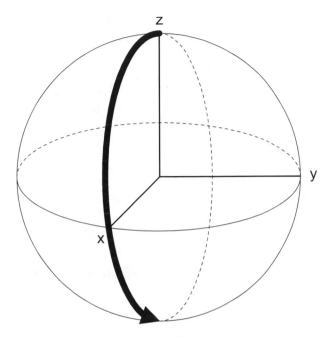

Figure 3-6. *A rotation around the y-axis on the Bloch sphere*

If you need to apply the Y-gate in your calculations, it is represented by the following unitary matrix:

$$\begin{pmatrix} 0 & -i \\ i & 0 \end{pmatrix}_Y$$

If you apply the Y-gate to the basis states $|0\rangle$ and $|1\rangle$, you map the $|0\rangle$ state to $i|1\rangle$ and the $|1\rangle$ state to $-i|0\rangle$:

$$|0\rangle \Rightarrow \begin{pmatrix} 1 \\ 0 \end{pmatrix}\begin{pmatrix} 0 & -i \\ i & 0 \end{pmatrix}_Y = \begin{pmatrix} 0 \\ i \end{pmatrix} = i|1\rangle$$

$$|1\rangle \Rightarrow \begin{pmatrix} 0 \\ 1 \end{pmatrix}\begin{pmatrix} 0 & -i \\ i & 0 \end{pmatrix}_Y = \begin{pmatrix} -i \\ 0 \end{pmatrix} = -i|0\rangle$$

If you apply the Y-gate to a superposition state, it maps the $|+\rangle$ superposition state into a $|-\rangle$ superposition state and vice versa, which still results in a 50% chance of collapsing to either $|0\rangle$ or $|1\rangle$:

$$|+\rangle \Rightarrow \begin{pmatrix} \dfrac{1}{\sqrt{2}} \\ \dfrac{1}{\sqrt{2}} \end{pmatrix} \begin{pmatrix} 0 & -i \\ i & 0 \end{pmatrix}_Y = \begin{pmatrix} -\dfrac{i}{\sqrt{2}} \\ \dfrac{1}{\sqrt{2}} \end{pmatrix} = \frac{-i\,|0\rangle + i\,|1\rangle}{\sqrt{2}} = |-\rangle$$

Z-Gate or Pauli Z

Finally, the third rotation-gate or Z-gate will rotate the state vector π radians or 180 degrees around the Z-axis.

Very similarly to the H-, X-, and Y-gate, the Z-gate is visualized in a circuit as a box with the capital letter Z inside. Figure 3-7 shows the Z-gate applied to a qubit $|q\rangle$.

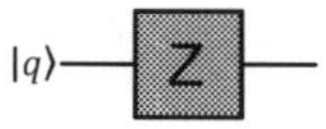

Figure 3-7. *A wire representing a qubit $|q\rangle$ and the Z-gate applied to it*

You can visualize the Z-gate on the Bloch sphere by thinking about a π radians or 180-degree rotation around the z-axis. Figure 3-8 shows this rotation if you start with a superposition $|+\rangle$ state making you end up with the superposition $|-\rangle$ state.

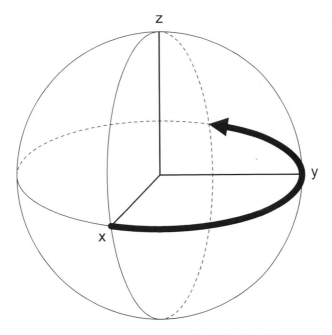

Figure 3-8. *A rotation around the z-axis on the Bloch sphere*

If you need to apply the Z-gate in your calculations, it is represented by the following unitary matrix:

$$\begin{pmatrix} 1 & 0 \\ 0 & -1 \end{pmatrix}_{Z}$$

If you apply the Z-gate to the basis states $|0\rangle$ and $|1\rangle$, nothing really happens. The $|0\rangle$ state maps to $|0\rangle$ and the $|1\rangle$ state maps to $-|1\rangle$:

$$|0\rangle \Rightarrow \begin{pmatrix} 1 \\ 0 \end{pmatrix} \begin{pmatrix} 1 & 0 \\ 0 & -1 \end{pmatrix}_{Z} = \begin{pmatrix} 1 \\ 0 \end{pmatrix} = |0\rangle$$

$$|1\rangle \Rightarrow \begin{pmatrix} 0 \\ 1 \end{pmatrix} \begin{pmatrix} 1 & 0 \\ 0 & -1 \end{pmatrix}_{Z} = \begin{pmatrix} 0 \\ -1 \end{pmatrix} = -|1\rangle$$

If you apply the Z-gate to a superposition state, it maps the $|+\rangle$ superposition state into a $|-\rangle$ superposition state and vice versa, which still results in a 50% chance of collapsing to either $|0\rangle$ or $|1\rangle$:

$$|+\rangle \Rightarrow \begin{pmatrix} \dfrac{1}{\sqrt{2}} \\ \dfrac{1}{\sqrt{2}} \end{pmatrix} \begin{pmatrix} 1 & 0 \\ 0 & -1 \end{pmatrix}_z = \begin{pmatrix} \dfrac{1}{\sqrt{2}} \\ -\dfrac{1}{\sqrt{2}} \end{pmatrix} = \dfrac{|0\rangle - |1\rangle}{\sqrt{2}} = |-\rangle$$

M-Gate or Measurement

The measurement gate is a bit different when compared to the other gates. The measurement gate does not apply a unitary transformation to the state vector, but it collapses the state to one of its basis states. Because of this, the measurement gate is not reversible because you lose complex state information and is therefore not an actual quantum gate. Measurement causes the quantum state to be observed and thus collapses the wave function. The quantum state will be projected to one of its basis states, $|0\rangle$ or $|1\rangle$.

The measurement gate bridges the gap between the quantum world and the classical Boolean world. You can use quantum state information to achieve logic that can otherwise not be achieved in the classical world, but you need to retrieve classical information in the end. A typical quantum algorithm will have its quantum state prepared by a classical computer, several quantum operations executed on that state by quantum hardware, and finally some measurements performed to return a piece of classical information.

Figure 3-9 shows the graphical visualization in a quantum circuit. A measurement is represented by a box with a measurement device and the capital letter M.

Figure 3-9. *A wire representing a qubit $|q\rangle$ and a measurement applied to it*

Multiple Qubit Gates

Some quantum gates have multiple input and output qubits. Because quantum gates are reversible, the number of input and output qubits is always equal.

To execute a single gate on multiple qubits, their state must be combined, and the multiple-qubit-gate should be applied to that combined state.

CNOT-Gate or Controlled X

The CNOT-gate is a very important quantum gate and is the base for the entanglement circuit which will be uncovered later in this chapter. The CNOT-gate is the controlled version of the X-gate, which means that it will apply the X-gate on one of two qubits, only if the other qubit is ONE. Figure 3-10 shows the visualization of a CNOT-gate, applied on two qubits. The CNOT-gate has a solid dot on the qubit that is the control qubit and a circle with a plus inside on the qubit where the X-gate is applied to. The solid dot and the circle are connected with a line to make it clear that both shapes belong to the same gate.

Figure 3-10. *The CNOT-gate, applied on two qubits, with the second qubit as the control qubit and the first qubit as the target qubit*

If you need to apply the CNOT-gate in your calculations, it is represented by the following unitary matrix:

$$\begin{pmatrix} 1 & 0 & 0 & 0 \\ 0 & 1 & 0 & 0 \\ 0 & 0 & 0 & 1 \\ 0 & 0 & 1 & 0 \end{pmatrix}_{CNOT}$$

This matrix has more elements, because it needs to be applied to the combined state of two qubits.

The CNOT-gate can be applied to four combinations of qubits in basis states $|0\rangle$ and $|1\rangle$. First, the state needs to be combined by calculating the tensor product of the individual states. Next, the CNOT-matrix can be applied to the combined state:

$$\left(\begin{pmatrix} 1 \\ 0 \end{pmatrix} \otimes \begin{pmatrix} 1 \\ 0 \end{pmatrix} \right) \begin{pmatrix} 1 & 0 & 0 & 0 \\ 0 & 1 & 0 & 0 \\ 0 & 0 & 0 & 1 \\ 0 & 0 & 1 & 0 \end{pmatrix}_{CNOT} = \begin{pmatrix} 1 \\ 0 \\ 0 \\ 0 \end{pmatrix} \begin{pmatrix} 1 & 0 & 0 & 0 \\ 0 & 1 & 0 & 0 \\ 0 & 0 & 0 & 1 \\ 0 & 0 & 1 & 0 \end{pmatrix}_{CNOT} = \begin{pmatrix} 1 \\ 0 \\ 0 \\ 0 \end{pmatrix} = \begin{pmatrix} 1 \\ 0 \end{pmatrix} \otimes \begin{pmatrix} 1 \\ 0 \end{pmatrix}$$

$$\left(\begin{pmatrix} 1 \\ 0 \end{pmatrix} \otimes \begin{pmatrix} 0 \\ 1 \end{pmatrix} \right) \begin{pmatrix} 1 & 0 & 0 & 0 \\ 0 & 1 & 0 & 0 \\ 0 & 0 & 0 & 1 \\ 0 & 0 & 1 & 0 \end{pmatrix}_{CNOT} = \begin{pmatrix} 0 \\ 1 \\ 0 \\ 0 \end{pmatrix} \begin{pmatrix} 1 & 0 & 0 & 0 \\ 0 & 1 & 0 & 0 \\ 0 & 0 & 0 & 1 \\ 0 & 0 & 1 & 0 \end{pmatrix}_{CNOT} = \begin{pmatrix} 0 \\ 1 \\ 0 \\ 0 \end{pmatrix} = \begin{pmatrix} 1 \\ 0 \end{pmatrix} \otimes \begin{pmatrix} 0 \\ 1 \end{pmatrix}$$

$$\left(\begin{pmatrix} 0 \\ 1 \end{pmatrix} \otimes \begin{pmatrix} 1 \\ 0 \end{pmatrix} \right) \begin{pmatrix} 1 & 0 & 0 & 0 \\ 0 & 1 & 0 & 0 \\ 0 & 0 & 0 & 1 \\ 0 & 0 & 1 & 0 \end{pmatrix}_{CNOT} = \begin{pmatrix} 0 \\ 0 \\ 1 \\ 0 \end{pmatrix} \begin{pmatrix} 1 & 0 & 0 & 0 \\ 0 & 1 & 0 & 0 \\ 0 & 0 & 0 & 1 \\ 0 & 0 & 1 & 0 \end{pmatrix}_{CNOT} = \begin{pmatrix} 0 \\ 0 \\ 0 \\ 1 \end{pmatrix} = \begin{pmatrix} 0 \\ 1 \end{pmatrix} \otimes \begin{pmatrix} 0 \\ 1 \end{pmatrix}$$

$$\left(\begin{pmatrix} 0 \\ 1 \end{pmatrix} \otimes \begin{pmatrix} 0 \\ 1 \end{pmatrix} \right) \begin{pmatrix} 1 & 0 & 0 & 0 \\ 0 & 1 & 0 & 0 \\ 0 & 0 & 0 & 1 \\ 0 & 0 & 1 & 0 \end{pmatrix}_{CNOT} = \begin{pmatrix} 0 \\ 0 \\ 0 \\ 1 \end{pmatrix} \begin{pmatrix} 1 & 0 & 0 & 0 \\ 0 & 1 & 0 & 0 \\ 0 & 0 & 0 & 1 \\ 0 & 0 & 1 & 0 \end{pmatrix}_{CNOT} = \begin{pmatrix} 0 \\ 0 \\ 1 \\ 0 \end{pmatrix} = \begin{pmatrix} 0 \\ 1 \end{pmatrix} \otimes \begin{pmatrix} 1 \\ 0 \end{pmatrix}$$

Because the CNOT-gate is applied on two qubits, we cannot represent it as a rotation on the Bloch sphere.

Quantum Circuits

Quantum circuits are the basic building blocks for your quantum algorithms. By combining one or multiple qubits and any number of quantum gates applied to those qubits, you can build useful quantum circuits.

Quantum circuits are visualized using the wires and boxes I've shown you on the previous pages. In the next paragraphs, I'll show you two very popular quantum circuits: the circuit for quantum entanglement and the circuit for quantum teleportation.

Quantum circuits can be used and reused like code in your favorite programming language. Many quantum algorithms are using entanglement, so the entanglement circuit can be reused within all those algorithms. In Part 2 of this book, you will be encouraged to implement some quantum circuits in Q#, where they are called quantum operations.

A quantum circuit can result in a quantum state, or a classical state, depending on your desired use. If you need to keep your complex quantum state at the end of your circuit because additional quantum operations need to be executed, you should not execute any measurements. If you measure your qubits at the end of your circuit, the complex quantum state collapses, and you are left with a classical bit-state.

Entanglement

In Chapter 1, you've learned about quantum entanglement. Thanks to some of the quantum gates from this chapter, I can show you how to build a circuit that entangles two qubits.

Figure 3-11 shows a circuit with two wires, representing two qubits that have been initialized to the $|0\rangle$ state. The first qubit is put in superposition with the help of the Hadamard gate. Next, the CNOT-gate is applied with the first qubit, which is in superposition, as the control qubit and the second qubit as the target qubit. The CNOT-gate will apply the X-gate to the target qubit if the control qubit is in the $|1\rangle$ state. Because the control qubit is in superposition, the two qubits participating in the CNOT-gate are entangled. Measuring the two qubits at the end of this circuit will have them collapse to $|00\rangle$ or $|11\rangle$ with a 50% chance each.

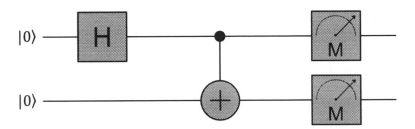

Figure 3-11. *The entanglement circuit using two qubits, a Hadamard and CNOT-gate*

You could try to calculate the process of this circuit using the mathematical matrix representation. Starting with two qubits in state $|0\rangle$ is easy; you need the following matrix for each qubit to begin our calculation:

$$\begin{pmatrix} 1 \\ 0 \end{pmatrix}$$

The first qubit is put through the Hadamard gate to put it in superposition. For this, you take the qubit state matrix and multiply it with the Hadamard matrix:

$$\begin{pmatrix} 1 \\ 0 \end{pmatrix} \begin{pmatrix} \dfrac{1}{\sqrt{2}} & \dfrac{1}{\sqrt{2}} \\ \dfrac{1}{\sqrt{2}} & -\dfrac{1}{\sqrt{2}} \end{pmatrix}_H = \begin{pmatrix} \dfrac{1}{\sqrt{2}} \\ \dfrac{1}{\sqrt{2}} \end{pmatrix}$$

For the next step, the two qubits need to be put through the CNOT-gate. To make the calculation work, the qubit state matrix needs to be compatible with the CNOT matrix. Since the CNOT-gate works on two qubits, it needs the combined qubit state. For this, you need to calculate the tensor product of the two-qubit state matrices:

$$\begin{pmatrix} \dfrac{1}{\sqrt{2}} \\ \dfrac{1}{\sqrt{2}} \end{pmatrix} \otimes \begin{pmatrix} 1 \\ 0 \end{pmatrix} = \begin{pmatrix} \dfrac{1}{\sqrt{2}} \\ 0 \\ \dfrac{1}{\sqrt{2}} \\ 0 \end{pmatrix}$$

Now that you have a combined state matrix, you can multiply it with the CNOT matrix:

$$\begin{pmatrix} \dfrac{1}{\sqrt{2}} \\ 0 \\ \dfrac{1}{\sqrt{2}} \\ 0 \end{pmatrix} \begin{pmatrix} 1 & 0 & 0 & 0 \\ 0 & 1 & 0 & 0 \\ 0 & 0 & 0 & 1 \\ 0 & 0 & 1 & 0 \end{pmatrix}_{CNOT} = \begin{pmatrix} \dfrac{1}{\sqrt{2}} \\ 0 \\ 0 \\ \dfrac{1}{\sqrt{2}} \end{pmatrix}$$

If you want to measure the qubits at the end of the circuit, you need to extract the single-qubit states from the combined state. This should be easy, because you know how to perform a tensor product using the following formula:

$$\begin{pmatrix} \dfrac{1}{\sqrt{2}} \\ 0 \\ 0 \\ \dfrac{1}{\sqrt{2}} \end{pmatrix} = \begin{pmatrix} a \\ b \end{pmatrix} \otimes \begin{pmatrix} c \\ d \end{pmatrix}$$

You can do some calculations and deduce the values for a, b, c, and d:

$$ac = \frac{1}{\sqrt{2}}$$
$$ad = 0$$
$$bc = 0$$
$$bd = \frac{1}{\sqrt{2}}$$

But what happened here? If you look closely, you can see that there is an issue. If a times d should equal zero and b times c should also equal zero, there is no chance that a times c or b times d are nonzero. At least a or d and b or c should be zero for these expressions to make sense, and that is not possible.

So, this combined qubit state is entangled and can't be extracted. The consequence is that if you measure one of the qubits, it collapses to the $|0\rangle$ or $|1\rangle$ state, and the other entangled qubit will collapse to the same state.

Teleportation

Quantum teleportation is about moving the quantum state from one qubit to another qubit. This quantum state is not just the $|0\rangle$ or $|1\rangle$ states but includes every kind of superposition state.

A very important word in the previous paragraph is the word move. Quantum teleportation will not copy the quantum state; it will move or teleport it. A very important rule in quantum mechanics is the non-cloning theorem. This rule makes quantum computing more difficult because it cannot use classical error correction. In Chapter 1, I talked about physical and logical qubits, where a single logical qubit is backed by many physical qubits to make sure the quantum state is as stable as possible using error correction. Since you are not able to copy a quantum state from one qubit to another, the only way to make that work is to repeat every operation you performed on a single qubit on the other qubits.

Because cloning a quantum state is not possible, teleporting a quantum state will invalidate the source qubit leaving it useless.

An example of this mind-boggling concept is the teleportation circuit visualized in Figure 3-12.

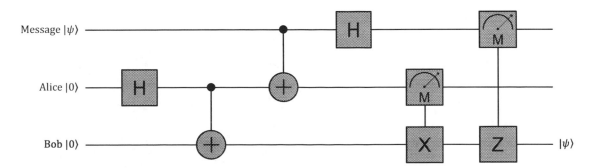

Figure 3-12. *The quantum teleportation circuit which uses entanglement on three qubits*

The simplest form of quantum teleportation can be executed using three qubits and the circuit in Figure 3-12. There are three qubits: the first qubit will be in an arbitrary state PHI and the second and third qubit will be in state $|0\rangle$.

In a hypothetical world where Alice and Bob want to teleport some information, they need some preparation. The teleportation circuit relies heavily on entanglement. Because of this, teleporting the quantum state can be instant, no matter how far apart Alice and Bob have traveled. First, the two qubits that are in state $|0\rangle$ need to be entangled using the Hadamard and CNOT-gates. After this process, Alice can take the message qubit and the first half of the entangled qubit-pair and take her two qubits wherever she wants. Second, Bob can take the second half of the entangled qubits and take it wherever he wants.

If Alice and Bob have reached their respective destinations, the actual teleportation process can begin. To teleport the state of the message qubit from Alice to Bob, Alice needs to entangle her message qubit to her already entangled half-qubit-pair which she shares with Bob. Next, Alice needs to use a classical technology to communicate with Bob, like a telephone or some texting application on a classical computer, and she needs to measure the states of her two qubits.

If the collapsed state of the qubit which was entangled with the qubit from Bob is $|1\rangle$, Alice needs to tell Bob to put his entangled qubit through the X-gate. If the collapsed state of the message qubit is $|1\rangle$, Alice needs to tell Bob to put his entangled qubit through the Z-gate.

The result will be that Alice now has two useless qubits, but the quantum state from the message qubit has been teleported to the qubit in Bobs possession. This doesn't sound all too exciting because Alice needs to get Bob on the phone to pass the two classical bits. Keep in mind though that the quantum state of the qubit that carries the message can be in a state of superposition and this complex state can be teleported by only passing the two classical bits of information. If you extend this circuit to support multiple qubits carrying messages, a lot more quantum state information can be teleported in the same way.

Exercises

The following two exercises will test the knowledge you have gathered from this chapter. You are free to work on these and compare your results with the exercise solutions at the end of this chapter.

EXERCISE 3-1

If you take a qubit in state $|0\rangle$ and put it through an X-gate, it will end up in state $|1\rangle$. If you take another qubit in state $|0\rangle$ and put it through the H-gate, then the Z-gate, and then again through the H-gate, it will also end up in the state $|0\rangle$. Figure 3-13 shows these two circuits and their result.

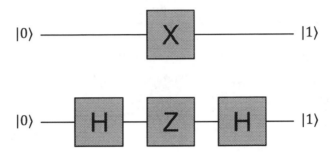

Figure 3-13. *Two different circuits with $|0\rangle$ input and $|1\rangle$ output*

For this exercise, it is up to you to prove, with both math and the Bloch sphere, why both circuits end up with a qubit in the state $|1\rangle$.

EXERCISE 3-2

While reading this chapter, you've learned about the circuit for entangling two qubits. Two qubits in state $|00\rangle$ will be entangled, and the result is a 50% chance of measuring the state $|00\rangle$ and a 50% chance of measuring the state $|11\rangle$.

Modify the entanglement circuit, with the same qubit input state $|00\rangle$, to make the measured state a 50% chance of $|01\rangle$ and a 50% chance of $|10\rangle$.

The Last Word

In this chapter, you learned about quantum gates and quantum circuits, the building blocks of your quantum algorithms.

This chapter concludes the first part of this introductory book on quantum computing and Microsoft Q#. In the next part, you'll use Microsoft Q# and the quantum gates discussed in this chapter to simulate some quantum circuits and algorithms on your own PC.

Solutions to Exercises

EXERCISE 3-1

If you take a qubit in state $|0\rangle$ and put it through an X-gate, it will end up in state $|1\rangle$. If you take another qubit in state $|0\rangle$ and put it through the H-gate, then the Z-gate, and then again through the H-gate, it will also end up in the state $|1\rangle$.

For this exercise, it is up to you to prove, with math and the Bloch sphere, why both circuits end up with a qubit in the state $|1\rangle$.

Solution

You can write down the matrix calculations to verify the outcome of both circuits, visualized in Figure 3-12 from Exercise 3-1. The top circuit only applies an X-gate to a qubit in state $|0\rangle$, so you need to multiply the X-gate matrix with the qubit state:

$$\begin{pmatrix} 1 \\ 0 \end{pmatrix}\begin{pmatrix} 0 & 1 \\ 1 & 0 \end{pmatrix}_X = \begin{pmatrix} 0 \\ 1 \end{pmatrix} = |1\rangle$$

This multiplication results in a matrix that is equal to the qubit state $|1\rangle$.

The bottom circuit applies an H-gate, a Z-gate, and another H-gate to a qubit in state $|0\rangle$. Just use matrix multiplication again, and calculate all operations one by one from left to right. First, multiply with the H-gate matrix, use that result, and multiply it with the Z-gate matrix, and finally use that result and multiply with the H-gate matrix again:

$$\begin{pmatrix} 1 \\ 0 \end{pmatrix}\begin{pmatrix} \dfrac{1}{\sqrt{2}} & \dfrac{1}{\sqrt{2}} \\ \dfrac{1}{\sqrt{2}} & -\dfrac{1}{\sqrt{2}} \end{pmatrix}_H = \begin{pmatrix} \dfrac{1}{\sqrt{2}} \\ \dfrac{1}{\sqrt{2}} \end{pmatrix}\begin{pmatrix} 1 & 0 \\ 0 & -1 \end{pmatrix}_Z = \begin{pmatrix} \dfrac{1}{\sqrt{2}} \\ -\dfrac{1}{\sqrt{2}} \end{pmatrix}\begin{pmatrix} \dfrac{1}{\sqrt{2}} & \dfrac{1}{\sqrt{2}} \\ \dfrac{1}{\sqrt{2}} & -\dfrac{1}{\sqrt{2}} \end{pmatrix}_H = \begin{pmatrix} 0 \\ 1 \end{pmatrix} = |1\rangle$$

You can verify the same two circuits by drawing the gate operations on the Bloch sphere. If you do this, you will end up with the solutions visible in Figure 3-14. On the left-hand side for the top circuit using only the X-gate, there is a single rotation around the x-axis. On the right-hand side for the bottom circuit using the H-gate, Z-gate, and second H-gate, there are a total of three rotations. The first rotation around the diagonal axis between the x- and z-axes, from applying the Hadamard gate, results in a superposition state of $\dfrac{|0\rangle + |1\rangle}{\sqrt{2}}$. The second rotation around the z-axis, from applying the Z-gate, results in a superposition state of $\dfrac{|0\rangle - |1\rangle}{\sqrt{2}}$. The third and final rotation around the same diagonal axis as before, from applying the second Hadamard gate, results in a state of $|1\rangle$.

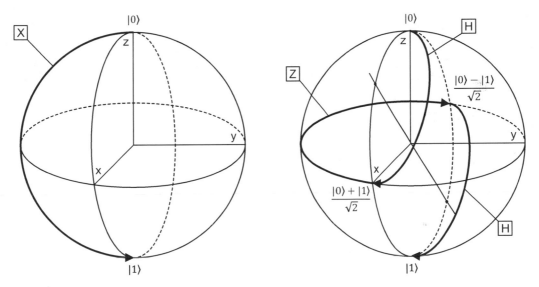

Figure 3-14. *The X-circuit on the left-hand side and the HZH-circuit on the right-hand side*

EXERCISE 3-2

While reading this chapter, you've learned about the circuit for entangling two qubits. Two qubits in state $|00\rangle$ will be entangled, and the result is a 50% chance of measuring the state $|00\rangle$ and a 50% chance of measuring the state $|11\rangle$.

Modify the entanglement circuit, with the same qubit input state $|00\rangle$, to make the measured state a 50% chance of $|01\rangle$ and a 50% chance of $|10\rangle$.

The entanglement circuit will bit-flip the second qubit from $|0\rangle$ to $|1\rangle$ if the first qubit is $|1\rangle$. If the second qubit is already $|1\rangle$, it will be flipped back to $|0\rangle$ if the first qubit is $|1\rangle$, creating the combined $|01\rangle$ and $|10\rangle$ states. Figure 3-15 shows an additional X-gate on the second qubit, before the CNOT-gate is applied, to get this behavior.

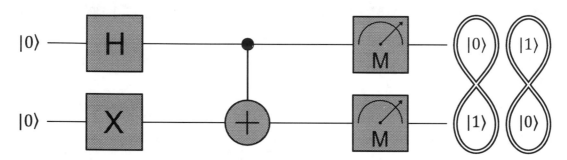

Figure 3-15. *The modified entanglement circuit where the second qubit is bit-flipped before the CNOT-gate is applied to create an entangled qubit-pair that measures to $|01\rangle$ or $|10\rangle$.*

PART II

The Microsoft Quantum Development Kit and Q#

## CHAPTER 4

Develop with the Microsoft Quantum Development Kit

After reading the previous chapters, you have gained just enough theoretical knowledge about quantum mechanics and quantum computing to get started with actual quantum software development. Different companies, cloud providers, and software vendors are preparing for a future where quantum computers will be generally available and used to solve real-world problems. One of these companies is Microsoft. To prepare for quantum computing, Microsoft has already invested in tools and a programming language that provides developers with an opportunity to play around with quantum software. The collection of these tools and programming language is named the Microsoft Quantum Development Kit.

Quantum Development Kit

In 2017, Microsoft released the Quantum Development Kit. This software development kit, or SDK for short, combines several important components to get you started with quantum software development:

- The Q# programming language (pronounced like Q-Sharp)
- APIs for quantum computing simulation using the .NET ecosystem and/or Python
- Tools to help you develop and simulate your quantum programs using command-line tools, Visual Studio Code, or Microsoft Visual Studio

71

© Johnny Hooyberghs 2022
J. Hooyberghs, *Introducing Microsoft Quantum Computing for Developers*,
https://doi.org/10.1007/978-1-4842-7246-6_4

Installing the Quantum Development Kit

You will have some flexibility when jumping into quantum development with Q#. Depending on your preferences or previous experiences, you will have to make a few choices regarding what development tools and supporting programming languages you are going to use.

Tip   If you are completely new to tools like Microsoft Visual Studio or Visual Studio Code, I would encourage you to follow all the steps from command-line development to Visual Studio Code development and, finally, to Microsoft Visual Studio Development. When you have reached the end of this chapter, you can select the environment that is most to your liking to continue working through the rest of this book.

Prepare Your .NET Environment

The Q# development tools are based on the Microsoft .NET ecosystem. Because of this, you will need to install the correct version of the .NET Software Development Kit, or .NET SDK for short.

At the time of writing, .NET Core SDK 3.1 is the required version that will be able to support your Q# development. Newer versions of the .NET platform are already available, but they are not yet supported by the Microsoft Quantum Development Kit. Verify the Microsoft Quantum documentation to make sure this is still relevant today. As you can see in Figure 4-1, you can download the .NET Core 3.1 SDK for free on the official Microsoft .NET website.[1]

---

[1] https://dotnet.microsoft.com/download

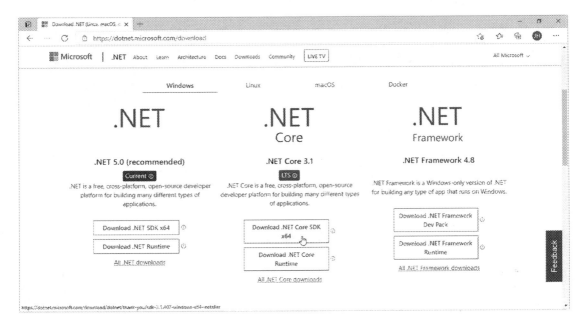

Figure 4-1. *The official website to download the latest .NET Core version*

After a successful download, you can go ahead and open the executable to start the installation wizard for the .NET SDK. The installation wizard will show you a welcome screen containing some links to get some additional information. You can click the "Install" button, visible in Figure 4-2.

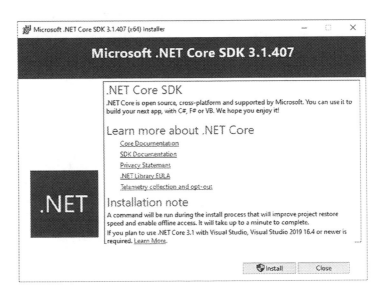

Figure 4-2. *The .NET SDK Installer welcome screen*

The .NET SDK contains both the .NET runtime and the SDK. The runtime will make your PC capable to run applications which are developed using the .NET SDK, and the SDK will provide you with the tools to develop these .NET applications. The installation wizard should now be progressing, and you should see a screen like what is presented in Figure 4-3.

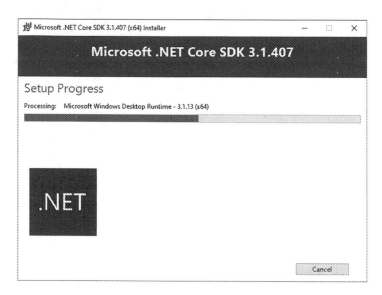

Figure 4-3. *The installation wizard is progressing*

After the installation process is completed, the wizard will show you a success screen and will again list several links to help you get started with the .NET SDK. You can go ahead and click the "Close" button, visible in Figure 4-4, to close the installation wizard.

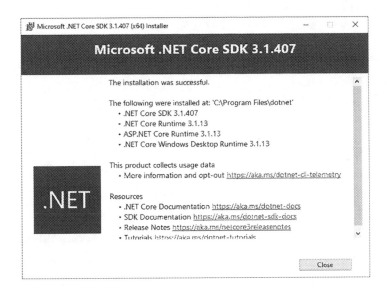

Figure 4-4. *The last page for the .NET SDK installation wizard*

The .NET SDK provides application development tools in the form of lightweight command-line utilities. After installation, you should be able to test these utilities by opening a command-line tool and typing the following command:

```
$> dotnet –version
```

Note   You can choose a command-line tool for your operating system. For Windows, CMD, PowerShell, and the Windows Terminal are some of many valid options.

If the installation was successful, the command should output the exact installed version of the .NET SDK, or higher, if that version was already preinstalled:

```
$> dotnet --version
5.0.201
```

If you have multiple versions of the .NET SDK installed on your system, the latest version will be the one that is used by default. You can force a specific version of the SDK to be used by putting a global.json file in your current directory or in a parent directory. Listing 4-1 shows you how to force the dotnet version using the global.json file.

Listing 4-1. The contents for global.json to force .NET SDK

```
01 {
02   "sdk": {
03     "version": "3.1.412"
04   }
05 }
```

If you are going to recreate the Q# experiments from this book on your own computer, you are best to create a dedicated directory on your local filesystem and put the global.json inside that directory. Make sure the directory will only be used for your Q# exercises. For every Q# project you want to create, create a child directory within your dedicated exercise directory.

If you look at the contents of your dedicated exercise directory, it could look something like this:

```
Directory: E:\MyQSharpExercises
  Mode     Name
  ----     ----
  d-----   04-01 Standalone Console From CommandLine
  d-----   04-02 Standalone Console From Visual Studio Code
  d-----   04-03 Standalone Console From Visual Studio
  d-----   04-04 QSharp From Python
  -a----   global.json
```

Now, from within your dedicated exercise directory, which contains the global.json file, rerun the dotnet command to get the correct .NET SDK used:

```
$> dotnet --version
3.1.412
```

Well done. This was the first step to getting your development environment ready for quantum software development using the Microsoft Quantum Development Kit and Q#.

Prepare for Command-Line Development

To write quantum code using the Q# programming language and the Microsoft Quantum Development Kit (QDK) tools, you need nothing more than a text editor and a command-line tool of your choice.

If you are happy with command-line and your favorite text editor, you can use the dotnet command-line commands to create the project structure, edit the files using your text editor, and use the commands again to run or simulate your quantum code.

Inside your dedicated exercise directory, create an empty directory that will contain your first Q# project. I like to order my directories using numbers, which makes this the first exercise from Chapter 4.

Microsoft .NET uses a command-line tool dotnet, which you already used to determine the installed version, to access many of its commands. To activate the Q# templates, you need to initialize it using the following command:

```
$> dotnet new -i Microsoft.Quantum.ProjectTemplates
```

The output from that command shows you a long list of supported templates and languages for creating new applications. Now, navigate to your newly created directory for this first exercise, and run the following command to create a new standalone console quantum application:

```
$> dotnet new console -lang Q# -o HelloQ
```

The first part of this command "dotnet new console" creates a .NET console executable application that can be used from command-line. The parameter "-lang Q#" tells the .NET SDK to use the Q# language as the programming language template. The parameter "-o HelloQ" will set HelloQ as the project name of your Q# console application.

After the command has executed successfully, a new folder HelloQ will be created containing a *.csproj file and a *.qs file. The HelloQ.csproj file contains some project-related information you can ignore for now. The Program.qs contains your Q# quantum code and is shown in Listing 4-2 for your reference.

Listing 4-2. The contents of Program.qs

```
01 namespace HelloQ
02 {
03     open Microsoft.Quantum.Canon;
04     open Microsoft.Quantum.Intrinsic;
05
06     @EntryPoint()
07     operation HelloQ() : Unit
```

```
08   {
09      Message("Hello quantum world!");
10   }
11 }
```

If you navigate inside of the HelloQ folder using the command-line tool and execute the following command, your quantum Q# application will be simulated on your local classical computer:

```
$> dotnet run
Hello quantum world!
```

This was the first option for you to create and run Microsoft Q# quantum applications on your local computer. Next up is preparing your computer for developing Q# applications using Visual Studio Code.

Prepare for Visual Studio Code Development

Visual Studio Code is a platform-independent and lightweight integrated development environment (IDE) from Microsoft. Visual Studio Code is only a few years old but has grown to be a popular tool in the Microsoft community and beyond. It is lightweight by default but supports a large range of extensions or plugins to enrich its experience and thus has support for many programming languages and application development tools.

Install Visual Studio Code

You can install Visual Studio Code for a wide range of operating systems by visiting its official website,[2] visible in Figure 4-5. Go ahead and click the download button to get the latest version for your operating system.

---

[2] https://code.visualstudio.com/

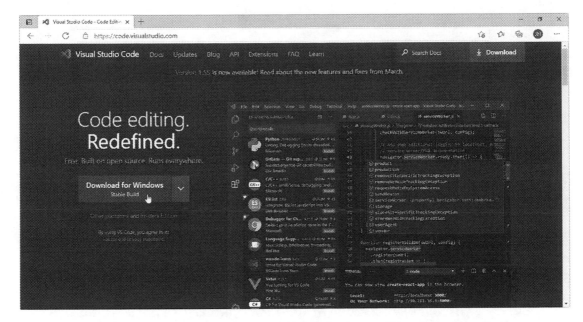

Figure 4-5. *The official website to download the latest Visual Studio Code*

If you launch the executable after download, you will be greeted with the Visual Studio Code Setup wizard. Read and accept the license agreement, displayed in Figure 4-6.

Figure 4-6. *The first step in the Visual Studio Code Setup wizard*

Next, review the additional installation options, and select or deselect the options you like or dislike. Figure 4-7 shows you these options. The "Open with Code" actions on files and folders inside Windows Explorer can be beneficial to quickly open projects in Visual Studio Code from Windows Explorer.

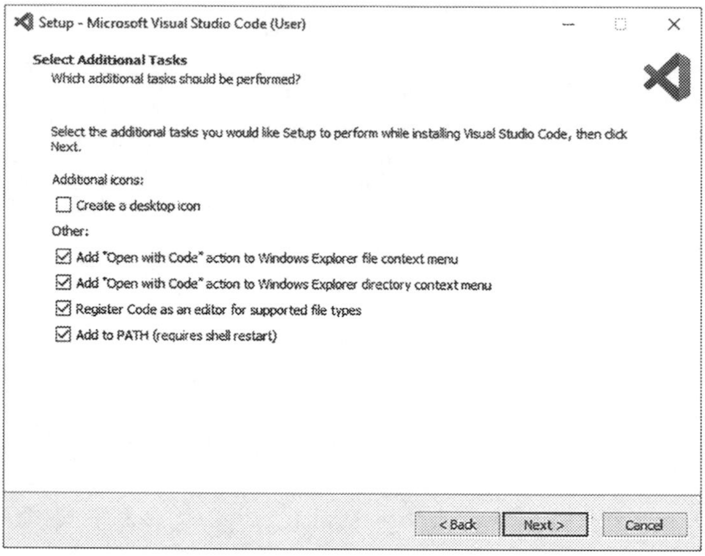

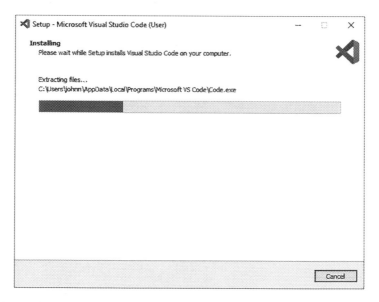

Figure 4-7. *A number of additional installation options for Visual Studio Code*

After this, the Visual Studio Code Setup wizard will start to execute the necessary tasks to install Visual Studio Code just like you can see in Figure 4-8.

Figure 4-8. *The installation wizard is progressing*

Finally, when the Visual Studio Code Setup wizard is complete, you have the option to immediately launch Visual Studio Code. Go ahead and do that so you can do some additional setup from there. Check out Figure 4-9 for your reference.

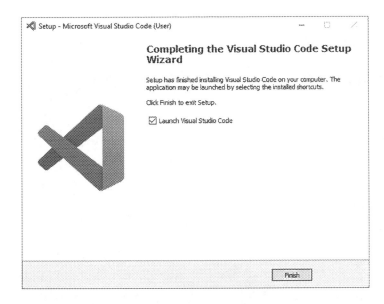

Figure 4-9. *The last page for the Visual Studio Code Setup wizard*

If Visual Studio Code is successfully installed, you will see the welcome screen, just like Figure 4-10.

Figure 4-10. *Visual Studio Code after its first launch, greeting you with its welcome screen*

Now that Visual Studio Code is installed, you can install several extensions or plugins to make it compatible with the Microsoft Quantum Development Kit.

Install the Microsoft Quantum Development Kit for Visual Studio Code

The Microsoft quantum team has created, and is actively maintaining, an extension or plugin for developing quantum applications using Q# for Visual Studio Code. Click the extensions tab on the left-hand side of Visual Studio Code to search for the Microsoft Quantum Development Kit for Visual Studio Code extension. Look at Figure 4-11 if you need some help to find it.

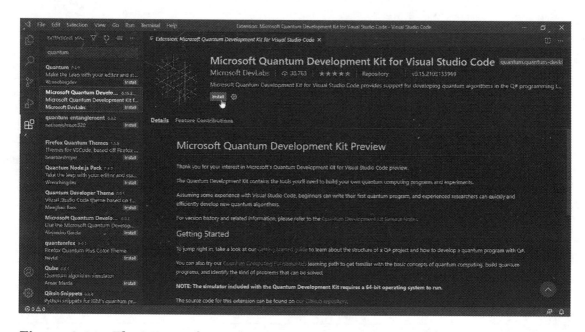

Figure 4-11. *The Microsoft Quantum Development Kit for Visual Studio Code extension*

If you found the extension, click the "Install" button below the title, right next to the icon, to add the extension to your installation of Visual Studio Code. You only need to do this once if you keep Visual Studio Code installed on your computer.

Next, for some additional .NET support, you can install the OmniSharp C# extension. This extension is normally used for C# development, but it can also help you during Q# development. Find it using the same method as before, and use Figure 4-12 if you need any help.

Figure 4-12. *The OmniSharp C# extension*

If both extensions are installed, you are now able to create and run Q# application from within Visual Studio Code. Visual Studio Code works with a combination of UI elements and commands to execute functionality that is added using extensions. To show all commands, you should use the following keyboard shortcut:

$$\boxed{\texttt{Ctrl}} + \boxed{\texttt{Shift}} + \boxed{\texttt{P}}$$

A dropdown list on the top will be available for you to find supported commands. Type "q#" to find any commands related to the Microsoft Quantum Development Kit, and select "Q#: Create new project...". Use Figure 4-13 if you need some help.

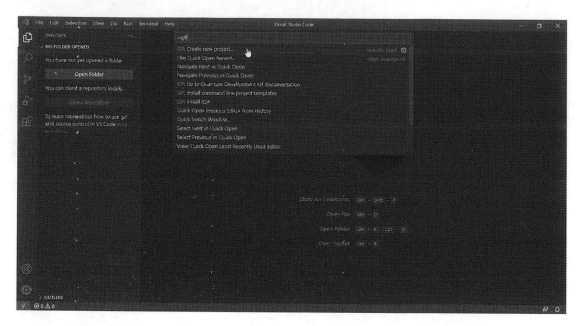

Figure 4-13. *Use the Visual Studio Code command palette to create a new Q#
project*

The Visual Studio Code command palette works like a wizard. Sometimes, you will
get some additional questions, and, in this case, you need to select what kind of Q#
application you would like to create. Just like the command-line option from before, you
can choose the "Standalone console application" to create a simulated quantum console
application. Figure 4-14 can help you if you don't know what option to click.

Figure 4-14. *The option to create different kinds of quantum applications*

The next step is to select a directory on your local filesystem to create the new Q# project. Choose an existing directory, or create a new one, fill in a name for your project, and click the "Create Project" button. Check Figure 4-15 if you need something to compare your situation with.

Figure 4-15. *Create a new standalone console application on your local filesystem*

After your project is created, Visual Studio Code will prompt you to open it. Answer this prompt in the bottom, and click the "Open new project…" button. This is visible in Figure 4-16.

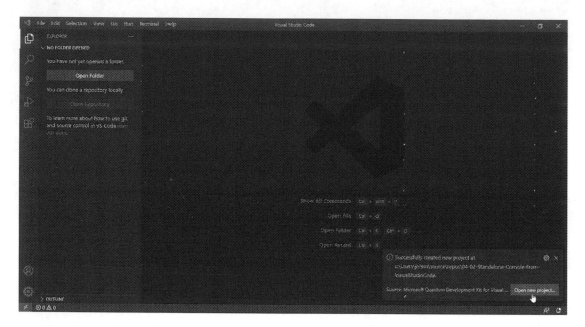

Figure 4-16. *Answer the prompt to open the new project*

The same kind of project from before has been created for you, and the folder containing that project is opened inside Visual Studio Code. If you click the Explorer tab on the left-hand side, you can see the *.csproj and the Program.qs files. Open the Program.qs file to verify its contents and compare it with Figure 4-17.

Figure 4-17. *The Program.qs source file, opened in Visual Studio Code*

You can run your quantum console application project by opening the Terminal window in the bottom. If this window is not visible, use the View menu and select Terminal. If the terminal window is visible, it should be located inside your project directory, and you can run your application by typing the `dotnet run` command. Compare your result with the result in Figure 4-18.

Figure 4-18. *Running your application inside the Terminal window in Visual Studio Code*

Visual Studio Code delivers a richer experience when developing your Q# applications. You get source code coloring and some help while typing.

Prepare for Microsoft Visual Studio Development

If you are used to the full-blown Microsoft Visual Studio, you have the option to use that and install the Microsoft Quantum Development Kit for Microsoft Visual Studio. If you are not familiar with Microsoft Visual Studio, I suggest to keep using Visual Studio Code, as it is much more lightweight than Microsoft Visual Studio.

Install Visual Studio

Microsoft Visual Studio is often used by professional developers and is available in many different versions. The Professional and Enterprise versions are not free and will cost you a subscription fee. There is, however, a free Community edition that you can use for personal projects, open-source projects, and learning.

Installing Microsoft Visual Studio is complex and gives you a plethora of options to choose from. Because of this, installing it is not part of this book, and we will skip to the installation of the QDK. You can try to install Microsoft Visual Studio by yourself or use your already preinstalled version to continue with the following guide.

Install the Microsoft Quantum Development Kit for Visual Studio

If you start Microsoft Visual Studio, you are greeted with its opening window. From this window, you can create new projects and open existing projects. There is, however, a small link in the bottom where you can start Microsoft Visual Studio without creating or opening a project. Check Figure 4-19 if you need some help.

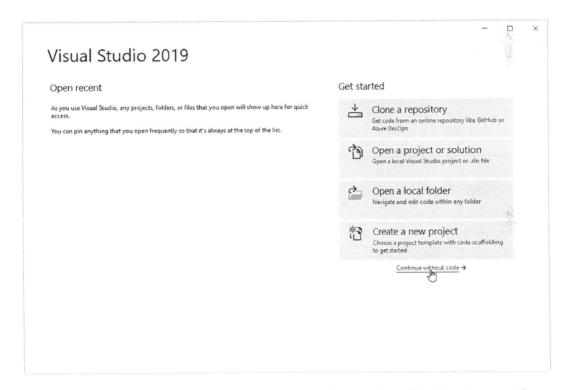

Figure 4-19. *The opening window for Microsoft Visual Studio. Continue without code*

If Microsoft Visual Studio has opened, use the Extensions menu, and select the Manage Extensions option to open the "Manage Extensions" window. Use this window to find the Microsoft Quantum Development Kit extension, and use Figure 4-20 if you need some help. Make sure you have the Online Visual Studio Marketplace selected on the left-hand side.

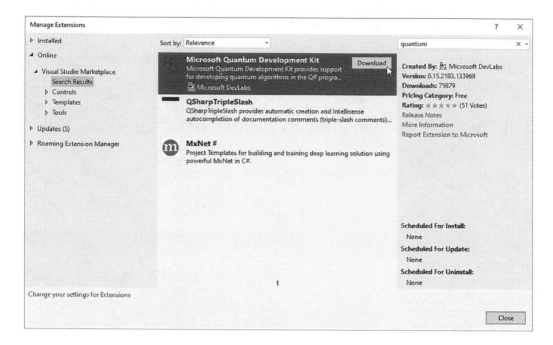

Figure 4-20. *Use the Manage Extensions window to download the extension*

If you click the Download button for the Microsoft Quantum Development Kit extension, it will be downloaded, and afterward, you will be prompted to close Microsoft Visual Studio to install the extension. After manually closing Microsoft Visual Studio, and being a little patient, you will get a small VSIX Installer window. In this window, click the Modify button. Use Figure 4-21 to compare with your situation.

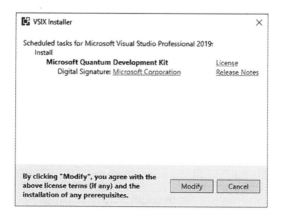

Figure 4-21. *Click Modify in the VSIX Installer to install the extension*

Figure 4-22 shows you the installation progress in the VSIX Installer.

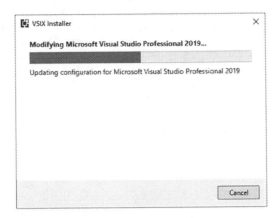

Figure 4-22. *The installation progress in the VSIX Installer*

If the installation has finished, you can close the VSIX Installer window by clicking the close button. Figure 4-23 shows you this final screen.

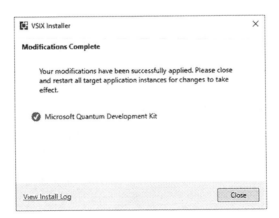

Figure 4-23. *The installation of the extension has completed*

You can now start Microsoft Visual Studio again, and on the welcome screen, you should create a new project by clicking the corresponding button. You can verify using Figure 4-24.

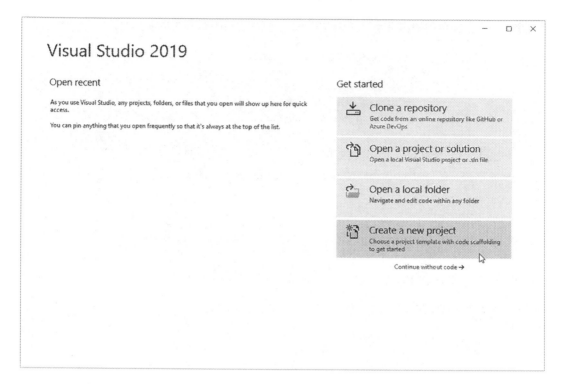

Figure 4-24. *Create a new project from the Microsoft Visual Studio welcome window*

In the next window, you should find the "Q# Application" template. Select this template, and click the "Next" button, just like Figure 4-25. The Q# Application template has an additional description and tells you that you can use it for creating a Q# command-line application. This template is equivalent to the standalone console application that you have used before from the command-line and Visual Studio Code.

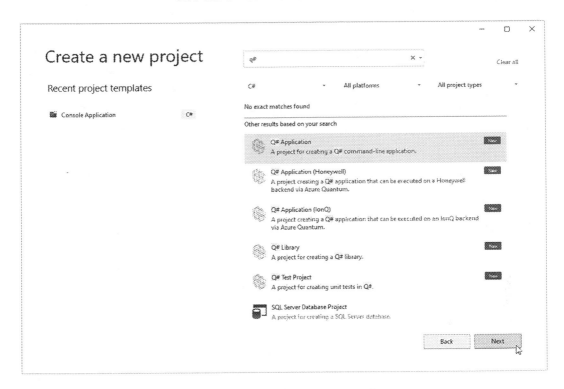

Figure 4-25. *Find and select the Q# Application template*

In the next window, you need to pick a name for your project and solution. Microsoft Visual Studio uses an encompassing solution file that holds your project. In this specific case, a solution is not really needed, so you can select the "Place solution and project in the same directory" option. Now you only need to pick a name and location for your project. Check Figure 4-26 for your reference.

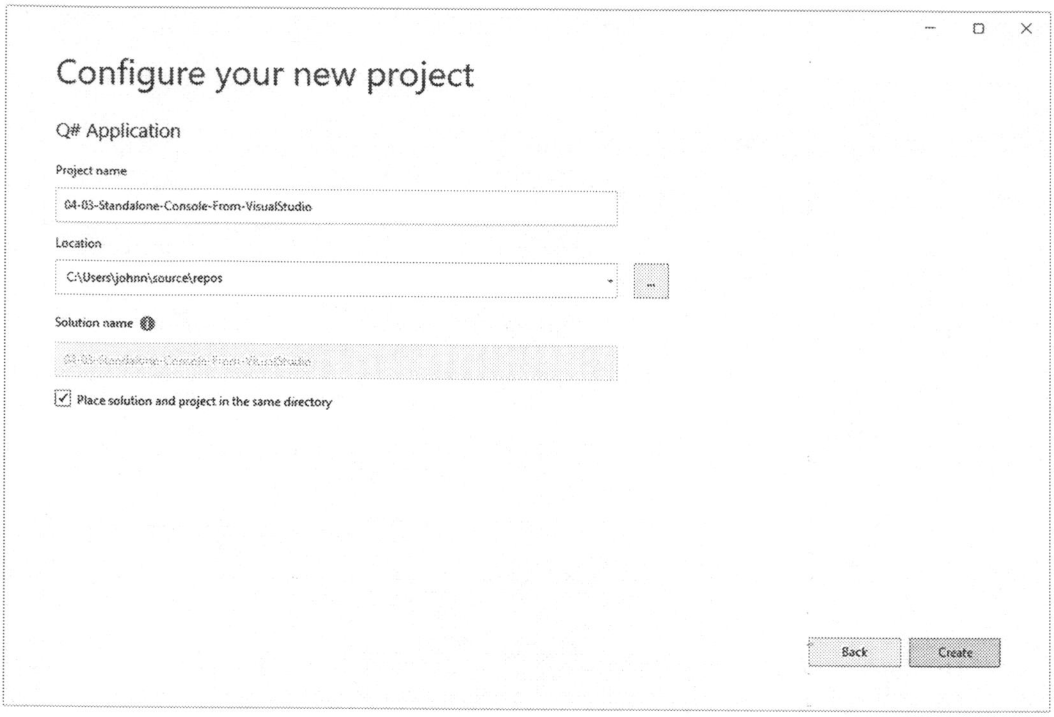

Figure 4-26. *Select a project name and location for your Q# Application*

When your project is created and Microsoft Visual Studio has fully loaded, you can find the Solution Explorer window on the right-hand side. This window shows the `*.csproj` and the `Program.qs` files. If the Solution Explorer window is not visible, you can find it using the View menu by selecting the Solution Explorer option. Your Visual Studio environment with the Solution Explorer should look like Figure 4-27.

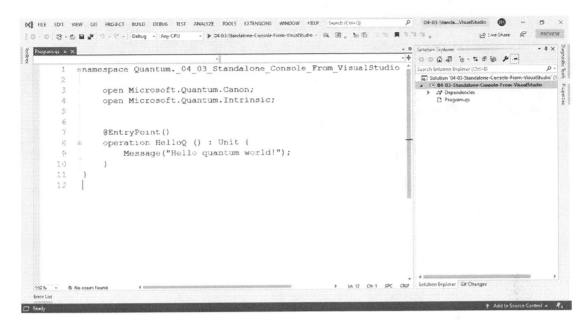

Figure 4-27. *Microsoft Visual Studio with the Program.qs file opened in the editor window*

Running your programs from Microsoft Visual Studio is easy. Just press the green play button in the top toolbar, and a console window should appear which will run your program. Compare your output with the output shown in Figure 4-28.

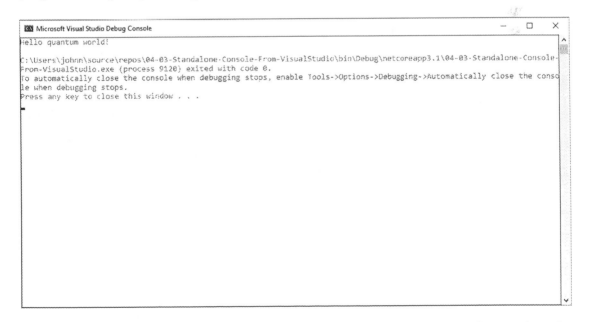

Figure 4-28. *Running your quantum console application from Microsoft Visual Studio*

Microsoft Visual Studio offers an even bigger advantage for writing software programs. There are many integrated tools for writing, running, and debugging your programs that are outside the scope of this book.

Prepare for Python Development

If you would like to simulate and support your Q# programs using Python, you will need to set up your environment to support it.

Install Python

You can visit the Python web page[3] to download the latest version of Python for your platform and operating system. See Figure 4-29 for an example of Python 3.9.4 for Windows.

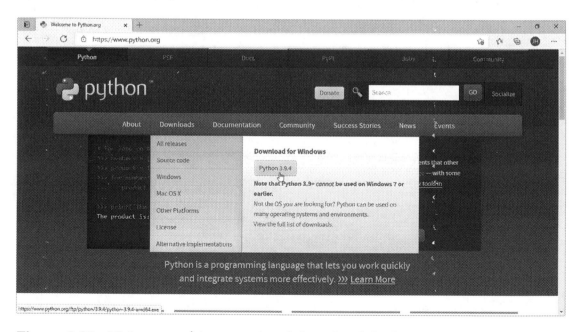

Figure 4-29. *Visit www.pyhton.org/ and download the latest version of Python*

---

[3] https://www.python.org/

If your download was successful, install the downloaded package by opening it. In the first step of the installation wizard, you should enable both the "Install launcher for all users" and the "Add Python to PATH" options. Adding Python to PATH will make sure your command-line utilities are able to recognize the Python commands. See Figures 4-30, 4-31, and 4-32 to have a sense of what the installation process will look like.

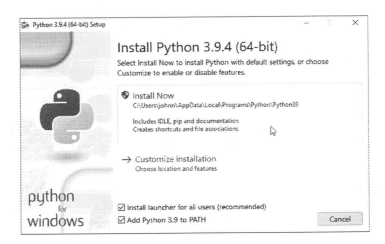

Figure 4-30. *Install Python for all users and add it to the PATH environment variable*

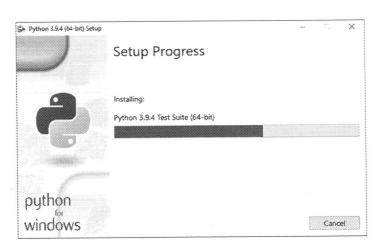

Figure 4-31. *The Python installation progress window*

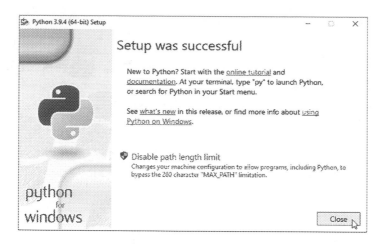

Figure 4-32. *The final step of the Python installation wizard where you can bypass the 260-character limitation for your computer*

Open a command-line interface on your computer, and type the Python command to check if the installation was successful:

```
$> python
```

If the python installation was successful and you added it to your PATH environment variable, you should see the following message:

```
$> python
Python 3.8.2 (tags/v3.8.2:7b3ab59, Feb 25 2020, 22:45:29) [MSC v.1916 32
bit (Intel)] on win32
Type "help", "copyright", "credits" or "license" for more information.
>>>
```

You are now inside the interactive Python environment. To leave this environment, just type exit() and press the Enter key.

Install the Microsoft Quantum Development Kit for Python

Python installs a package manager by default. With a package manager, you can easily install additional tools, features, and frameworks to enrich your programming experience with Python. For Q# specifically, there is also a package available.

Open a command-line and execute the following command to install the Python Q# package:

```
$> pip install qsharp
```

The qsharp package for Python provides interoperability with the Microsoft Quantum Development Kit and the Q# language for easy simulation of Q# applications from within Python. The previous command installs that package.

Now that Python has a way of interacting with Q#, you need to install and configure IQ#, a kernel used by Python and Jupyter that provides the core functionality for compiling and running Q# applications. Run the following command to install that IQ# kernel as a .NET global tool:

```
$> dotnet tool install -g Microsoft.Quantum.IQSharp
```

Next, exit your command-line tool and reopen it to execute the following command. This command will make sure the IQ# kernel installs and configures itself correctly.

```
$> dotnet iqsharp install
```

Get a copy of the program.qs that you have used before, and put it inside a new subdirectory of your dedicated exercise directory. The Q# source is repeated in Listing 4-3 for your reference.

Listing 4-3. The contents of Program.qs

```
01 namespace _04_04_QSharp_From_Python
02 {
03   open Microsoft.Quantum.Canon;
04   open Microsoft.Quantum.Intrinsic;
05
06   @EntryPoint()
07   operation HelloQ() : Unit
08   {
09     Message("Hello quantum world!");
10   }
11 }
```

Now, open your favorite text editor, and create a host.py file in the same directory as your program.qs. Listing 4-4 shows you the contents for this Python host. Please make sure that the namespace inside the program.qs is the same as the import from the Python host.

Listing 4-4. The contents of host.py

```
01 import qsharp
02 from _04_04_QSharp_From_Python import HelloQ
03
04 print(HelloQ.simulate())
```

Finally, open your terminal, navigate to the directory that contains both program.qs and host.py, and run the python file by using the following command:

```
$>python ./host.py
```

If all goes well, you should get the following output:

```
Preparing Q# environment...
Hello quantum world!
```

The Last Word

You have finished the first chapter for Part 2 of this book. Now that you have some theoretical knowledge and you have installed the tools needed, you are ready to continue. In the next chapter, you will create your first quantum application where you are going to generate random numbers using quantum superposition.

## CHAPTER 5

Your First Quantum Program

Now that you have a working development environment, you are ready to start and write your first working quantum program.

Note   Keep in mind that the Microsoft Quantum Development Kit contains Q# as a quantum programming language and the tools and frameworks to simulate a quantum program on your PC. The programming language Q# itself is meant to run on an actual quantum computer, but when you are running it on your local PC, you are only simulating a quantum computer. The available memory of your PC will limit the number of qubits you can use and, therefore, determine the maximum complexity of your program.

A True Random Number Generator

One of the benefits of a quantum computer is the ability to generate truly random numbers. A classical computer does not have the ability to generate these. Generating a truly random number is a very difficult thing to do for a deterministic computer system. If you are using a programming language of your choice on a classical computer and you are requesting a random number, you are not actually getting a random number but a pseudo-random number.

Pseudo-random numbers are numbers generated by an algorithm that generates a sequence of numbers that approximate the properties of sequences of random numbers. A mathematical function and a seed value, an initial value to initialize this mathematical

© Johnny Hooyberghs 2022
J. Hooyberghs, *Introducing Microsoft Quantum Computing for Developers*,
https://doi.org/10.1007/978-1-4842-7246-6_5

function, determines the sequence of numbers generated. Selecting a mathematical function and seed is very important for creating a high-quality and unpredictable sequence of pseudo-random numbers. Most programming languages use a time-based seed by default. Because of this, generating pseudo-random numbers from two separate instances of the random number generator at the same time will generate the same sequence of numbers.

Quantum computers, however, can take advantage of superposition to implement true randomness. Putting a qubit in superposition and measuring its value will result in zero or one with an equal probability. Because a real quantum computer uses real-life components and their properties in superposition, the measured value will always be truly random.

Note   For some years now, classical Intel and AMD CPUs have support for generating truly random numbers with the addition of the RDRAND and RDSEED instructions. These instructions use an on-chip hardware random number generator that generates random numbers from physical, low-level, statistically random noise signals. Many programming languages and runtimes will still use pseudo-random number generators and only use the dedicated RDRAND and RDSEED instructions for very specific use-cases, like randomness for security-related implementations.

For quantum programs, creating a random bit or number is the equivalent of the world-famous "Hello World" example application. This is exactly what you will do in the next exercises. So, power on that classical computer of yours and let's go!

Tip   Q# is the focus of this book, but to simulate the algorithms you write in Q#, you can use several other supporting programming languages. This book will provide you with examples in C# and Python. You can, but are not required to, learn both programming languages. If you are already proficient in one, please use that. If not, choose the one that looks the least threatening to you.

Generating a Random Bit

In your first exercise, you will create a quantum program that generates a single, random bit, a bit that will result in the value zero or one. Figure 5-1 shows you a diagram of how this process unfolds. A single qubit, prepared in a superposition will collapse to either zero or one with an equal probability of 50% when measured.

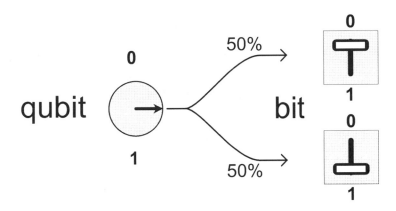

Figure 5-1. *A single qubit, prepared in a superposition state, collapses to zero or one with a 50–50% chance*

I will provide this exercise in three variations. Because the program is simple enough, the first variation will only use Q# and will run as a standalone console application. The second variation will use a host application, written in the popular .NET language C#. A host application gives you more flexibility to work with the quantum part of your application. The third and last variation will exchange C# for Python when writing the host application.

Note   The exercises in this chapter will generate a truly random bit or number if they were to be run on an actual quantum computer. Because you don't have a quantum computer in your immediate vicinity, you are running Q# on your classical computer using a simulator provided by the Quantum Development Kit. Putting a qubit in superposition is something that is not possible on a classical computer, so measuring the result from a simulated superposed qubit will just use a pseudo-random number generator.

Only Q#

Open Visual Studio Code, and enter command-mode by pressing the following keyboard shortcut:

$$\boxed{\texttt{Ctrl}} + \boxed{\texttt{Shift}} + \boxed{\texttt{P}}$$

Find the command "Q#: Create new project...", execute it, and choose the option "Standalone console application." Visual Studio Code will now ask you to select a location to create and store your project and source files. Choose a destination path, and type a name for your project in the filename box. For this exercise, you can choose the name "05-01" to mark it the first exercise of the fifth chapter. Finish the template wizard by clicking the "Create Project" button.

Visual Studio Code will create the project and will show you a pop-up in the lower-right corner of your screen prompting you to open that new project. Click the "Open new project..." button to perform this action.

A Q# project is just like any other Microsoft .NET project and will contain your source files, accompanied by a project file. The project file, which is automatically generated by the .NET software development kit or SDK, contains the XML code from Listing 5-1 and should not be edited by you right now.

Listing 5-1. The contents of the generated project file which you should not edit

```
01 <Project Sdk="Microsoft.Quantum.Sdk/0.21.2111177148">
02   <PropertyGroup>
03     <OutputType>Exe</OutputType>
04     <TargetFramework>netcoreapp3.1</TargetFramework>
05   </PropertyGroup>
06 </Project>
```

The project file contains the following important information:

- On line 01, the .NET SDK that should be used to compile this project. In this case, a specific version of the Microsoft Quantum SDK is used.

- On line 03, the output type that should be used to compile this project. In this case, a Windows executable will be produced.

- On line 04, the target framework and runtime that should be used to run the compiled application. In this case, the .NET Core 3.1 framework will be targeted.

Next to the project file, a single Q# source file is created called "Program.qs". This source file contains the minimum Q# source code that is required to make your program execute and should look like Listing 5-2.

Listing 5-2. The contents of the generated "Program.qs" file

```
01 namespace _05_01
02 {
03   open Microsoft.Quantum.Canon;
04   open Microsoft.Quantum.Intrinsic;
05
06   @EntryPoint()
07   operation HelloQ() : Unit
08   {
09     Message("Hello quantum world!");
10   }
11 }
```

Just like many other programming languages, Q# uses curly braces to define scope. The topmost scope within this generated Q# is called a namespace and is a concept from .NET. The .NET base class library is organized using a collection of namespaces, just like you would organize the files on your hard disk using folders and subfolders. For namespaces, different sub namespaces are delimited with dots instead of the slashes that go with a directory structure. In order to be able to use predefined types and functions, you will need to include the necessary namespaces by opening them, just like on lines 03 and 04 of Listing 5-2.

Within the namespace scope, on line 07, there is an operation called HelloQ. This operation is a function that can be executed. The HelloQ operation is decorated with the @EntryPoint() attribute and will, therefore, be executed automatically when your compiled application is started. The HelloQ operation defines its own scope and uses a built-in function Message to print a user-friendly message to the console.

You should be able to run this Q# application by opening the Terminal within Visual Studio Code and typing the command dotnet run. Make sure the terminal is pointing to the directory that contains your source files and project file, which it should by default.

```
$> dotnet run
```

The terminal will show the message "Hello quantum world" and will then exit your Q# application automatically, returning you to its prompt.

Your next step will be to change the automatically generated Q# code and generate a random bit. Go ahead and open the "Program.qs" file in the Visual Studio Code editor if you have not already done so, and make the necessary changes. Your result should resemble Listing 5-3.

Listing 5-3. The modified version of "Program.qs", which will generate a random bit

```
01 namespace _05_01
02 {
03    open Microsoft.Quantum.Canon;
04    open Microsoft.Quantum.Intrinsic;
05
06    @EntryPoint()
07    operation HelloQ() : Unit
08    {
09      Message("Hello quantum world!");
10
11      use qubit = Qubit();
12
13      H(qubit);
14
15      let measuredResult = M(qubit);
16
17      if( measuredResult == Zero )
18      {
19        Message("0");
20      }
```

```
21    else
22    {
23      Message("1");
24    }
25  }
26 }
```

On line 11 of Listing 5-3, a single qubit will be allocated. This qubit will be your base for generating a random bit. Thanks to the H operation, which corresponds with the Hadamard gate on line 13, the qubit will be put in superposition. If you measure a result from this qubit using the M operation on line 15, you can store that result in an immutable variable called measuredResult. If that measured result equals Zero, the user-friendly message 0 is printed to the console on line 19. In any other case, decided by the else statement on line 21, the measured result equals One and the user-friendly message 1 is printed to the console on line 23.

Just like before, you can use the built-in Visual Studio Code terminal to execute your application and be excited to witness your first quantum program.

$› dotnet run

You should see the same message "Hello quantum world!" followed by the number one or zero. You will get the value zero or one at random with an equal chance. So run the application multiple times by executing the same command repeatedly. Sometimes, you will see the number zero; sometimes, you will see the number one.

Figure 5-2 shows you the graphical Bloch sphere representation of the three-step process for the quantum program you just wrote. Your qubit starts in its neutral $|0\rangle$ state on the left-hand side picture. Applying the Hadamard operation rotates your qubit to the $|+\rangle$ superposition state in the center picture. Finally, measuring your qubit using the Measure operation collapses your qubit state with an equal chance toward the $|0\rangle$ or $|1\rangle$ state on the right-hand side picture.

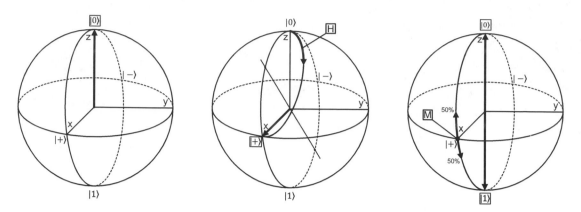

Figure 5-2. *The three-step process of putting a qubit in superposition and measuring it*

Congratulations! You just wrote your first quantum program.

Q# with a C# Host

Q# contains a rich base to create a large range of quantum algorithms, including quantum operators, mathematical functions, and very specific scientific libraries. For creating full-blown applications, Q# will probably fall a bit short because it is purely focussed on quantum and maths.

Writing a real-life application that uses quantum will most likely be a combination of a classical piece of software and one or more quantum algorithms. When learning Q#, you can always use any .NET programming language as a host and call into your quantum algorithm which uses Q#. Possible .NET languages are C#, Visual Basic .NET or F#. In the following exercise, you are going to rewrite the Q# application from before and print the result to the console from C# and not Q#.

Again, open Visual Studio Code and enter command-mode by pressing the following keyboard shortcut:

`Ctrl` + `Shift` + `P`

Find the command "Q#: Create new project...", execute it, and choose the option "Quantum library." Visual Studio Code will again ask you to select a location to create and store your project files. Because you'll end up with two separate projects, a quantum library and a C# host, you'll need to create an extra directory that will contain those two projects. Create a directory named "05-02", and within that directory, type the project name "05-02-Quantum" in the filename box. Finish the template wizard by clicking the "Create Project" button.

The project will be created by Visual Studio Code, and you can click the "Open new project..." button to actually open it.

Copy or replicate the code from Listing 5-4 into the "Library.qs" source file. You probably notice that it is very much like the previous exercise. Only now, it will not use the Message operation to print a result to the console. The operation GenerateRandomBit on line 6 of Listing 5-4 will be called from our yet-to-be-created host application and will return a Boolean value True or False. On line 14, the measuredBit variable is compared with the possible value One to convert its value to a Boolean.

Listing 5-4. The entire contents of the source file "Library.qs"

```
01 namespace _05_02_Quantum
02 {
03   open Microsoft.Quantum.Canon;
04   open Microsoft.Quantum.Intrinsic;
05
06   operation GenerateRandomBit () : Bool
07   {
08     use qubit = Qubit();
09
10     H(qubit);
11
12     let measuredBit = M(qubit);
13
14     return measuredBit == One;
15   }
16 }
```

With that, you have the Q# part of the exercise finished. You can go ahead and continue with the creation of the C# host application. Once more, enter the command-mode of Visual Studio Code by pressing the following shortcut keys:

Ctrl + Shift + P

Find the command "dotnet new," and choose the template "Console Application." Use the same directory "05-02" from before, and create an additional subdirectory "05-02-Host" next to the "05-02-Quantum" you created before. Inside the "05-02-Host" directory, you can go ahead and finish the prompt by typing the name "05-02-Host". Visual Studio Code will create a second project containing a project file that looks very much like the one from the previous exercise and a source file called "Program.cs". Open the "Program.cs" file, and copy or replicate the code from Listing 5-5.

Listing 5-5. The entire contents of the source file "Program.cs"

```
01 using System;
02 using System.Threading.Tasks;
03 using Microsoft.Quantum.Simulation.Simulators;
04
05 namespace _05_02_Host
06 {
07   class Program
08   {
09     static async Task Main(string[] args)
10     {
11       using var simulator = new QuantumSimulator();
12       var result = await _05_02_Quantum
13             .GenerateRandomBit.Run(simulator);
14
15       Console.WriteLine(result ? "0" : "1");
16     }
17   }
18 }
```

In C#, you'll see some of the same concepts return. There is a namespace on line 05 of Listing 5-5. There are scopes, defined by curly braces. There is a class called Program on line 07, and there is a method called Main on line 09. Just like Q#, there is also the need to open, or use, several namespaces if we have the need to use functionality from them.

The Main method in a C# Console Application is always the entry-point of the application. It is the method that will be called when the application starts. Within this method, you declare a QuantumSimulator object and assign it to the simulator variable

on line 11. On lines 12 and 13, you use the simulator to run the Q# operation named
_05_02_Quantum.GenerateRandomBit. This name corresponds with the name of your Q#
operation, combined with the name of its namespace. Because the Q# operation returns
a Boolean value, you can store that value in a variable called result at the start of line 12.

Finally, on line 15, you write the value zero or one to the console based on the
Boolean value of the result variable. C# can use a specific operator for this: if whatever
comes before the question mark equals True, use the value before the colon. Otherwise,
use the value after the colon.

To test the C# host application, open the terminal inside of Visual Studio Code and
navigate to the folder "05-02-Host". Within that folder, you can execute the well-known
command:

```
$> dotnet run
```

You should see the exact same output as before but without the welcome message
this time. The application will just write the value zero or one. Run it multiple times to
see that the value randomly changes.

Q# with a Python Host

As an alternative to .NET and C#, you can use Python to write a classical host application
for calling into quantum programs using Q#. A Python application is somewhat different
from a .NET application and cannot be compiled into an executable. Python is an
interpreted language and runs using the Python interpreter which you installed in the
previous chapter. Because of this, it is a lot easier and more accessible to create a project
containing a Python host. Go ahead and create a new folder called "05-03", and create
two empty source files in that folder:

- "host.py", containing the Python code that will call into the Q# code

- "quantum.qs", containing the Q# code from Listing 5-6

For the "quantum.qs" file, you can copy the contents from the previous exercise,
or copy the contents from Listing 5-6. Since the only thing you are changing is the host
application, the Q# part of the application is exactly the same as in the previous exercise.

Listing 5-6. The entire contents of the source file "quantum.qs"

```
01 namespace _05_03_Quantum
02 {
03   open Microsoft.Quantum.Canon;
04   open Microsoft.Quantum.Intrinsic;
05
06   operation GenerateRandomBit () : Bool
07   {
08     using( qubit = Qubit() )
09     {
10      H(qubit);
11
12       let measuredBit = M(qubit);
13
14       Reset(qubit);
15
16       return measuredBit == One;
17     }
18   }
19 }
```

For the "host.py" source file, you can copy or reproduce the contents from Listing 5-7. Just like Q# and C#, Python needs to import some external dependencies. First, on line 01, you should import the **qsharp** dependency to make Python understand how to communicate with Q#. Next, on line 02, you should import the Q# operation GenerateRandomBit from the _05_03_Quantum namespace. On line 04, you can call that Q# operation by simulating it using the Python Q# simulator. Finally, on line 05, you will convert the Boolean value to an Integer value and print it to the console.

Listing 5-7. The entire contents of the source file "host.py"

```
01 import qsharp
02 from _05_03_Quantum import GenerateRandomBit
03
04 result = GenerateRandomBit.simulate()
05 print( int(result) )
```

Inside Visual Studio Code or your favorite terminal window, use the following command to run the Python host application:

```
$> py host.py
```

Before outputting the actual random bit value, you will see the message "Preparing Q# environment...", which will take some time.

That's it. You have now created three variations of a quantum program that generate a single random bit thanks to quantum superposition.

Generating a Random Number

Generating a random bit is not a very exciting exercise. Because of that, I would like to improve the quantum algorithm and generate a bunch of random bits that together make up a larger integer. An integer is a number in base-10 that can be represented by a computer using the base-2 or binary system. The number 5 in base-10 equals the number 101 in binary. Because we can represent numbers using binary, we can use a qubit to randomly generate each bit in the binary representation in a loop. Q# helps us with converting from base-2 to base-10, so generating a random number should be easy. In Figure 5-3, you can see a graphical representation of what you will try to achieve. Three qubits, prepared in superposition, will collapse to all possible variations of three bits with an equal chance, equal to 100% divided by eight variations.

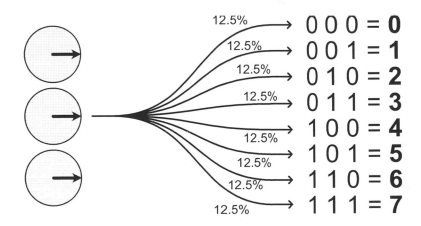

Figure 5-3. *Three qubits, prepared in a superposition state, will collapse to every three-bit combination with an equal chance of 12.5%*

Only Q#

For this exercise, I would like to ask the user for a number. This number will be the upper bound for the random number that is generated. If the user inputs the value 10, the randomly generated number should range from zero to nine, so excluding the upper bound.

Q# is a domain-specific language for quantum-related algorithms and does not provide functions to ask for user input. Thanks to the Quantum Development Kit and its support for host applications in .NET or Python, you can ask the user for input from the host application and forward that input to your Q# operation.

For starters, you will hardcode a number that will determine the upper bound and you will not create a host application just yet. Go ahead and use Visual Studio Code to create a Q# Console Application, just like you did before. Use the code from Listing 5-8, and run the application using the terminal.

Listing 5-8. The entire contents of the source file "Program.qs"

```
01 namespace _05_04
02 {
03    open Microsoft.Quantum.Canon;
04    open Microsoft.Quantum.Convert;
05    open Microsoft.Quantum.Intrinsic;
06    open Microsoft.Quantum.Math;
07
08    @EntryPoint()
09    operation HelloQ() : Unit
10    {
11     let maximum = 10;
12
13      let bitSize = BitSizeI(maximum);
14     mutable resultArray = new Result[0];
15      mutable randomNumber = 0;
16
17      repeat
18      {
19        set resultArray = new Result[0];
20
```

```
21        for( index in 0..bitSize-1 )
22        {
23          using( qubit = Qubit() )
24          {
25            H(qubit);
26            set resultArray += [M(qubit)];
27            Reset(qubit);
28          }
29        }
30
31        set randomNumber = ResultArrayAsInt(resultArray);
32      }
33      until(randomNumber < maximum);
34
35      Message($"{randomNumber}");
36    }
37 }
```

Line 11 contains the hardcoded upper bound. Use whatever value you like for testing, and try to run the application multiple times to make sure all generated values are within the correct range. On line 13, you can use the built-in function BitSizeI to calculate the number of bits required to represent a given integer and store the result in an immutable variable called bitSize. On lines 14 and 15, you declare an array of Result values containing zero elements and a randomNumber variable to store the final result. On line 21, you start a loop that will execute a number of times, based on the number of bits that need to be generated. A new qubit is allocated on line 23, and it is put in superposition on line 25. On line 26, the measurement of that superposed qubit is added to the array of results, and on line 27, the qubit is reset to its default zero state. Finally, on line 31 the binary representation inside the array of results can be converted to an integer by using the built-in function ResultArrayAsInt.

On lines 17 and 33, an outer loop is used to retry the whole process if the generated integer is larger than the specified upper bound. This is necessary because the upper bound can be any number, but a binary number represented by a certain number of bits will always have a maximum that is a power of two minus one. If the generated number is larger or equal to the upper bound, the whole process should be retried.

115

Q# with a C# Host

For this exercise, you will use .NET and C# to create a host application. Now, the user can input an upper bound, and that upper bound should be sent to the Q# operation.

The code in Listing 5-9 has been changed from the code in Listing 5-8 and does not hardcode the upper bound. This value is expected as a parameter maximum, which is an integer, for the GenerateRandomNumber operation. At the end of the code, on line 32, the generated number will be returned instead of printed to the console.

Listing 5-9. The entire contents of the source file "Library.qs"

```
01  namespace _05_05_Quantum
02  {
03    open Microsoft.Quantum.Canon;
04    open Microsoft.Quantum.Convert;
05    open Microsoft.Quantum.Intrinsic;
06    open Microsoft.Quantum.Math;
07
08    operation GenerateRandomNumber( maximum: Int ) : Int
09    {
10      let bitSize = BitSizeI(maximum);
11      mutable resultArray = [Zero, size = 0];
12      mutable randomNumber = 0;
13
14    repeat
15      {
16        set resultArray = [Zero, size = 0];
17
18        for( index in 0..bitSize-1 )
19        {
20          using( qubit = Qubit() )
21          {
22            H(qubit);
23            set resultArray += [M(qubit)];
24            Reset(qubit);
```

```
25          }
26        }
27
28      set randomNumber = ResultArrayAsInt(resultArray);
29    }
30    until(randomNumber < maximum);
31
32    return randomNumber;
33  }
34 }
```

For the C# host application, the upper bound is read from the console on line 12 of Listing 5-10. On line 13, that value is converted to an integer, because input from the console is always treated as text. Just like before, on lines 15, 16, and 17, a QuantumSimulator is created to call into the GenerateRandomNumber operation. This time, the maximum value is passed as a parameter.

On line 16, the result from the GenerateRandomNumber operation is stored in a variable that can be written to the console on line 19.

Listing 5-10. The entire contents of the source file "Program.cs"

```
01 using System;
02 using System.Threading.Tasks;
03 using Microsoft.Quantum.Simulation.Simulators;
04
05 namespace _05_05_Host
06 {
07   class Program
08   {
09     static async Task Main(string[] args)
10     {
11       Console.Write("Maximum: ");
12       string input = Console.ReadLine();
13       int maximum = Convert.ToInt32(input);
14
```

```
15      using var simulator = new QuantumSimulator();
16      var result = await _05_05_Quantum
17        .GenerateRandomNumber.Run(simulator, maximum);
18
19      Console.WriteLine(result);
20    }
21  }
22 }
```

To test the C# host application, open the terminal, navigate to the folder "05-05-Host", and execute the well-known command:

```
$> dotnet run
```

The terminal will prompt you to input a number to use as the upper bound. Provide a value, and press the enter key. The application will now allocate a qubit, put it in superposition, and generate a random bit. This will be repeated for each bit that is needed to generate the random integer. If the resulting random number exceeds the upper bound, the whole process is repeated.

Q# with a Python host

For the last exercise and variation of this chapter, you are using Python for the host application. Listing 5-11 contains the Q# code for the quantum part of the application and is an exact copy of Listing 5-9 from the previous exercise.

Listing 5-11. The entire contents of the source file "quantum.qs"

```
01 namespace _05_06_Quantum
02 {
03   open Microsoft.Quantum.Canon;
04   open Microsoft.Quantum.Convert;
05   open Microsoft.Quantum.Intrinsic;
06   open Microsoft.Quantum.Math;
07
```

```
08    operation GenerateRandomNumber( maximum: Int ) : Int
09    {
10      let bitSize = BitSizeI(maximum);
11      mutable resultArray = new Result[0];
12      mutable randomNumber = 0;
13
14      repeat
15      {
16        set resultArray = new Result[0];
17
18        for( index in 0..bitSize-1 )
19        {
20          using( qubit = Qubit() )
21          {
22            H(qubit);
23            set resultArray += [M(qubit)];
24            Reset(qubit);
25          }
26        }
27
28        set randomNumber = ResultArrayAsInt(resultArray);
29      }
30      until(randomNumber < maximum);
31
32      return randomNumber;
33    }
34 }
```

Listing 5-12 contains the necessary Python code to ask the user for input and send that input to the quantum operation. On line 04, the function input gets the upper bound value from the console. On line 05, the upper bound value is sent as an input for the GenerateRandomNumber operation. Because Python is a dynamic language, you don't need to convert the text from the console to an integer. The Python interpreter is smart enough to do that for you automatically.

Listing 5-12. The entire contents of the source file "host.py"

```
01 import qsharp
02 from _05_06_Quantum import GenerateRandomNumber
03
04 max = input( 'Maximum: ')
05 result = GenerateRandomNumber.simulate( maximum = max )
06 print( result )
```

Once more, you should use the terminal and execute the following command to run the Python host application:

```
$> py host.py
```

If everything works out, you will need to enter a number, press the Enter key, and the application should show you a random number ranging from zero to the number you have entered. Don't forget to run the application multiple times to see the generated number change with every run.

Congratulations! You have finished six exercises which showed you the very basics of the Microsoft Quantum Development Kit, Q#, C#, and Python.

The Last Word

In the previous chapter, you installed all necessary tools. In this chapter, you immediately started with the Q# programming language, and you wrote your first quantum applications. You learned how to use Q# by itself, as a self-contained console application, how to use Q# hosted with a .NET programming language like C#, and how to use Q# with a more dynamic programming language like Python.

You delved into creating Q# operations, the allocation of qubits, and putting qubits through the Hadamard quantum gate to put them into superposition. You finished this chapter by extending your first quantum application, you used some built-in Q# functions for getting the number of required bits to represent an integer, and you used loops that execute a piece of code multiple times.

In the next chapter, you will encounter a lot more details about the specifics of the Q# programming language and its available types and functions. You will also dive deeper into the world of quantum computing by working on some more exercises.

## CHAPTER 6

Q# Language Overview and the Quantum Simulator

The Q# language, pronounced as q-sharp, is part of Microsoft's QDK, or Quantum Development Kit, which also provides tools and IDE or Integrated Development Environment support. The goal of the Q# quantum programming language is not only to support early learnings on quantum computing and quantum hardware but also to support development of future large-scale applications.

The Q# language, and its underlying type-system, gives you the power to combine classical computations and quantum computations within the same program. A Q# program can perform classical computations based on the results of quantum measurements. It is possible that not all current hardware implementations support these features, but thanks to the QDK, you as a developer can specify an explicit target machine, and the tools will notify you to what is possible and what is not.

Much like many other classical programming languages, Q# allows you to write programs using statements and expressions. In this chapter, you will get an overview of many Q# language features and how to use them.

Q# Project Structure

Most programming languages and their corresponding SDKs help you to structure your development experience by allowing you to create multiple text-based files containing code and configuration. Those files will eventually be compiled into a binary executable file.

121

© Johnny Hooyberghs 2022
J. Hooyberghs, *Introducing Microsoft Quantum Computing for Developers*,
https://doi.org/10.1007/978-1-4842-7246-6_6

Q# works very similar to other Microsoft .NET platform programming languages like Visual Basic .NET and C#. Your project will be located inside a directory on your file system; it will contain a project configuration file and one or multiple source code files.

The most basic Q# project will contain a minimum of two files: A `*.csproj` file and a `*.qs` file. The `*.csproj` file contains the configuration information to compile your project into an executable program. Listing 6-1 shows you the contents of such a project file.

Listing 6-1. *A* `*.csproj` *file containing Q# project configuration*

```
01 <Project Sdk="Microsoft.Quantum.Sdk/0.18.2106148911">
02   <PropertyGroup>
03     <OutputType>Exe</OutputType>
04     <TargetFramework>netcoreapp3.1</TargetFramework>
05     <ExecutionTarget>ionq.qpu</ExecutionTarget>
06   </PropertyGroup>
07 </Project>
```

A Q# project file is basically a .NET project file, and it uses the XML-format to encode its configuration data. Line 1 from Listing 6-1 tells the compiler which version of the Q# SDK, or QDK, it needs to use to compile your entire project. Lines 3 and 4 configure the binary output format that is supported to simulate your application on a classical computer. The only supported use-case today is to create an executable on the .NET Core 3.1 platform. Optionally, line 5 instructs the compiler to also target the physical quantum processing unit (QPU) from a company called IonQ. Depending on the physical hardware you are targeting, not all Q# language features will be available. The compiler will help you by throwing errors to let you know that some of your constructs will not be executed on your hardware target.

Note   Targeting physical quantum hardware is relatively new to Q# at the time of writing and works through Microsoft's cloud offering Azure Quantum. Chapter 11 will touch on Azure Quantum briefly. Because Azure Quantum is currently still in public preview and functionality changes quite often, it will not be the focus of this book.

Next to the project file, one, or multiple files, organized into folders, can be part of your project. For Q# specifically, these files will always have a `*.qs` extension which is shorthand for q-sharp.

Q# Application Structure

For most of its functionality and features, Q# is very similar to many programming languages. Q# uses files and, in addition to that, namespaces to organize and categorize your code. Code is based on syntax and grammar using literals, statements, and expressions. There is support for immutable and mutable variables, types, custom types, callables, loops, conditional branching, and more.

Comments

You can add comments anywhere in your source code. Comments are used to help readers to understand the full context and meaning of your code. Sometimes, the Q# language can look a bit abstract. In this case, comments can provide helpful insight into a line of code.

Comments always start with two forward slashes and continue until the end of the line. If you are using the Visual Studio Code or Microsoft Visual Studio IDE, comments will be colored green by default. Listing 6-2 shows you an operation that puts a qubit in superposition and adds some comments to that operation.

Listing 6-2. The HelloQuantum operation containing comments

```
01 operation HelloQuantum() : Result
02 {
03   // Allocate a single qubit and assign it
04   // to the immutable variable 'qubit'.
05   use qubit = Qubit();
06
07   // Apply the Hadamard transformation to that qubit.
08   H(qubit);
09
10   // Perform a measurement of the qubit in the Pauli-Z
11   // basis and return the result of that measurement.
12   return M(qubit);
13 }
```

Additionally, comments can also be formatted using Markdown for documentation purposes. This is often used to document callables like operations and functions. Documentation comments can be added by using three forward slashes instead of just two. Listing 6-3 shows the same HelloQuantum operation from Listing 6-2, but this time, it contains documentation comments.

Listing 6-3. The HelloQuantum operation containing documentation comments

```
01 /// # Summary
02 /// Puts a qubit in superposition and measures its
03 /// state to return as a result from this operation.
04 ///
05 /// # Output
06 /// A result, Zero or One, after qubit measurement.
07 ///
08 /// # See Also
09 /// - Microsoft.Quantum.Intrinsic.H
10 operation HelloQuantum() : Result
11 {
..  //...
..  }
```

Documentation comments above operations and functions can be extracted by a tool to generate documentation files, but they can also be used by IDEs like Visual Studio Code or Microsoft Visual Studio. Figure 6-1 shows you what happens if you hover your mouse over a call to an operation or function that has documentation comments.

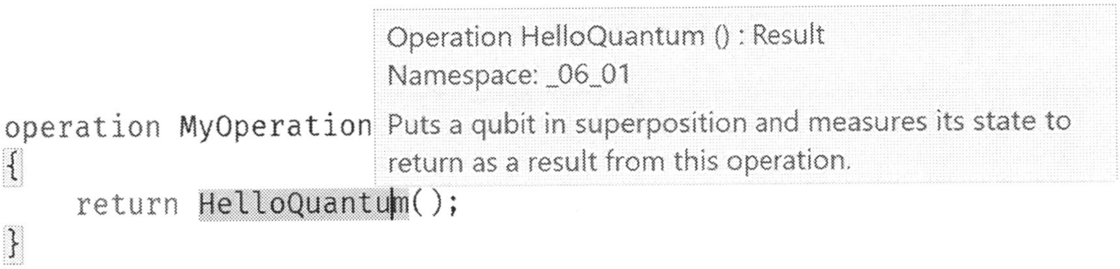

```
                          Operation HelloQuantum () : Result
                          Namespace: _06_01
operation MyOperation     Puts a qubit in superposition and measures its state to
{                         return as a result from this operation.
    return HelloQuantum();
}
```

Figure 6-1. *Pop-up in Visual Studio Code with documentation comments on a call to an operation*

Namespaces

At the uppermost hierarchical level, Q# supports namespaces. Except for comments, nothing else can live outside of a namespace. Namespaces are used to structure your code and are typically, but not obligatorily, related to a directory structure that contains your source code files.

A namespace block is built using the namespace keyword, followed by the fully qualified name of the namespace and the namespace contents within a block delimited by curly braces:

```
namespace My.Quantum.Examples
{
    // ...
}
```

Namespace names consist of a sequence of names, separated by a dot, and can only use letters, numbers, and underscores. Namespace names cannot start with a number, but they can contain numbers anywhere else. Namespaces cannot be nested, but you can create the sense of hierarchy by creating multiple namespaces that share a part of their fully qualified name.

```
namespace My.Quantum
{
    // ...
}
```

```
namespace My.Quantum.Examples
{
    // ...
}
```

You are not limited to use one namespace for one source code file. You can use as many namespaces within a single file as you need. Namespaces can also span multiple source code files if you declare the same namespace in multiple files. Typically, you want to create a hierarchy to organize your source code and have one file per namespace, or maybe multiple files that share the same namespace if the number of operations or functions within a namespace grows large.

You can use operations and functions from within the same namespace automatically, even if they are spread among multiple source code files. If you need to use operations and functions that are declared in another namespace, you need to use the fully qualified namespace name or open the namespace beforehand. Listing 6-4 shows you these two approaches on lines 8, 12, and 13.

Listing 6-4. Multiple namespaces and callables

```
01 namespace My.Quantum
02 {
03   operation Foo() : Unit { }
04 }
05
06 namespace My.Quantum.Examples
07 {
08   open My.Quantum;
09
10   operation Bar() : Unit
11   {
12     My.Quantum.Foo();
13     Foo();
14   }
15 }
```

Line 12 from Listing 6-4 uses the fully qualified name for the Foo operation and includes its namespace. Line 13 omits the namespace because it was opened on line 8 beforehand.

To improve readability, you can create aliases for your namespaces. This may also be helpful if you want to avoid conflicts if you use multiple operations that share the same name but exist in different namespaces. Listing 6-5 shows you an alias to the My.Quantum namespace on line 8 and how to use it on line 12.

Listing 6-5. Creating namespace aliases and using them

```
01 namespace My.Quantum
02 {
03   operation Foo() : Unit { }
04 }
05
06 namespace My.Quantum.Examples
07 {
08   open My.Quantum as My;
09
10   operation Bar() : Unit
11   {
12     My.Foo();
13   }
14 }
```

Namespaces, or namespace aliases, can also help you to discover operations and functions thanks to IDEs like Visual Studio Code and Microsoft Visual Studio. These IDEs support a code completion feature when you add a dot in the end of a namespace or alias and will provide you with a list of all possible operations and functions from that namespace. Figure 6-2 shows you what this looks like in Visual Studio Code.

```
open Microsoft.Quantum.Intrinsic as Q;
```

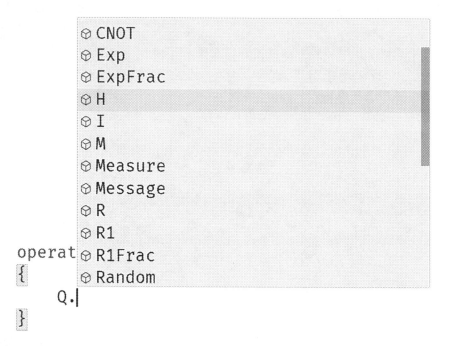

Figure 6-2. *Code completion when using namespaces or namespace aliases*

Variable Declarations and Assignments

Variables can be declared by a unique name using the let and mutable statements. Additionally, the set statement allows you to change the value of a mutable variable. Listing 6-6 shows you these three statements in action.

Listing 6-6. The let, mutable, and set statements in action

```
01 let text = "Hello";
02 mutable number = 4;
03 set number = 7;
```

Line 1 shows you how to declare a variable text and immediately assign it the value "Hello". The variable text is immutable and cannot be changed after its initial assignment. Line 2 shows you how to declare a mutable variable number and assign it the value 4. On line 3, you can see that the set statement is able to change the value of mutable variables.

Scopes

Q# uses statement blocks, and just like other programming languages like C#, Java, or C++, these blocks are delimited by curly braces.

```
function CalculateSum(x: Int, y: Int) : Int
{
    return x + y;
}
```

Variables declared in outer blocks are visible and defined in inner blocks and can only be bound once per block. Variables declared in inner blocks are not defined in the outer blocks. Listing 6-7 shows you some correct uses of blocks and scope.

Listing 6-7. Correct use of variables and scopes

```
01 operation First() : Unit
02 {
03    let (x, y) = (1, 2);
04
05    if (x == y)
06    {
07       let n = 4;
08       // n is 4
09    }
10
11    let n = 9;
12    // n is 9
13 }
14
15 operation Second() : Unit
16 {
17    let (x, y) = (1, 2);
18
```

```
19   if (x == y)
20   {
21     let n = 4;
22     // n is 4
23   }
24   else
25   {
26     let n = 9;
27     // n is 9
28   }
29
30   // n does not exist
31 }
```

The variables x and y, declared and assigned on lines 3 and 17, are only valid within their scope, which is the body of the outer operations First and Second. The variable n, declared and assigned on line 7, goes out of scope at line 9 and can be declared and assigned again on line 11. The variable n, declared and assigned on lines 21 and 26, is only valid within its scope and does not exist from line 29 onward.

Listing 6-8 shows you some invalid uses where variable declarations conflict with others within the same scope.

Listing 6-8. Incorrect use of variables and scopes

```
01 operation First() : Unit
02 {
03    let n = 1;
04
05    let n = 2; // compile error
06 }
07
08 operation Second() : Unit
09 {
10    let (x, y) = (1, 2);
11    let n = 1;
12
```

```
13    if (x == y)
14    {
15        let n = 2; // compile error
16    }
17 }
```

Declaring the variables n on lines 5 and 15 will cause compile-time errors. The variable n on line 5 cannot be declared because it is already declared in the same scope on line 3. The variable n on line 15 cannot be declared because it is already declared in the outer scope on line 11.

Quantum Data Types

Most programming languages know the concept of variables and data types to store information. Since Q# allows you to combine both quantum and classical programming concepts, there are also data types related to quantum processing and classical processing. The most important, and effectively only, quantum data type is the qubit, or Qubit as it is defined in Q#.

Qubit

The qubit data type treats qubits as opaque items that can be passed around and can only be interacted with by passing them to instructions that are native to quantum processors. Physical quantum hardware needs to represent these qubits internally by physical carriers, and intrinsic quantum instructions need to be implemented on a hardware level and should modify the quantum state stored by the qubit.

The Microsoft.Quantum.Intrinsics namespace contains many intrinsic quantum instructions that do not have a defined implementation within the language. If the Q# compiler targets a physical quantum QPU, those operations need to be translated to native instructions within that QPU. Thanks to namespaces and operations, you as a developer can create higher-level operations to express quantum computations by using the underlying quantum intrinsic instructions.

In a simulated environment, by running your program using the .NET platform on your local machine for example, the Qubit data type is implemented by storing all the mathematical information about the quantum state. Intrinsic quantum operations are implemented by performing transformations on that quantum state. This is the reason that simulating quantum programs on classical hardware in a simulated environment becomes difficult if you need many qubits. The classical information that needs to be stored for a combined quantum state grows exponentially for every additional qubit you add to that combined state.

Quantum Memory Management

Since Qubit is a quantum data type and relies heavily on hardware implementation, it needs to be allocated explicitly using the Qubit statement. There are different approaches to do this. Qubits can be allocated as individual qubits, or as arrays of qubits, or as a combination of both.

The following is an example of allocating a single qubit and assigning it to the variable q:

```
use q = Qubit();
```

Allocating multiple qubits and assigning them to individual variables q1 and q2 can be achieved by using the tuple syntax:

```
use (q1, q2) = (Qubit(), Qubit());
```

Allocating an array of qubits can be achieved by using the array syntax:

```
use register = Qubit[5];
```

Using the tuple syntax, you can allocate a combination of single qubits and arrays of qubits:

```
use (temp, register) = (Qubit(), Qubit[5]);
```

You probably noticed the use keyword when you allocate and assign qubits. This keyword makes sure that the allocated and assigned qubits are only available in the current block. The use keyword can be used with an optional statement block to fine-tune the availability scope of your qubits.

If you are familiar with the C# language, it uses the same concept with the using keyword that automatically disposes the object if it goes out of scope.

```
use q = Qubit()
{
    // ...
}
```

Qubits that are allocated via the use statement are guaranteed to be in a $|0\rangle$ state. When the assigned qubit variable goes out of scope at the end of the current block, it is automatically released and requires to be reset to the $|0\rangle$ state or to have been measured beforehand. This requirement is not enforced by the compiler but can throw a runtime error or lead to incorrect behavior when you forget.

On physical quantum hardware, allocating qubits is very costly since qubits are difficult to create and maintain. The use statement allocates qubits from the quantum processor's free qubit heap and returns them to the heap if they are released.

If you need temporary qubits and they do not need to be in a specific state, you can use the borrow statement and corresponding borrow keyword:

```
borrow q = Qubit();
borrow (q1, q2) = (Qubit(), Qubit());
borrow register = Qubit[5];
borrow (temp, register) = (Qubit(), Qubit[5]);
```

Just like the use statement, the borrow statement can also use the optional statement block to fine-tune its scope:

```
borrow q = Qubit()
{
    // ...
}
```

Some quantum algorithms can use qubits without relying on their exact state. This can help quantum computers to temporarily reuse already allocated qubits and thus help to minimize the total number of necessary qubits.

If you borrow qubits, the quantum runtime will make sure to provide you with qubits that are guaranteed to not be used from the moment you borrow them until your last usage. At that moment in time, you are required, and you need to make sure that you revert their state back to its state from when you first borrowed them.

If there are not enough unused qubits available, the borrow statement will allocate new qubits from the heap and release them back to the heap, just like the use statement.

Result Literals

The Result data type specifies the result of a quantum measurement. It is a classical data type, but it is closely related to the Qubit because you get it after quantum measurement. Its possible values are represented by the two literals Zero and One.

Listing 6-9 shows you how to use the Zero and One literals in comparison expressions on lines 6 and 11.

Listing 6-9. Creating namespace aliases and using them

```
01 use q = Qubit();
02 H(q);
03 mutable message = "";
04 let result = M(q);
05
06 if (result == Zero)
07 {
08     set message = "|0⟩";
09 }
10
11 if (result == One)
12 {
13     set message = "|1⟩";
14 }
```

Pauli Literals

The default M operation from the Microsoft.Quantum.Intrinsic namespace performs a measurement of a single qubit in the Pauli Z basis for |0⟩ and |1⟩ outcomes.

You can specify another Pauli basis for measurement if you use the Measure operation from the same Microsoft.Quantum.Intrinsic namespace. The Measure operation takes an additional argument where you can specify the Pauli I, Pauli X, Pauli Y, or Pauli Z basis.

Listing 6-10 shows you how to measure a qubit using a custom Pauli basis.

Listing 6-10. Meauring a qubit using a custom Pauli basis

```
use qubit = Qubit();
let result = Measure([PauliX], [qubit]);
```

The square brackets in Listing 6-10 are used to describe arrays. Arrays will be handled a little further down this chapter, but for now, it is good to know that the Measure operation takes an array of Pauli literals and an array of qubits. If you only want to pass a single item, you can use the square brackets to create a new array on the fly with only a single element.

Types

The current type-system in Q# is relatively basic. There are no object-oriented concepts like classes or interfaces, and all types are immutable value types. Because of this, there are no pointers or references.

The list of supported types is very comprehensive:

- **Unit**: A singleton type with value ()

- **Int**: A 64-bit signed integer ranging from -9,223,372,036,854,775,808 to 9,223,372,036,854,775,807

- **BigInt**: A signed integer of any size

- **Double**: A double precision 64-bit floating-point number ranging from -1.79769313486232e308 to 1.79769313486232e308 as well as NaN (not a number)

- **Bool**: Boolean values true and false

- **String**: Text encoded using UTF-16

Arrays

An array is a sequence of one or more values, separated by commas and enclosed in square brackets. All values in an array must have a common base type which will be the type of the array.

Listing 6-11 shows you different kinds of arrays and how to use them.

Listing 6-11. Different kinds of arrays and how to use them

```
01 use qubits = Qubit[10];
02 let q = qubits[0];
03 mutable numbers = new Result[10];
04
```

```
05 for index in 0..Length(qubits)
06 {
07   set numbers w/= index <- M(qubits[index]);
08 }
```

Line 1 from Listing 6-11 declares and assigns an array of ten qubits. Line 2 assigns the first element from that array, at index zero, to the immutable variable q. Line 3 declares and assigns an array of ten Result values. Lines 5 through 8 iterate through the array of qubits by using an index and sets the result in the array of results for each qubit measurement. If you are mystified by the w/= operator, please hold on. It will be discussed further down this chapter.

Ranges

Arrays not only have support for indexes when accessing items, but they also have support for ranges. Ranges are expressions that describe a range of indices and are written in the form of start..step..stop where start, step, and stop are expressions of type Int. The step expression in a range is optional. If it is omitted, the default step is one. If start and stop can be inferred by the compiler, they can be replaced with a single dot, and they will be replaced with the default values for the array that you use them on.

You can use ranges to slice arrays. Listing 6-12 shows you a few examples of ranges.

Listing 6-12. Example ranges to slice arrays

```
let array = [10, 20, 30, 40, 50];

let slice1 = array[0..4]; // [10, 20, 30, 40, 50]
let slice2 = array[0..2..4]; // [10, 30, 50]
let slice3 = array[...2...]; // [10, 30, 50]
let slice4 = array[...-1...]; // [50, 40, 30, 20, 10]
let slice5 = array[...-2...]; // [50, 30, 10]
```

User-Defined Types

Q# supports user-defined types by combining multiple named or anonymous items based on existing data types or other user-defined types.

User-defined types can only be declared directly in a namespace and not within an operation or function. User-defined types can be used within the same namespace or in other namespaces by using the fully qualified name or by opening the correct namespace beforehand.

A simple user-defined type for complex numbers could look something like

```
newtype Complex = (Real: Double, Imaginary: Double);
```

You can think of the `Complex` user-defined type as a data type that can store a complex number with a `Real` inner-item and an `Imaginary` inner-item that are both of type `Double`.

The `newtype` keyword is used to define a user-defined type by providing a name and assigning a tuple of inner items. Values can be assigned by using constructors which are automatically generated by the compiler and need the inner items in the same order as defined by the `newtype` keyword.

```
let c = Complex(2.0, 3.0);
```

Note   Custom user-defined constructors, which are supported in other classical programming languages like C#, are not supported right now.

The inner items of user-defined types can be anonymous and have no name. User-defined types can also contain a combination of named and anonymous items.

```
newtype TupleOfFour = (Int, Int, Int, Int);
newtype Combination = (A: Int, B: Int, Bool);
```

User-defined types can also contain nested inner items by defining the inner items using nested tuples.

```
newtype Nested = (A: Int, (B: Bool, Text: String));
```

Assigning values for nested user-defined types can be achieved by using the automatically generated constructor and providing the same tuple-style arguments.

```
let n = Nested(6, (true, "Hello"));
```

Inner items for user-defined types can be accessed by deconstructing the entire type using the unwrap operator ! or by accessing named inner items directly using the item access operator ::.

```
let c = Complex(2.0, 3.0);
let (real, imaginary) = c!;
// or
let imaginary = c::Imaginary;

let n = Nested(6, (true, "Hello"));
let (number, (boolean, text)) = n!;
// or
let text = n::Text;
```

While deconstructing user-defined types, inner items can be ignored by using the discard operator _ inside the target tuple.

```
let n = Nested(6, (true, "Hello"));
let (number, (boolean, _)) = n!;
```

The concept of user-defined types can also help you to leverage the static type-system in Q# to make your quantum programs more readable and decrease the chance of making errors when using high-level operations and functions. For example, The Q# language library contains user-defined types like BigEndian and LittleEndian that are used in the quantum arithmetic library:

```
newtype BigEndian = Qubit[];
newtype LittleEndian = Qubit[];
```

Both BigEndian and LittleEndian only have a single anonymous inner item which is an array of qubits, and they are basically the same user-defined type with another name. Because both exist, they can be used as input and output types for operations and functions and, therefore, provide a meaningful description of what is expected without the need for extra documentation. The type-system forces you to only be able to use BigEndian or LittleEndian values.

Operators

Expressions in Q# can be built using operators. The following sections teach you about some of the popular operators and how to use them in expressions and statements.

Copy-and-Update Expressions

Copy-and-update expressions are supported for value types with item access. User-defined types and arrays fall into this category. User-defined types allow access to items via name, and arrays allow access to items via index or ranges.

A copy-and-update expression instantiates a new value of which all items are set from the values of the original expression, except for certain specified items, which are set to the values defined on the right-hand side of the expression. These new values are constructed using the ternary w/ <- operator. The w/ syntax resembles the commonly used short notation for "with."

If you are familiar with the C# language, it has something similar using the with keyword to copy records and mutate them.

Listing 6-13 shows you how to set an item of an array using its index and setting an item of a user-defined type using its name.

Listing 6-13. Setting the item of an array using its index and the item.of a user-defined type using its name

```
mutable array = new String[3];
set array w/= 0 <- "Hello";
set array w/= 1 <- "Quantum";
set array w/= 2 <- "World";

mutable complex = ComplexNumber(1.0, 2.0);
set complex w/= Imaginary <- 3.0;
```

The statements from Listing 6-13 that use the w/= operator are nothing but a shorthand for the more verbose syntax:

```
set complex = complex w/ Imaginary <- 3.0;
```

The copy-and-update operator allows for easy chaining of copy-and-update expressions. Listing 6-14 shows you how to chain copy-and-update expressions to set more than one item using a single statement.

Listing 6-14. Chaining copy-and-update expressions to set multiple items at once

```
let array = new String[3]
    w/ 0 <- "Hello"
    w/ 1 <- "Hello"
    w/ 2 <- "Hello";

let complex = Default<ComplexNumber>()
    w/ Real <- 1.0
    w/ Imaginary <- 2.0;
```

The variables `array` and `complex` from Listing 6-14 are declared as immutable variables because they are performing an in-place modification using the copy-and-update expression.

Tip   The `Microsoft.Quantum.Arrays` namespace provides many convenient functions for array creation and manipulations.

Comparative Expressions

Q# supports equality comparison using the == operator and inequality comparison using the != operator. These operators are limited to the `Int`, `BigInt`, `Double`, `String`, `Bool`, `Result`, `Pauli`, and `Qubit` data types.

Additionally, Q# has support for quantitative comparison using the less-than <, less-than-or-equal <=, greater-than >, and greater-than-or-equal >= operators. These operators can only be used with operands of type `Int`, `BigInt`, and `Double`.

Comparative and quantitative comparison operators always evaluate to a Boolean result.

Listing 6-15 shows you some comparative expressions.

Listing 6-15. Several comparative expressions

```
let (x, y) = (5, 6);
let bool1 = x == y;
let bool2 = x != y;
let bool3 = x <= y;
let bool4 = bool1 == bool2 == bool3;
```

Note   There is currently no support for equality comparison for arrays, tuples, ranges, user-defined types, or callables.

Logical Expressions

Q# uses the Bool type to define Boolean logic values. Logical operators are expressed as predefined keywords like and, or, and not. As it is common in most programming languages, evaluation of and expressions will not evaluate the second expression if the first expression evaluates to false, and evaluation of or expressions will not evaluate the second expression if the first expression evaluates to true.

Listing 6-16 shows you a few trivial logical expressions where you can combine logical keywords with Boolean literals, logical keywords with comparative operators and Int literals, and logical keywords with functions or operations and variables.

Listing 6-16. Several logical expressions

```
let result1 = true and false;
let result2 = 5 == 5 or 6 < 7;
let result3 = Callable1() and Callable2();
let result = result1 and result2 and result3;
```

Note   There is currently no operator for the logical XOR operation.

Conditional Expressions

Q# has support for a conditional expression that consist of three sub-expressions, where the leftmost expression is of type Bool and determines if the second or third sub-expression is evaluated. The first, leftmost, sub-expression is separated from the second and third sub-expressions with the ? operator, and the second sub-expression is separated from the third sub-expression with the | operator.

Listing 6-17 shows you an example of a conditional expression.

Listing 6-17. The conditional expression

```
let (x, y) = (5, 6);
let text = x < y ? "less-than" | "greater-than-or-equal";
```

In the previous example, a variable text is declared and assigned the "less-than" value if the expression x < y evaluates to true, or assigned the "greater-than-or-equal" value if the expression x < y evaluates to false.

The first sub-expression should always evaluate to the Bool type, and the second and third sub-expressions should have matching types, String in this case.

Arithmetic Expressions

Q# supports arithmetic operators like + for addition, - for subtraction, * for multiplication, / for division, - for negation, and ^ for exponentiation. All these operators can be applied to operands of type Int, BigInt, and Double. There is the additional % operator for calculating the modulus, which is available for types Int and BigInt only.

Listing 6-18 shows you all these operators in action.

Listing 6-18. Arithmetic expressions in action

```
let addition = 3 + 4;
let subtraction = 9.6 - 6.3;
let multiplication = 3 * 6;
let division = 10 / 2;
let negation = -33.999;
let exponentiation = 2 ^ 8;
let modulus = 9 % 2;
```

Except for the exponentiation operator, the type for the operands must match. The exponent, or right-hand side operand for the exponentiation operator, should be of type Int if the value, or the left-hand operand, is of type BigInt. The type of the entire expression matches the type of the left-hand operand.

Note   Q# does not support automatic or implicit conversions between arithmetic data types.

Concatenations

Concatenation is only supported for values of type String and arrays. Concatenation for these types is always expressed using the + operator.

Listing 6-19 shows you how to concatenate String and arrays.

Listing 6-19. Concatenation of string and arrays

```
let text1 = "Hello";
let text2 = "Quantum";
let text3 = "Word";
let text = text1 + " " + text2 + " " + text3;

let array1 = [1, 2, 3];
let array2 = [7, 8, 9];
let array = array1 + [4, 5, 6] + array2;
```

For arrays, the + operator expects both operands are of the same type because the type of the entire expression should match the type of the operands.

Statements

Q# supports a mixture of classical and quantum computations, and the implementation looks a lot like other well-known classical programming languages.

Conditional Branching

Q# allows your code to branch, based on an expression of type Bool. To achieve conditional branching, you need a single if-statement, followed by zero or more elif-clauses and an optional else-clause.

Listing 6-20 shows you conditional branching using the if-statement and its corresponding elif and else clauses.

Listing 6-20. Conditional branching

```
let condition = true;
let (x, y) = (5, 6);

if condition
{
  Message("Something should happen!");
}
elif x == y
{
  Message("This is unexpected...");
}
else
{
  Message("Whatever :)");
}
```

Note   Conditional expressions allow you to express simple conditional branching in the form of a single expression.

Iterations

Iterations are loops that iterate over a sequence of values and are expressed using the for statement. Q# supports the for statement on arrays and ranges. The statement body, the contents of the loop, is executed multiple times, and the defined symbol is bound to each value in the array or range. The iteration symbol that is bound to these values is immutable and cannot be reassigned within the body of the loop and go out of scope when the loop finishes.

Listing 6-21 shows you an example of an iteration over an array of qubits and puts each qubit in superposition. These newly allocated qubits are all in the $|0\rangle$ state. The bound variable q in this iteration represents every qubit within the array of qubits.

Listing 6-21. An iteration over an array

```
use qs = Qubit[5];

for q in qs
{
  H(q);
}
```

Listing 6-22 shows you an example of an iteration over a range and puts every odd qubit in an array in superposition. The bound variable `index` in this iteration represents every possible index within the array of qubits.

Listing 6-22. An iteration over a range

```
use qs = Qubit[5];

for index in 0..2..Length(qs)-1
{
  H(qs[index]);
}
```

Note   There is no support for `break` or `continue` in Q#. This makes the loop iteration count predictable, and `for`-loops can be executed on all quantum hardware. If the number of iterations is predictable, the quantum operations inside the loop can vectorized.

Conditional Loops

Next to iterations, Q# supports loops that break based on a condition. Q# supports two kinds of conditional loops: classical conditional loops that do not depend on quantum measurements and quantum conditional loops that depend on quantum measurements.

While Loops

The Q# while loop is very similar to while loops in other classical programming languages. The while loop will continue as long as the expression of type Bool evaluates to true.

Listing 6-23 shows an example of a while loop.

Listing 6-23. A while loop

```
mutable number = 100;

while number > 0
{
    set number -= 2;
}
```

Note   For now, while loops are not supported outside of functions to make sure that the condition cannot depend on the outcomes of quantum measurements. Furthermore, while loops are discouraged because loops that break on a condition are difficult to translate to runtimes on quantum hardware.

Repeat Loops

Repeat loops are syntactically similar to while loops, but they execute a least once, evaluate an expression of type Bool using the until statement, and have an additional fixup block. The repeat-statement block executes repeatably until the until-expression evaluates to false and the fixup-block is executed after each iteration if the until condition is not met.

Listing 6-24 shows you an example of the repeat loop with fixup block where two qubits are put in superposition and measured until the measurement results in the combined |11⟩ state. The fixup block just displays a message to show you what happens, but it could perform some additional cleanup logic for your quantum state.

Listing 6-24. A repeat loop with fixup block

```
use (q1, q2) = (Qubit(), Qubit());

repeat
{
  H(q1);
  let result1 = M(q1);
  H(q2);
  let result2 = M(q2);
  Message($"({result1},{result2})");
}
until result1 == One and result2 == One
fixup
{
  Message("Fixup...");
}
```

A possible output from the repeat loop in Listing 6-24 is shown in Listing 6-25.

Listing 6-25. A possible output for the repeat loop in Listing 6-24

```
(Zero,Zero)
Fixup...
(Zero,One)
Fixup...
(One,One)
```

The output in Listing 6-25 makes it clear that the `fixup`-block is executed after each iteration, except for the last one, where the `until` expression does not evaluate to `true`.

The complete `repeat`-statement is treated as a single scope, and symbols declared inside the `repeat`-block are available to the `until`-condition and within the optional `fixup`-block. Symbols declared inside the `fixup`-block are not available inside the `repeat`-block because that would be the next iteration.

Note   Repeat loops are supported inside operation and can depend on the outcomes of quantum measurements. They are, however, still a challenge to execute on quantum hardware and are not supported by many of them.

Conjugations

Due to the particularities of quantum memory, the conjugation pattern is often used in quantum computations. Q# supports a dedication statement for expressing computation that requires a subsequent cleanup using the `within apply` statement.

The statements in the within block are applied first, followed by the statements in the apply-block, and finally, the automatically generated adjoint of the entire within block is applied to cleanup.

Listing 6-26 shows you an example for the within-apply statement. Two qubits are allocated, and the first qubit is put through the X-gate, putting it in the $|1\rangle$ state. Next, both qubits are put through a CNOT-gate, putting also the second qubit in the $|1\rangle$ state. Finally, the automatically generated adjoint for the within-block will be performed, putting the first qubit back into its original $|0\rangle$ state.

Listing 6-26. The within-apply statement

```
01 use (q1, q2) = (Qubit(), Qubit());
02
03 within
04 {
05   X(q1);
06 }
07 apply
08 {
09   CNOT(q1, q2);
10 }
```

Conjugations are a language-feature of Q# and are translated to a series of intrinsic quantum operations by the compiler.

Tip   The following section provides you with some more technical background
information about the Q# language and its compiler. Feel free to skip it if you're not
interested in this kind of deep dive.

Applications compiled for the .NET platform are compiled to an intermediate, lower-level language before they are compiled to machine code by the runtime and Q# uses the same mechanism. Thanks to this mechanism, you can use a tool to decompile your code back into its original source code. That tool is called ILSpy, short for Intermediate Language Spy. ILSpy does not have support for Q# specifically but is able to decompile your Q# programs into C#. If you create and compile a Q# project and copy the code from Listing 6-26, you should be able to use ILSpy to decompile it and look at the result.

If you download, install, and open ILSpy, you can open your compiled DLL file which you can find in your project directory in the bin/Debug/netcoreapp3.1 subfolder. There will be an executable with your project name, which is just a bootstrapper to be able to execute your quantum simulated program, and a DLL file with the same name. That is the DLL file you need to open in ILSpy. Figure 6-3 shows you what this looks like.

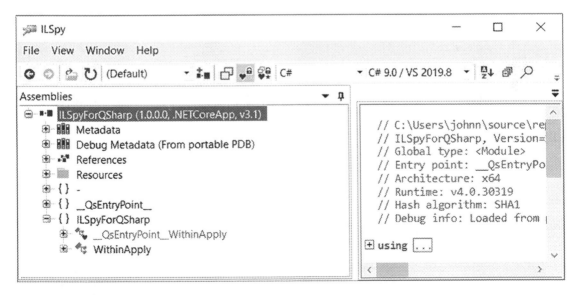

Figure 6-3. *The main window for ILSpy with your within-apply operation inside*

On the left-hand side of the ILSpy main window, you should recognize your DLL file, and if you open it up, you will see a list of namespaces you declared. Find your default namespace and expand it. You should see the name of your operation inside. Expand that and find the __Body__ item, after which you can click it. On the right-hand side, you will find the decompiled code for your operation that executes the within apply statement. Listing 6-27 shows a copy of that decompiled code for your reference.

Listing 6-27. The decompiled body for your apply within operation

```
01 public override Func<QVoid, QVoid> __Body__ => delegate
02 {
03   Qubit qubit = Allocate__.Apply();
04   Qubit qubit2 = Allocate__.Apply();
05   Qubit qubit3 = qubit;
06   Qubit qubit4 = qubit2;
07   bool flag = true;
08   try
09   {
10     Quantum__Intrinsic__X.Apply(qubit3);
11     Quantum__Intrinsic__CNOT.Apply((qubit3,qubit4));
12     Quantum__Intrinsic__X.Adjoint.Apply(qubit3);
13   }
14   catch
15   {
16     flag = false;
17     throw;
18   }
19   finally
20   {
21     if (flag)
22     {
23       Release__.Apply(qubit3);
24       Release__.Apply(qubit4);
25     }
26   }
27   return QVoid.Instance;
28 };
```

On lines 3 through 6 from Listing 6-27, you can see the allocation of the two qubits with some weird additional steps. There are four qubits declared, and two qubits are allocated and referenced by `qubit3` and `qubit4`. These four lines of code represent line 1 from Listing 6-26.

On line 10 from Listing 6-27, you can see the X-operation applied to the first qubit. This represents the X-operation inside the within statement on line 5 from Listing 6-26.

On line 11 from Listing 6-27, you can see the `CNOT` operation applied on the two qubits. This represents the `CNOT` operation inside the apply statement on line 9 from Listing 6-26.

On line 12 from Listing 6-27, you can see the adjoint for the X-operation applied on the first qubit. This operation is invisible in the original code because it implicitly defined by the `within apply` statement. A conjugation automatically applies the adjoint of the first operations after the last operations.

The section you just read shows you how a programming language can introduce higher-level abstractions for popular concepts to simplify development. The compiler and the SDK tools help you to translate the high-level code you write into the much more verbose machine code that is needed to run your programs.

Callables

Q# supports callable declarations, or callables, and they are declared at a global scale, within a namespace only. There are two kinds of callables, operations and functions.

Both operations and functions are declared using a unique name, within the current namespace, and a single input and output. Both input and output can be a single value, or a tuple of multiple values. The following examples show you an operation and a function with one or more arguments as input and an output type or a tuple of output types:

```
operation Foo(b: Bool, q: Qubit) : String { return ""; }
function Bar(q: Qubit) : (Bool, Bool) { return (true, true); }
```

Declaring a callable is very similar to functions or methods in other programming languages. You can break it down into its distinct parts:

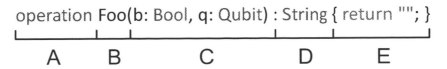

- **A**: Callable declaration keyword: operation, or function

- **B**: Unique name for the operation or function

- **C**: List of input arguments as a tuple. Can be empty or contain one or multiple arguments

- **D**: Output type. Can be a singleton tuple or a tuple with one or multiple types. Cannot be empty

- **E**: Scope and body of the callable

Using a callable from your code is straightforward. You call it by its name, provide its input arguments, and assign its output to a variable.

```
function CalculateSum(x: Int, y: Int) : Int
{
    return x + y;
}

let sum = CalculateSum(4, 5);
```

Syntactically, there is no difference between operations and functions except for the keywords `operation` and `function`. Obviously, there is a difference in semantics.

Functions

In Q#, functions are what you would expect from a function. Calling a function is deterministic, and there are no side effects. Because Q# uses immutable classic data types, calling a function with the same input will always produce the same output.

Operations

Quantum computations are natively supported on the targeted quantum hardware and are executed in the form of side effects on the qubits. Because of this, callables that operate on the state of a qubit should be declared as operations.

Operations can call other operations but can also call functions. Functions can call other functions, but because they should be kept deterministic, they cannot call operations. Qubits can still be provided as input parameters for functions, but because operations cannot be called from functions, changing the quantum state or executing quantum measurements is not possible. All intrinsic quantum operations are declared in Q# as operations.

One more difference between operations and functions is that operations can contain additional information about the characteristics of an operation. These characteristics are a set of built-in labels or functors.

Functors

Many quantum algorithms and quantum computing hardware often need the adjoint or a controlled variant of a given transformation. Q# supports functors to declare these specializations for operations, and these specializations can be automatically generated or explicitly declared in code. Functions do not have support for functors and only contain one body implementation and no further specializations.

Operations have a body specialization declared implicitly, but you can also declare it explicitly. The following operation

```
operation OP(q : Qubit) : Unit
{
    Ry(PI() / 2.0, q);
}
```

is equivalent to

```
operation OP(q : Qubit) : Unit
{
    body(...)
    {
        Ry(PI() / 2.0, q);
    }
}
```

The three dots after the body keyword correspond to the list of arguments that should be copied from the operation declaration by the compiler.

The Adjoint Specialization

If you want your operation to support the Adjoint functor, which is the inverse for unitary operations, you need to add the is Adj characteristic to your operation. Adding the is Adj characteristic tells the compiler to automatically generate support for the Adjoint functor. Listing 6-28 shows you how to declare and use an operation with support for the Adjoint functor using the Is Adj characteristic.

Listing 6-28. An operation with support for the Adjoint functor using the Is Adj characteristic

```
01 @EntryPoint()
02 operation AdjointFunctor() : Unit
03 {
04   use qubit = Qubit();
05
06     MyCustomOperation(qubit);
07     Adjoint MyCustomOperation(qubit);
08 }
09
10 operation MyCustomOperation(q: Qubit) : Unit is Adj
11 {
12     X(q);
13 }
```

Lines 10 through 13 from Listing 6-28 declare a custom operation that just executes the intrinsic X-operation from Q#. The signature for this operation on line 10 contains the Is Adj characteristics which tells the compiler to automatically generate support for the Adjoint functor. Line 6 executes the operation normally, and line 7 executes the adjoint variant using the Adjoint functor.

Another option to define the adjoint for the operation is to add it manually. Listing 6-29 shows you an alternative where you can omit the Is Adj characteristic if you tell the operation to autogenerate the adjoint next to its body specialization.

Listing 6-29. An alternative implementation for the operation from Listing 6-28

```
01 operation MyCustomOperation(q: Qubit) : Unit
02 {
03     body(...)
04     {
05       X(q);
06     }
07     adjoint auto;
08 }
```

Because your custom operation only executes the intrinsic X-operation from Q#, which is self-adjoint, you don't need to make the compiler automatically generate the adjoint. You know that executing the Pauli X rotation a second time automatically inverts it, so you can instruct the compiler to create a self-adjoint, which will call the same operation a second time. Listing 6-30 shows you how to instruct the compiler to do this.

Listing 6-30. A self-adjoint version for the operation from Listing 6-28

```
01 operation MyCustomOperation(q: Qubit) : Unit
02 {
03   body(...)
04   {
05     X(q);
06   }
07   adjoint self;
08 }
```

Finally, if you really want to customize the adjoint specialization, you can write it yourself. Listing 6-31 shows you how to do this.

Listing 6-31. Write your own adjoint specialization

```
01 operation MyCustomOperation(q: Qubit) : Unit
02 {
03   body(...)
04   {
05     X(q);
06   }
07   adjoint(...)
08   {
09     Adjoint X(q);
10   }
11 }
```

In most cases, the automatically generated specializations are the easiest way to implement them. In some cases, it can be more beneficial or more performant to implement a custom specialization.

Tip   If you read the optional section on ILSpy earlier, you may want to get some extra information on these specializations by looking at the decompiled source code. If you skipped the earlier section on ILSpy, you could still go back, have a look, and come back to investigate how the specializations are automatically generated.

If you compile the last two variants for the adjoint specialization and investigate the decompiled source code using ILSpy, you will clearly see the difference.

Listing 6-32 shows you the decompiled source code for the automatically generated specialization from Listing 6-29.

Listing 6-32. The decompiled source code for the adjoint auto specialization

```
01 public override Func<Qubit, QVoid> __Body__
02    => delegate(Qubit __in__)
03 {
04   Microsoft__Quantum__Intrinsic__X.Apply(__in__);
05   return QVoid.Instance;
06 };
07
08 public override Func<Qubit, QVoid> __AdjointBody__ =>
09   delegate(Qubit __in__)
10 {
11   Microsoft__Quantum__Intrinsic__X.Adjoint.Apply(__in__);
12   return QVoid.Instance;
13 };
```

Lines 1 through 6 from Listing 6-32 contain the decompiled source code for the body specialization, and lines 8 through 13 contain the decompiled source code for the adjoint specialization. The Q# compiler autogenerated this source code and calls the Adjoint functor for the intrinsic X-operation.

Listing 6-33 shows you the decompiled source code for the self-adjoint specialization from Listing 6-30.

Listing 6-33. The decompiled source code for the `adjoint self` specialization

```
01 public override Func<Qubit, QVoid> __Body__
02    => delegate(Qubit __in__)
03 {
04    Microsoft__Quantum__Intrinsic__X.Apply(__in__);
05    return QVoid.Instance;
06 };
07
08 public override Func<Qubit, QVoid> __AdjointBody__
09    => __Body__;
```

Lines 8 and 9 from Listing 6-33 show you that in this case, the `Adjoint` functor just redirects the call to the implementation for the body specialization. The adjoint for this operation is the operation itself.

The Controlled Specialization

If you need a controlled variant for your operation, you can use the `Is Ctl` characteristic to support the `Controlled` functor. The controlled variant gives you the possibility to apply your operation only if all control qubits are in the $|1\rangle$ state.

Listing 6-34 shows you an operation that adds support for the `Controlled` functor using the `Is Ctl` characteristic.

Listing 6-34. An operation with support for the `Controlled` functor using the `Is Ctl` characteristic

```
01 @EntryPoint()
02 operation ControlledFunctor() : Unit
03 {
04    use (c, qubit) = (Qubit(), Qubit());
05
06    MyCustomOperation(qubit);
07    Controlled MyCustomOperation([c], qubit);
08 }
09
```

```
10 operation MyCustomOperation(q: Qubit) : Unit is Ctl
11 {
12   X(q);
13 }
```

Line 10 from Listing 6-34 shows you how to use the Is Ctl characteristic to instruct the compiler to automatically generate support for the Controlled functor. Line 7 shows you how to use the Controlled functor. The operation, called with the Controlled functor, also needs an array of control qubits and will only be applied if all the control qubits are in the $|1\rangle$ state.

Listings 6-35 and 6-36 show you how to define the controlled specialization manually using the specialization syntax.

Listing 6-35. The controlled specialization, automatically generated, without the Is Ctl characteristic

```
01 operation MyCustomOperation(q: Qubit) : Unit
02 {
03   body(...)
04   {
05     X(q);
06   }
07   controlled auto;
08 }
```

Listing 6-36. The controlled specialization, implemented manually

```
01 operation MyCustomOperation(q: Qubit) : Unit
02 {
03   body(...)
04   {
05     X(q);
06   }
07   controlled(cs, ...)
08   {
09     Controlled X(cs, q);
10   }
11 }
```

Line 7 from Listing 6-36 shows you how to define a manual controlled specialization. The cs argument contains the control qubits and are followed by the original arguments, copied from the operation on line 1.

Combining Specializations

You can combine specializations. Listings 6-37, 6-38, and 6-39 show you examples of how to combine support for multiple functors.

Listing 6-37. Autogenerated support for the Controlled and Adjoint functors using the Is Adj + Ctl characterization

```
01 @EntryPoint()
02 operation CombiningFunctors() : Unit
03 {
04   use (c, qubit) = (Qubit(), Qubit());
05
06   MyCustomOperation(qubit);
07   Controlled Adjoint MyCustomOperation([c], qubit);
08 }
09
10 operation MyCustomOperation(q: Qubit) : Unit is Adj + Ctl
11 {
12   X(q);
13 }
```

Listing 6-38. Autogenerated support for the Controlled and Adjoint functors using specializations

```
01 operation MyCustomOperation(q: Qubit) : Unit
02 {
03   body(...)
04   {
05     X(q);
06   }
```

```
07    adjoint auto;
08    controlled auto;
09    controlled adjoint auto;
10 }
```

Listing 6-39. Manually implemented support for the Controlled and Adjoint functors using specializations

```
01 operation MyCustomOperation(q: Qubit) : Unit
02 {
03    body(...)
04    {
05      X(q);
06    }
07    adjoint(...)
08    {
09      Adjoint X(q);
10    }
11    controlled(qs, ...)
12    {
13      Controlled X(qs, q);
14    }
15    controlled adjoint(qs, ...)
16    {
17      Controlled Adjoint X(qs, q);
18    }
19 }
```

Caution   If you are not autogenerating the adjoint or controlled specializations, Q# will not check if your implementation is correct. You should make sure and not rely on the compiler.

Returns and Termination

All callables, both operations and functions, can be exited by using the return statement. If a callable is exited, it always returns a value to its callee. The return statement can be wherever, and there can even be multiple return statements in the same callable. There should always be a return statement for every possible code path within a callable, except if the callable returns a value of type Unit. For callables that have Unit as its output type, control is returned to its callee automatically when all statements have been executed.

Listing 6-40 shows you a function that returns zero, an operation that does nothing and implicitly returns the Unit literal and an operation that does almost nothing and explicitly returns the Unit literal.

Listing 6-40. Return control from a callable to the callee

```
01 function ReturnZero() : Int
02 {
03   return 0;
04 }
05
06 operation DoNothing() : Unit
07 {
08
09 }
10
11 operation DoAlmostNothing() : Unit
12 {
13   return ();
14 }
```

You can return from a callable from different locations if your code has multiple branches. Listing 6-41 shows you a recursive function that calculates the Fibonacci number at position n in the Fibonacci array.

Listing 6-41. Return control from a callable with multiple branches

```
01 function Fibonacci(n: Int) : BigInt
02 {
03   if( n == 0 )
04   {
05     return IntAsBigInt(0);
06   }
07   elif( n == 1 or n == 2 )
08   {
09     return IntAsBigInt(1);
10   }
11   else
12   {
13     return Fibbonacci(n - 1) + Fibbonacci(n - 2);
14   }
15 }
```

You can terminate your entire program by calling the `fail` operation. This operation is used to immediately stop your computation if a fatal error happened that you cannot recover from. The `fail` statement takes a `string` argument to provide meaningful information about why the execution is halted:

```
fail "Oops, that shouldn't have happened!";
```

Operations and Functions As First-Class Objects

A callable itself can also be assigned to a variable. In this case, the callable will not be called, but a reference to it will be stored. Because of this, the callable can be provided as input to or retrieved as output from other operations and functions. In Listing 6-42, you can see how to reference a function from a variable.

Listing 6-42. Assigning a reference to a callable, a function in this case

```
01 function CalculateSum(x: Int, y: Int) : Int
02 {
03     return x + y;
04 }
```

```
05
06 let sum = CalculateSum(4, 5);
07 let calculateSumCall = CalculateSum;
08 let anotherSum = calculateSumCall(6, 7);
```

Lines 1 through 4 declare a function `CalculateSum` that adds the two input arguments x and y and returns their sum as output. Line 6 just calls the `CalculateSum` function normally, adds 4 and 5, and assigns the result to the variable `sum`. Line 7 assigns a reference to the `CalculateSum` function to the variable `calculateSumCall` without calling it. Line 8 calls the `CalculateSum` function by calling it indirectly using the reference variable `calculateSumCall`.

If you want to pass a reference to a callable as input or if you want to declare it as output in another callable, you need to use a very specific syntax. Listing 6-43 shows you how to do this.

Listing 6-43. Callable types in arguments and return types

```
01 operation ExecuteManyTimes(
02    q: Qubit, op: Qubit => Unit, n: Int) : Unit
03 {
04    for _ in 1..n
05    {
06        op(q);
07    }
08 }
09
10 ExecuteManyTimes(qubit, H, 2);
```

An operation `ExecuteManyTimes` is declared on lines 1 through 8. This operation takes a tuple containing a qubit q, an operation op, and an integer n as input. The operation op is declared using type `Qubit => Unit`, which states that it is an operation with a `Qubit` input and a `Unit` output. On lines 4 through 7, you can see a loop that iterates a range from 1 to the number n provided. The body of that loop will call the operation op and provides the qubit q as input. This is how the operation is called multiple times. On line 10, the `ExecuteManyTimes` operation is called using the qubit and the H operation as its input parameters. The final input parameter 2 will make sure that the H operation is executed twice for that qubit.

Caution   The type syntax for callables is very specific to operations and functions. Use the => operator for operations and the -> operator for functions.

Partial Application

A very cool and powerful mechanism in Q# is the ability to construct new callables, based on existing ones, on the fly, by using the discard operator. Listing 6-44 shows you how to use partial applications.

Listing 6-44. How to use partial applications

```
01 function Multiply(number: Int, factor: Int) : Int
02 {
03     return number * factor;
04 }
05
06 let twice = Multiply(_, 2);
07 let result = twice(10);
```

A normal function Multiply is declared on lines 1 through 4. On line 6, a partial application is applied to the Multiply function by ignoring the first argument number and hard coding the second argument factor as the value 2. In this case, Q# will automatically generate an anonymous function that calls the Multiply function with the value 2 for the factor argument. Because the first argument named number is ignored using the discard operator, the new anonymous function still needs this discarded argument as input and is, therefore, a function with a single argument. This new anonymous function is assigned to the twice variable and can then be called on line 7 by providing a single argument for the number argument.

You can imagine the powerful nature of callables and partial application when you start to combine them with in arguments. Listing 6-45 shows you an alternative use for the ExecuteManyTimes operation from Listing 6-43.

Listing 6-45. Combining callables as arguments and partial application

```
01 operation ExecuteManyTimes(
02    q: Qubit, op: Qubit => Unit, n: Int) : Unit
03 {
04    for _ in 1..n
05    {
06        op(q);
07    }
08 }
09
10 ExecuteManyTimes(qubit, Ry(PI() / 4.0, _), 2);
```

Lines 1 through 8 declare the ExecuteManyTimes operation which has not changed since Listing 6-43. Calling the ExecuteManyTimes operation on line 10 looks different and applies partial application of the Ry operation. The ExecuteManyTimes operation only takes an operation that has a single argument of type Qubit. The Ry operation takes two arguments, an angle to rotate the qubit state and the qubit itself. You can hard-code the rotation angle and discard the qubit argument to call that Ry operation multiple times using the ExecuteManyTimes operation.

Type Parameterizations

Q# has support for type parameterizations for both operations and functions. Thanks to this concept, templates for operations and functions can be created to support multiple data types. In combination with callables, this can also be a very powerful feature. Type parameterization is somewhat comparable with the concept of generics in both C# and Java.

As an example, maybe you have an array of variables that you need to project to another data type. The input will be an array of a specific type, and the output will be an array of another type. This kind of functionality can be built very flexible by also providing the function that performs the actual projection. Listing 6-46 shows you a possible implementation for a function that does just this.

Listing 6-46. Using type parameterization on a function that projects from one
data type to another

```
01 function Project<'TIn, 'TOut>(
02   input: 'TIn[], projection: 'TIn -> 'TOut) : 'TOut[]
03 {
04   let arrayLength = Length(input);
05   mutable projected = new 'TOut[arrayLength];
06
07   for i in 0..arrayLength-1
08   {
09     set projected w/= i <- projection(input[i]);
10   }
11
12   return projected;
13 }
14
15 let values = [true, false, true, false];
16 let results = Project<Bool, Result>(values, BoolAsResult);
```

The function `Project` is implemented on lines 1 through 13 and uses type
parameterization for its input and output. On line 1, the type parameterization template
is part of the function name. In this case there are two type parameters: `'TIn` and
`'Tout` – a type that comes in and a type that goes out. If this function is called, these
types should be specified. On line 16, you can see that the Project function is called
with Bool as the `'TIn` type parameter and Result as the `'Tout`. Therefore, we can think
of type parameterization as declaring templates for callables. `'TIn` and `'TOut` are only
placeholders that will eventually be replaced by concrete data types when we use them.
On line 2, the first input argument is an array of type `'Tin`, and the second argument is
a function that gets a `'TIn` value as its input and outputs a `'TOut` value. Next, the output
type for the `Project` function is an array of `'TOut` values. Line 4 gets the length of the
input array, and line 5 declares a new output array with the same length. Lines 7 through
10 iterate through the input array and call the `projection` function to map the input
array values from `'TIn` to `'TOut`. Finally, line 15 declares an array of Bool values, and line
16 calls the `Project` function to map the array to an array of type Result. The function

that actually performs the mapping is an existing Q# API function called `BoolAsResult` and exists in the `Microsoft.Quantum.Convert` namespace. The `BoolAsResult` function takes a `Bool` value as input and outputs a `Result` value, just the thing we need!

The Last Word

This chapter helped you with the Q# language and many of its constructs. If you have experience with other programming languages like C#, F#, Java, C++, or others, you will feel mostly comfortable. Q# adds some additional features that are very specific to quantum computing like the difference between operations and functions, functors, and conjugations.

You can go ahead and explore the language. Try things! Use the Visual Studio Code or Microsoft Visual Studio debugging tools to see what happens when you execute a piece of code. Maybe even use the ILSpy tool to investigate what the Q# compiler does to translate your code and generate your functors.

## CHAPTER 7

Testing and Debugging Your Quantum Programs

Writing your quantum programs should not be a whole lot different from writing your classical programs. To be able to check that your quantum programs are running as intended, you are able to watch their behavior and check their inner workings.

This chapter will guide you through some testing and debugging features, provided by the Microsoft Quantum Development Kit.

Simulators

When you are running your quantum applications on your local PC and not on an actual quantum computer, you are running them in a simulated environment. By default, a Q# program runs using the full-state simulator which runs using the .NET platform.

The Full-State Simulator

The default simulator that is used out of the box when running your Q# on your local PC is called the full-state simulator. It can simulate quantum programs with up to 30 qubits, give or take. This limitation exists because the possible complex quantum state of multiple qubits, stored in memory by the simulator, is represented by its mathematical representation and will, therefore, consume a lot of memory. Calculating the effects of quantum operations on a large collection of qubits also needs a lot of classical processing power because a lot of linear algebra needs to be used to calculate the state transformations. If you remember from Chapter 2, every additional qubit you add to a system doubles the amount of state you can represent. A 3-qubit system can represent a linear combination of 4 basis states, and a 4-qubit system can represent a linear

© Johnny Hooyberghs 2022
J. Hooyberghs, *Introducing Microsoft Quantum Computing for Developers*,
https://doi.org/10.1007/978-1-4842-7246-6_7

combination of 16 basis states. With this information, you can calculate that the full-state simulator needs to store 2 to the power of 30 basis states to fully represent a 30-qubit system.

Just for fun, I did some tests on my own laptop which has 64GB of RAM. I could see that allocating 21 qubits in Q# was consuming about 48 megabytes of data. If I allocate an additional qubit, so 22 in total, I could see the memory usage go up to 80 megabytes, which is almost double. If I continue this path and reach 31 qubits, I could see the memory usage reaching 32,778 megabytes and the application crashing when I try to allocate 32 qubits. Figure 7-1 shows you the evolution of memory usage while allocating qubits in Q#.

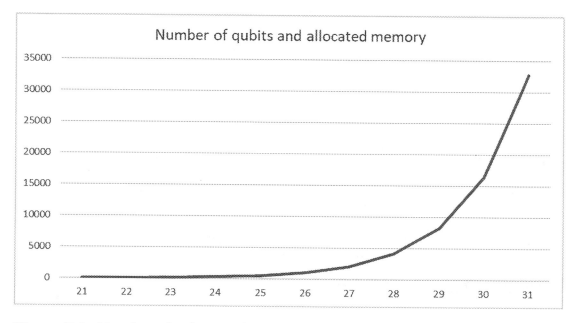

Figure 7-1. *Number of qubits and allocated memory*

For educational purposes or research, it can be beneficial to implement multiple simulators that fill specific needs. The Q# team at Microsoft has implemented several different simulators to help you out in different scenarios. If you revisit the random number generator program from Chapter 4 and recreate it with some minor changes from Listing 7-1, you can test some of these quantum simulators.

Note   Please remember that when you run your Q# code on your local machine, you need to add the `global.json` file to direct the .NET command-line tools (CLI) to use the correct SDK that is compatible with the Microsoft Quantum Development Kit. Refer to Chapter 4 if you need assistance with creating this file.

Listing 7-1. Your slightly modified quantum random number generator

```
01 namespace _07_01_FullStateSimulator_QSharp
02 {
03   open Microsoft.Quantum.Canon;
04   open Microsoft.Quantum.Convert;
05   open Microsoft.Quantum.Intrinsic;
06   open Microsoft.Quantum.Math;
07
08   @EntryPoint()
09   operation FullStateSimulator() : Unit
10   {
11     let maximum = 1023;
12
13     let bitSize = BitSizeI(maximum);
14     mutable resultArray = [Zero, size = 0];
15
16     set resultArray = [Zero, size = 0];
17     for index in 0..bitSize-1
18     {
19       use qubit = Qubit();
20       H(qubit);
21       set resultArray += [M(qubit)];
22       Reset(qubit);
23     }
24
25     let randomNumber = ResultArrayAsInt(resultArray);
26     Message($"{randomNumber}");
27   }
28 }
```

The code from Listing 7-1 generates a random number ranging from 0 to 1023 and needs 10 random bits to represent such a number. Remember that 10 bits can represent a number ranging from 0 to 2 to the power of 10 minus 1. The additional `Reset` operation on line 22 is not strictly needed because the qubit was already measured, but it will show us something interesting later when doing resource estimations.

You can run this quantum program using the full-state simulator by explicitly stating this requirement in the `dotnet run` command. Go ahead and try it from the terminal window within Visual Studio Code:

```
dotnet run -s QuantumSimulator
```

Since this full-state quantum simulator is the default for running quantum programs using the Microsoft Quantum Development Kit, you can omit the name of the simulator by just running

```
dotnet run
```

The result from running this code is what you expect because you did this before. You will get a random number between 0 and 1024. The full-state simulator tries to run your program like it would on an actual quantum computer, and in the background, it will try to represent the quantum superposition state in a mathematical way. If we measure the quantum state, the full-state simulator will use a pseudo-random number generator to determine the actual basis state.

The Resources Estimator

Sometimes, it would be nice to know some additional information about your quantum program. Maybe you need to know how many resources are needed from an actual quantum computer before you run your application on one. Try running the same application, but replace the argument that explicitly asks for the full-state simulator with the simple resource estimator:

```
dotnet run -s ResourcesEstimator
```

As a result, you will get a random generated number of 0, followed by a textual representation of the analysis of the resources needed to run your quantum program. Listing 7-2 displays the output here for your convenience.

Listing 7-2. The analysis output from the ResourcesEstimator if you run your quantum random number generator

```
0
Metric          Sum          Max
CNOT            0            0
QubitClifford   10           10
R               0            0
Measure         20           20
T               0            0
Depth           0            0
Width           1            1
QubitCount      1            1
BorrowedWidth   0            0
```

The first thing you notice is that the random number that was generated is always 0. This happens because your quantum program is not actually being executed but rather being analyzed. Because of this, the resource estimator is not limited as much by your PC's memory and processing power. You can use the resource estimator with thousands of qubits. The control flow of your program is analyzed, and the analysis data is collected.

Upon further examining this output, you should recognize some of these metrics:

- **CNOT**: The total count of controlled Pauli X (also known as CNOT) operations. In this case, none of them were used.

- **QubitClifford**: The total count of single-qubit Clifford and Pauli operations. In this case, 10 Hadamard or H operations were executed, one H operation for each bit that needed to be randomly generated.

- **R**: The total count of single-qubit rotations. In this case, no rotations were used.

- **Measure**: The total count of qubit measurements. In this case, you measured your qubit ten times to randomly generate each bit. The additional 10, to make 20 in total, is related to the Reset operation. The reset operation executes one more measurement and decides if it needs to execute an X-operation to reset the qubit to the $|0\rangle$ state.

- **QubitCount**: The minimum number of qubits that would be needed
  to execute your quantum program. In this case only one, because the
  qubit is allocated and reused for all consecutive bits that need to be
  randomly generated.

Just for fun, you're going to rewrite your random generator and make it allocate
multiple qubits at once instead of only one. Listing 7-3 shows you an alternate approach
and introduces some more Q# operations that you haven't used before.

Listing 7-3. Some additional modifications to use with the ResourceEstimator

```
01 namespace _07_03_ResourceEstimator_QSharp
02 {
03    open Microsoft.Quantum.Canon;
04    open Microsoft.Quantum.Convert;
05    open Microsoft.Quantum.Intrinsic;
06    open Microsoft.Quantum.Measurement;
07    open Microsoft.Quantum.Math;
08
09    @EntryPoint()
10    operation ResourceEstimator() : Unit
11    {
12        let maximum = 1023;
13
14        let bitSize = BitSizeI(maximum);
15        mutable randomNumber = 0;
16
17        use qubits = Qubit[bitSize];
18        ApplyToEach(H, qubits);
19        let resultArray = MultiM(qubits);
20        ResetAll(qubits);
21        set randomNumber = ResultArrayAsInt(resultArray);
22        Message($"{randomNumber}");
23    }
24 }
```

First, run this alternative random number generator using the full-state simulator. It should output a different random number with each execution. Next, run it again using the resource estimator, and compare the output which I copied underneath in Listing 7-4 with the output from the previous version in Listing 7-2.

Listing 7-4. The analysis output from the ResourceEstimator if you run your modified quantum random number generator

```
0
Metric          Sum           Max
CNOT            0             0
QubitClifford   10            10
R               0             0
Measure         20            20
T               0             0
Depth           0             0
Width           10            10
QubitCount      10            10
BorrowedWidth   0             0
```

As you would expect, the minimum number of qubits needed to run your quantum number generator has now increased to 10 because you are allocating all the qubits at once causing them to not be reused by the simulator.

The Toffoli Simulator

Another simulator I want you to know about is the Toffoli simulator. This simulator is a simulator that has a limited scope and only supports the X-operation, CNOT-operation, and multi-controlled X-operations. Because these operations can all be simulated using classical Boolean logic, the Toffoli simulator can simulate a very large number of qubits. Some parts of your quantum programs possibly only use these Boolean functions and can, therefore, be simulated on classical hardware and with large numbers of qubits.

Listing 7-5 shows you a quantum program that executes a multi-controlled X-operation on a large number of qubits.

Listing 7-5. A quantum program that allocates around 65,000 qubits for the Toffoli simulator

```
01 namespace _07_05_ToffoliSimulator_QSharp
02 {
03   open Microsoft.Quantum.Canon;
04   open Microsoft.Quantum.Intrinsic;
05
06   @EntryPoint()
07   operation ToffoliSimulator() : Unit
08   {
09     Perform(AllQubitsOne);
10     Perform(AllQubitsOneExceptLast);
11   }
12
13   operation AllQubitsOne(qs: Qubit[]) : Unit
14   {
15     ApplyToEach(X, qs);
16   }
17
18   operation AllQubitsOneExceptLast(qs: Qubit[]) : Unit
19   {
20     ApplyToEach(X, qs);
21     ApplyToTail(X, qs);
22   }
23
24   operation Perform(op: (Qubit[] => Unit)) : Unit
25   {
26     use qubits = Qubit[65535];
27     op(qubits);
28     use qResult = Qubit();
29     Controlled X(qubits, qResult);
30
31     let bResult = M(qResult);
32
```

```
33      ResetAll(qubits);
34      Reset(qResult);
35
36      Message($"{op}: {bResult}");
37    }
38 }
```

If you run this quantum program using the full-state simulator, you will notice a very quick increase of your PC's memory usage, extending to your page file on disk, which will eventually cause your quantum program to crash. The program from Listing 7-5 allocates 65,535 qubits plus one additional qubit, which needs too much RAM for your PC to handle. If you know from before that 29 qubits need about 8,200 megabytes of RAM, and each additional one requires about twice as much RAM, then you can imagine that 65,536 qubits will need a lot more RAM than all of the classical hardware in the world combined.

Try to run the program again, but this time, use the Toffoli simulator:

```
dotnet run -s ToffoliSimulator
```

The execution will succeed, and the program will run two scenarios. The first scenario, called on line 9 from Listing 7-5, allocates 65,535 qubits and executes an X-operation on all of them. After this, a controlled multi-qubit X-operation will flip an additional qubit on line 29. The additional qubit will be flipped, because all 65,535 qubits that are used as control qubits are in the $|1\rangle$ state. The second scenario, called from line 10 from Listing 7-5, allocates 65,535 qubits and executes an X-operation on all of them, except for the last. This is achieved on line 21 by only flipping the last qubit of the 65,535 qubits to return it back to the $|0\rangle$ state. This causes the controlled multi-qubit X-operation to not flip the additional qubit, because not all 65,535 qubits are in $|1\rangle$ state.

The output of running this quantum program will be determined by the `Message` function on line 36 from Listing 7-5:

```
AllQubitsOne: One
AllQubitsOneExceptLast: Zero
```

The Toffoli simulator defaults to a maximum of 65,536 allocatable qubits. Therefore, I suggested to allocate a 65,535 plus 1 additional qubit. Each allocated qubit requires one byte of memory, so the Toffoli simulator can simulate a significant number of qubits. You can use additional arguments to specify the number of qubits you need to increase this maximum of 65,536 allocatable qubits.

If you are trying to be bad and change the ApplyToEach operation in the AllQubitsOne operation to use the H operation instead of the X-operation and run the application again, you will see it fail because the H operation is not supported by the Toffoli simulator:

```
Unhandled exception: System.NotImplementedException:
The method or operation is not implemented.
```

Testing Your Quantum Programs

If you are a software developer, you already know that a software developer likes to have fast feedback on the work that's being done. Many classical programming languages include tools that can run source code in an environment that makes it easy to test and find bugs.

A special kind of quantum application, called a unit test project, can be used to write some code that is used specifically for testing. This code will never be executed in a production environment. It is just there for us developers to quickly test our actual code. You can create a standalone application or a quantum library that contains some code that you need to run on an actual quantum computer in production situations. In addition to these source code projects, you can write a unit test project that contains some tests that test your quantum code.

Go ahead and use Visual Studio Code to create a new unit test project. Listing 7-6 contains the entire source code for some example tests.

Listing 7-6. Three example unit tests

```
01 namespace _07_06_QuantumUnitTest_QSharp
02 {
03     open Microsoft.Quantum.Canon;
04     open Microsoft.Quantum.Diagnostics;
05     open Microsoft.Quantum.Intrinsic;
06
07     @Test("QuantumSimulator")
08     @Test("ToffoliSimulator")
```

```
09    operation Qubit_In_Zero_State() : Unit
10    {
11        // Arrange
12        use q = Qubit();
13
14        // Act
15        NoOp(q);
16
17        // Assert
18        AssertQubit(Zero, q);
19
20        // Cleanup
21        Reset(q);
22    }
23
24    @Test("QuantumSimulator")
25    @Test("ToffoliSimulator")
26    operation Qubit_In_One_State() : Unit
27    {
28        // Arrange
29        use q = Qubit();
30
31        // Act
32        X(q);
33
34        // Assert
35        AssertQubit(One, q);
36
37        // Cleanup
38        Reset(q);
39    }
40
```

```
41    @Test("QuantumSimulator")
42    operation Qubit_In_Superposition_State() : Unit
43    {
44        // Arrange
45        use q = Qubit();
46
47        // Act
48        H(q);
49
50        // Assert
51        AssertMeasurementProbability(
52            [PauliZ], [q], Zero, 0.5, "fail message", 0.1);
53
54        // Cleanup
55        Reset(q);
56    }
57 }
```

Listing 7-6 contains a total of three unit tests. These unit tests are very straightforward and will give you a basic idea on how to write your own tests. I like to write my unit tests using the triple-A methodology: arrange, act, assert. I use the same approach for classical unit tests. First, you arrange everything that is needed to make the test possible. Second, you act on something, and you often call the code that you want to test. Finally, you assert that all the results from your act phase are correct and as expected. In this case, there is an additional clean-up phase because qubits need to be reset to the $|0\rangle$ state after use.

The three unit tests from Listing 7-6 have some Test-attributes on top of them. These attributes will make sure the test runs on your preferred quantum simulator and can even be stacked. In this case, the two first unit tests will run twice – once on the full-state simulator and once on the Toffoli simulator. The last unit test will only run on the full-state simulator.

The .NET platform has built-in command-line tools to run unit test projects. Just like executing a quantum program, you can use these tools to run your quantum unit tests:

```
dotnet test
```

As a result, you will get a small analysis, and in your case, the tests will all succeed. Check Listing 7-7 to compare the output. Remember: Three unit tests will run on a combination of quantum simulators. This is why the output states that there are a total of five unit tests.

Listing 7-7. The output after running your unit test project

```
Microsoft (R) Test Execution Command Line Tool Version 16.7.1
Copyright (c) Microsoft Corporation.  All rights reserved.

Starting test execution, please wait...

A total of 1 test files matched the specified pattern.

Test Run Successful.
Total tests: 5
     Passed: 5
 Total time: 4,0076 Seconds
```

When you write your own quantum programs, you should try to write some unit tests to verify all the expected outcomes. This will help you to avoid creating bugs based on mistakes you make when writing quantum operations. Each unit test is explained in further detail on the next few pages.

Testing Qubit in the |0⟩ State

This unit test is very straightforward and only tests if the state of a newly allocated qubit is |0⟩. Listing 7-8 repeats only this test for your reference.

Listing 7-8. A unit test that tests the state of an allocated qubit

```
09 operation Qubit_In_Zero_State() : Unit
10 {
11     // Arrange
12     use q = Qubit();
13
14     // Act
15     NoOp(q);
16
```

```
17     // Assert
18     AssertQubit(Zero, q);
19
20     // Cleanup
21     Reset(q);
22 }
```

As part of the arrange-phase, on line 12 from Listing 7-8, you just assign a single qubit, and you don't need to make any additional changes to that qubit to test if it is in the $|0\rangle$ state. For consistency, the act-phase executes a NoOp operation, which doesn't do anything. Another option would be to replace the NoOp operation with the identity operation I or to skip the act phase altogether. The assert phase checks if the state of the qubit is equal to $|0\rangle$. If it is, the test succeeds. If it is not, the test fails.

Testing Qubit in the $|1\rangle$ State

This unit test checks if a newly allocated qubit is in the $|1\rangle$ state after it was put through an X-operation. Listing 7-9 repeats the code for this test for your reference.

Listing 7-9. A unit test that tests the state of a qubit after being changed by the X-operation

```
26 operation Qubit_In_One_State() : Unit
27 {
28     // Arrange
29     use q = Qubit();
30
31     // Act
32     X(q);
33
34     // Assert
35     AssertQubit(One, q);
36
37     // Cleanup
38     Reset(q);
39 }
```

The only difference from the first test is that in this case, the qubit is flipped using the X-operation on line 32 from Listing 7-9. On line 35, you need to assert the expected $|1\rangle$ state and not the previous $|0\rangle$ state.

Testing Qubit in the Superposition State

This final unit test checks if a newly allocated qubit is in a superposition state after putting it through an H operation. Listing 7-10 repeats the code for this test for your reference.

Listing 7-10. A unit test that tests the state of a qubit after being changed by the H operation

```
42 operation Qubit_In_Superposition_State() : Unit
43 {
44     // Arrange
45     use q = Qubit();
46
47     // Act
48     H(q);
49
50     // Assert
51     AssertMeasurementProbability(
52         [PauliZ], [q], Zero, 0.5, "fail message", 0.1);
53
54     // Cleanup
55     Reset(q);
56 }
```

During the act-phase of this unit test, you should use the H operation on your qubit. Because of this, the state of your qubit is based on probabilities. Therefore, the assert-phase looks a bit different than before. The function AssertMeasurementProbability measures the qubit state for a specific basis and expects a probability with a certain tolerance. In your case, you need to measure in the default basis, called the Pauli Z basis, and we expect zero with a 0.5 probability and tolerance of 0.1. The tolerance could also be a smaller value in this case, but you should experiment. Classical computers are bad with mathematics and can encounter some rounding errors.

Debugging Your Quantum Programs

Probably one of the most important features of a modern programming language is the debugger. A debugger allows you to run your application line by line and allows you to investigate the application state at any time. Q# supports using a debugger if you run your quantum program on a simulated environment like your local PC.

Create a new Q# application using Visual Studio Code, and choose the standalone console application template. Go ahead and copy the contents of Listing 7-11 to get started.

Listing 7-11 contains the DebugYourQuantumProgram operation, which is marked as the entry-point. This operation allocates three qubits and applies the X-gate on the first qubit, the H-gate on the second qubit, and the Ry-gate on the third qubit by calling three separate operations called DebugX, DebugH, and DebugRy.

Listing 7-11. Use this code to learn about debugging Q# inside Visual Studio Code

```
01 namespace _07_11_QuantumDebugging_QSharp
02 {
03     open Microsoft.Quantum.Measurement;
04     open Microsoft.Quantum.Canon;
05     open Microsoft.Quantum.Intrinsic;
06     open Microsoft.Quantum.Math;
07
08     @EntryPoint()
09     operation DebugYourQuantumProgram() : Unit
10     {
11         use (q1, q2, q3) = (Qubit(), Qubit(), Qubit());
12
13         let b1 = DebugX(q1);
14         let b2 = DebugH(q2);
15         let b3 = DebugRy(q3);
16
17         let bits = [b1, b2, b3];
18         Message($"{bits}");
19
20     }
21
```

```
22    operation ExecuteX(q : Qubit) : Result
23    {
24        X(q);
25        let b = M(q);
26        Reset(q);
27        return b;
28    }
29
30    operation ExecuteH(q : Qubit) : Result
31    {
32        H(q);
33        let b = M(q);
34        Reset(q);
35        return b;
36    }
37
38    operation ExecuteRy(q : Qubit) : Result
39    {
40        Ry(2.0 * PI() / 3.0, q);
41        let b = M(q);
42        Reset(q);
43        return b;
44    }
45 }
```

Using Visual Studio Code, you can click the empty space before each line of source code, just before the line number, to place a marker that is called a breakpoint. You can also use the F9 key on your keyboard to add breakpoints to the line you have your cursor at. A breakpoint looks like a red dot and marks that line of code. In Figure 7-2, you can see a breakpoint on line 11, just as the three qubits get allocated.

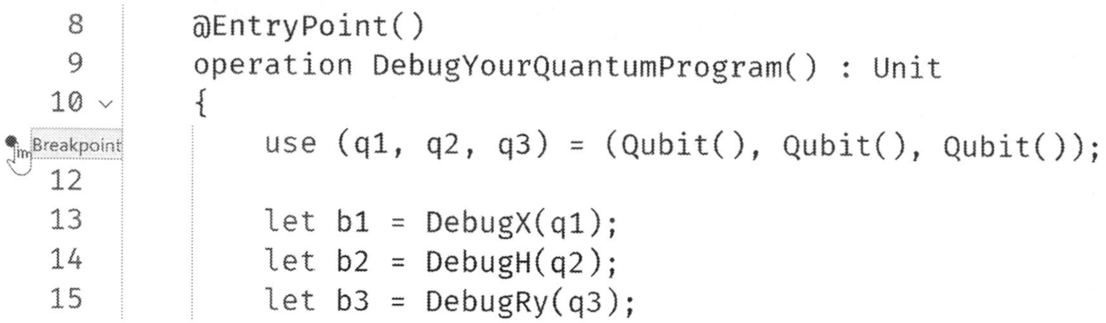

```
8        @EntryPoint()
9        operation DebugYourQuantumProgram() : Unit
10 ∨     {
Breakpoint   use (q1, q2, q3) = (Qubit(), Qubit(), Qubit());
12
13           let b1 = DebugX(q1);
14           let b2 = DebugH(q2);
15           let b3 = DebugRy(q3);
```

Figure 7-2. *Add a breakpoint by clicking the empty space before the line number*

Now, use the Visual Studio Code menu to click Run and Start Debugging. This will run your quantum program with debugging enabled. You can also use the shortcut key F5 instead of clicking the menu. Visual Studio Code will enter into debugging mode, and after some time, line 11 will be highlighted in yellow. The debugger has now encountered your breakpoint and paused the execution of your program at that breakpoint. It is very important to understand that the code highlighted by the debugger has not yet been executed but is about to be executed. Figure 7-3 shows you the highlighted code at line 11, which allocates the three qubits.

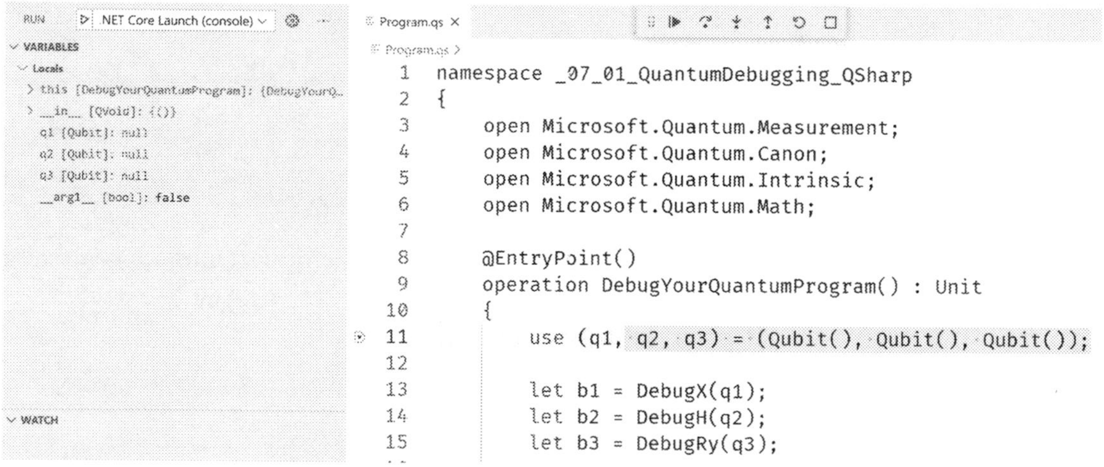

```
RUN    ▷ NET Core Launch (console) ∨  ⚙  ⋯     Program.qs ×
∨ VARIABLES                                    Program.qs >
  ∨ Locals                                1  namespace _07_01_QuantumDebugging_QSharp
    > this [DebugYourQuantumProgram]: {DebugYourQ...   2  {
    > __in__ [QVoid]: {()}                   3      open Microsoft.Quantum.Measurement;
      q1 [Qubit]: null                       4      open Microsoft.Quantum.Canon;
      q2 [Qubit]: null                       5      open Microsoft.Quantum.Intrinsic;
      q3 [Qubit]: null                       6      open Microsoft.Quantum.Math;
      __arg1__ [bool]: false                 7
                                             8      @EntryPoint()
                                             9      operation DebugYourQuantumProgram() : Unit
                                            10      {
                                          ▷ 11          use (q1, q2, q3) = (Qubit(), Qubit(), Qubit());
                                            12
                                            13          let b1 = DebugX(q1);
∨ WATCH                                      14          let b2 = DebugH(q2);
                                            15          let b3 = DebugRy(q3);
```

Figure 7-3. *Your program will stop at the breakpoint and has not yet executed the line highlighted in yellow*

Your application has stopped executing, and Visual Studio Code now waits for your input before continuing. When Visual Studio Code is in debugging mode, it displays a small toolbar at the top of your Q# document. This toolbar, displayed in Figure 7-4, contains several buttons you can use to direct the execution of your application.

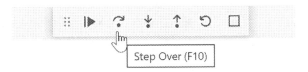

Figure 7-4. *Use the debug toolbar to step over the highlighted line of code and execute it*

The following actions are possible:

- **Continue (F5)**: If you click this button, or press the shortcut key F5, your application will resume execution and will continue until the end or until the next breakpoint is encountered.

- **Step Over (F10)**: If you click this button, or press the shortcut key F10, your application will execute the current highlighted line of code and will pause again on the next line of code. This is useful if you want to investigate the effect of executing a single line of code.

- **Step Into (F11)**: If you click this button, or press the shortcut key F11, your application will navigate into the line of code. This only makes sense if that line of code contains a call to a function or operation. The function or operation will not get executed, but the debugger will pause at the first line of code within that function or operation.

- **Step Out (F12)**: If you click this button, or press the shortcut key Shift+F11, your application will navigate out of the current function or operation. It doesn't matter which line of code inside the function or operation is currently highlighted: all remaining lines of code inside the current function or operation are executed immediately, and the line of code that called the current function or operation is highlighted.

- **Restart (Ctrl+Shift+F5):** If you click this button or press the shortcut key Ctrl+Shift+F5, your application will be terminated immediately and will restart with the debugger. This can be useful if you made a mistake while navigating your code or if you forgot to look at something and you want to retry.

- **Stop (Shift+F5):** If you click this button, or press the shortcut key Shift+F5, your application will be terminated immediately.

Go ahead and try all these different actions. You should probably run the application a few times to be able to try out all of the different debugging actions.

If the debugger has paused executing your code and has highlighted a line of code, you are able to investigate the context of your application at that moment in time. Restore the breakpoint on line 11 if you made any changes during your experiments, and restart the debugging process. Again, the debugger will pause at line 11, highlighting it in yellow. You can now use your mouse cursor and investigate the allocated qubits by hovering their names. You will notice that q1, q2, and q3 will show you a pop-up containing the value null. The reason for this is that the highlighted line of code has not yet executed, so the qubits have not yet been allocated.

Press the Step Over button on the debugger toolbar, or press the F10 shortcut key to execute line 11 and pause the debugger on the next line of code, line 13. Notice that the debugger skips empty lines.

If you try again and hover one of the qubit variables, you will get some information about that allocated qubit. Figure 7-5 shows you what should happen if you hover q1.

When debugging your quantum application inside of the quantum simulator, a qubit is represented by some properties that describe its state. In this case, the q1 qubit has a unique identifier, or index, of zero because it was allocated first. The qubit q1 knows if it has been measured or not, and it has a probability, which is a decimal value between 0 and 1. A probability of 0 means that it has a 100% probability of collapsing to $|0\rangle$ after measurement, and a probability of 1 means that it has a 100% probability of collapsing to $|1\rangle$ after measurement. This makes sense because an allocated qubit always starts out in state $|0\rangle$.

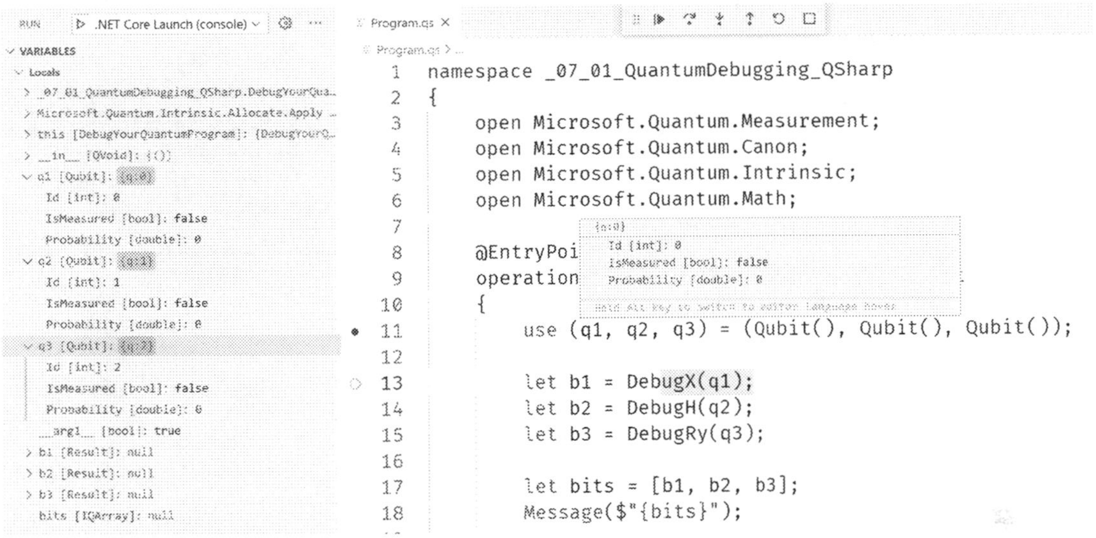

Figure 7-5. *Debugging is peeking at all the variables that are currently loaded into memory*

Note   Remember that debugging quantum programs is only possible in a simulated environment. Simulators can keep track of qubit states and probabilities. Qubits on real quantum computers cannot be measured without irreversibly damaging the quantum state.

Let's focus some more on the three different operations ExecuteX, ExecuteH, and ExecuteRy. First, take a close look at the operation ExecuteX from Listing 7-12. First, you put the qubit q through the X-gate, and second, you measure its state and store the binary result in an immutable variable called b. Finally, the qubit is reset to its clean $|0\rangle$ state, and the binary result b is returned.

Listing 7-12. The focus is now on the ExecuteX-operation

```
22 operation ExecuteX(q : Qubit) : Result
23 {
24     X(q);
25     let b = M(q);
26     Reset(q);
27     return b;
28 }
```

Put a breakpoint on line 25 and start to debug your application. You should see that putting your qubit through the X-gate changes its probability to 1 and that it has not yet been measured. Figure 7-6 shows what you should see in your Visual Studio Code debugger.

```
21
22          operation Debu    {q:0}
23          {                   Id [int]: 0
                                IsMeasured [bool]: false
24              X(q);           Probability [double]: 1
25              let b = M(q);   Hold Alt key to switch to editor language hover
26              Reset(q);
27              return b;
28          }
```

Figure 7-6.   Debugging is peeking at all the variables that are currently loaded into memory

If you tell your debugger to Step Over, it will execute the measurement. You can again investigate the qubit by hovering your mouse over it, and you will see that the probability has not changed because there was a 100% chance of collapsing to $|1\rangle$ after measurement. What has changed is that the qubit now knows that it has been measured. Figure 7-7 shows what you should see in your Visual Studio Code debugger.

```
21
22          operation Debu    {q:0}
23          {                   Id [int]: 0
                                IsMeasured [bool]: true
24              X(q);           Probability [double]: 1
25              let b = M(q);   Hold Alt key to switch to editor language hover
26              Reset(q);
27              return b;
28          }
```

Figure 7-7.   Debugging is peeking at all the variables that are currently loaded into memory

Now, let's look at the ExecuteH operation from Listing 7-13. This operation is very similar with the only difference being that the qubit is put through the H-gate and not the X-gate.

Listing 7-13. The focus is now on the DebugH operation

```
30 operation ExecuteH(q : Qubit) : Result
31 {
32     H(q);
33     let b = M(q);
34     Reset(q);
35     return b;
36 }
```

Put a breakpoint on line 33 and start to debug your application. If the qubit has not been measured, you will notice a probability of 0.5. This means that the qubit is in superposition with a 50% probability of collapsing to $|0\rangle$ and a 50% probability of collapsing to $|1\rangle$. Figure 7-8 shows you the expected result in Visual Studio Code.

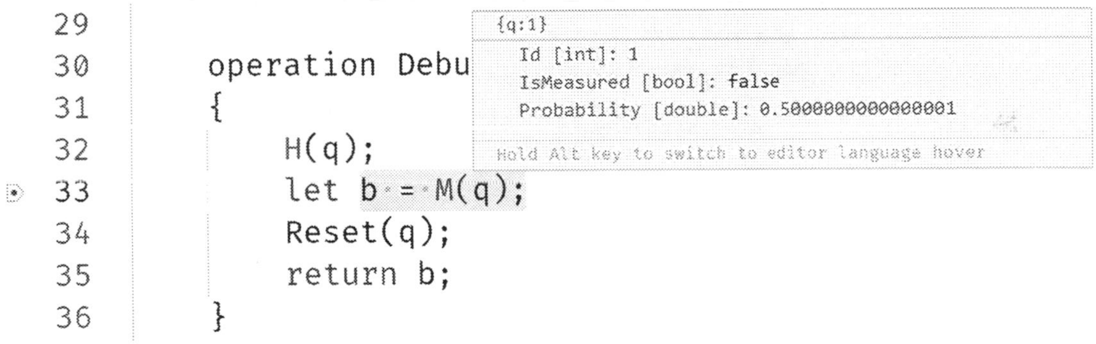

Figure 7-8. *Debugging is peeking at all the variables that are currently loaded into memory*

Again, use the Visual Studio Code debugger toolbar to Step Over once, and look at the qubit once more. After measurement, the probability has changed to either 0 or 1. In Figure 7-9, the probability collapsed to 0, but in your case, it could be different. If you try to debug this multiple times, you will see that sometimes the probability is 0 and sometimes it is 1.

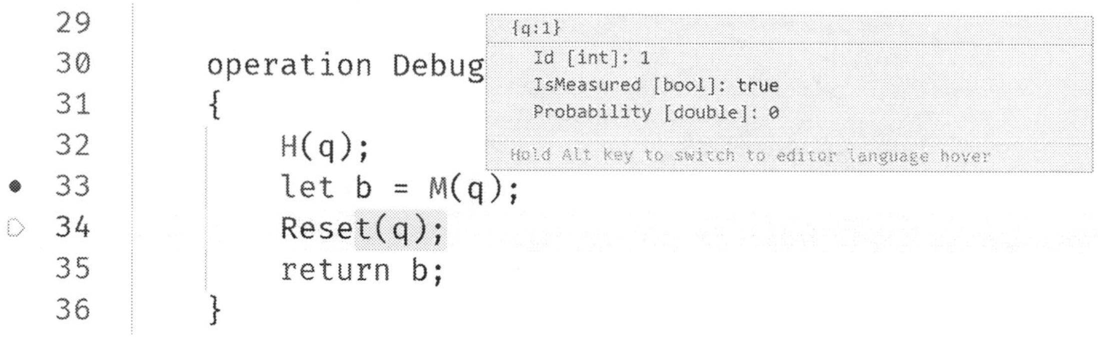

```
29
30          operation Debug          {q:1}
31          {                          Id [int]: 1
32              H(q);                  IsMeasured [bool]: true
•  33           let b = M(q);          Probability [double]: 0
▷  34           Reset(q);              Hold Alt key to switch to editor language hover
35              return b;
36          }
```

Figure 7-9. *Debugging is peeking at all the variables that are currently loaded into memory*

Finally, look at the ExecuteRy operation from Listing 7-14. The state of the qubit will be rotated around the y-axis by $2\pi/3$ radians. Thanks to some trigonometry knowledge, you should be able to figure out the probability beforehand.

Listing 7-14. The focus is now on the ExecuteRy operation

```
38 operation ExecuteRy(q : Qubit) : Result
39 {
40     Ry(2.0 * PI() / 3.0, q);
41     let b = MResetZ(q);
42     Reset(q);
43     return b;
44 }
```

One last time, debug your application after you have set a breakpoint on line 41. As you expected, the probability will now be 0.75, meaning the qubit has a 25% probability of collapsing to $|0\rangle$ and a 75% probability of collapsing to $|1\rangle$. Figure 7-10 shows you the expected result in Visual Studio Code.

```
 37
 38        operation Debu    {q:2}
 39        {                   Id [int]: 2
 40            Ry(2.0 * P      IsMeasured [bool]: false
                              Probability [double]: 0.7499999999999999
 41            let b = M(q);   Hold Alt key to switch to editor language hover
 42            Reset(q);
 43            return b;
 44        }
```

Figure 7-10. *Debugging is peeking at all the variables that are currently loaded into memory*

Stepping Over and measuring the qubit also changes the state of the qubit. In Figure 7-11, the probability has changed to 1. Again, in your case, it could be different, but the chances are now higher, 75% to be exact, that you'll get a 1 and not a 0.

```
 38        operation    {q:2}
 39        {             Id [int]: 2
 40            Ry(2.0    IsMeasured [bool]: true
                        Probability [double]: 1
 41            let b    Hold Alt key to switch to editor language hover
 42            Reset(q);
 43            return b;
 44        }
```

Figure 7-11. *Debugging is peeking at all the variables that are currently loaded into memory*

When you are learning about quantum computing, the debugger feature of Q# can really help you to understand what happens with the state of your qubits.

DumpMachine

As part of the Q# language and API, you can use some diagnostic functions that help you investigate the state of your qubits without using a debugger. One of these diagnostic functions is DumpMachine, which is part of the Microsoft.Quantum.Diagnostics namespace. DumpMachine writes the entire quantum state of all your qubits to the console window or into a text file on disk.

Listing 7-15 shows you a quantum application that dumps this information for two qubits in superposition and two entangled qubits.

Listing 7-15. A quantum prgram that dumps the qubit states for two scenarios to a text file

```
01 namespace _07_15_DumpMachine_QSharp
02 {
03     open Microsoft.Quantum.Canon;
04     open Microsoft.Quantum.Intrinsic;
05     open Microsoft.Quantum.Diagnostics;
06
07     @EntryPoint()
08     operation SayHello() : Unit
09     {
10         Superposition();
11         Entanglement();
12     }
13
14     operation Superposition() : Unit
15     {
16         use qubits = Qubit[2];
17
18         H(qubits[0]);
19         H(qubits[1]);
20
21         DumpMachine("superposition.txt");
22
23         Reset(qubits[0]);
24         Reset(qubits[1]);
25     }
26
27     operation Entanglement() : Unit
28     {
29         use qubits = Qubit[2];
30
```

```
31        H(qubits[0]);
32        CNOT(qubits[0], qubits[1]);
33
34        DumpMachine("entanglement.txt");
35
36        Reset(qubits[0]);
37        Reset(qubits[1]);
38    }
39 }
```

If you create a standalone Q# console application from Visual Studio Code and add the code from Listing 7-15, you will not see any console output. In this case, on lines 21 and 34, the DumpMachine function will write the output to two files on disk. The output from those files is shown in Listings 7-16 and 7-17.

Listing 7-16. Output from the superposition.txt file that was written to disk

```
# wave function for qubits with ids(least to most significant): 0;1
|0>: 0,500000 + 0,000000 i == ******    [ 0,250000 ]   --- [ 0,00000 rad ]
|1>: 0,500000 + 0,000000 i == ******    [ 0,250000 ]   --- [ 0,00000 rad ]
|2>: 0,500000 + 0,000000 i == ******    [ 0,250000 ]   --- [ 0,00000 rad ]
|3>: 0,500000 + 0,000000 i == ******    [ 0,250000 ]   --- [ 0,00000 rad ]
```

The file superposition.txt from Listing 7-16 shows the qubit states for the two qubits in superposition. DumpMachine will list all possible states for these two qubits. If you remember Chapter 2, you know that two qubits can represent a linear combination of four basis states, and you can write that down as

$$\alpha|00\rangle + \beta|01\rangle + \gamma|10\rangle + \delta|11\rangle$$

The text file that's generated from DumpMachine contains these four basis states as four separate lines. It, however, uses a the slightly different decimal notation instead of the binary notation:

$$\alpha|0\rangle + \beta|1\rangle + \gamma|2\rangle + \delta|3\rangle$$

195

You also know that the **α, β, γ**, and **δ** values are complex numbers. These values are also in the text file and are all equal to

$$0.5 + 0.0i$$

From these complex numbers, you can calculate the probabilities, but those probabilities are also part of the text file. A graphical representation using star-characters shows the magnitude and is proportionate to the probability of measuring that specific state. Just to be clear, each line also contains the numeric value of that magnitude, and in this case, they are all equal to 0.25.

Listing 7-17. Output from the entanglement.txt file that was written to disk

```
# wave function for qubits with ids (least to most significant): 0;1
|0⟩: 0,707107 + 0,000000 i == ********** [ 0,500000 ] --- [ 0,00000 rad ]
|1⟩: 0,000000 + 0,000000 i ==              [ 0,000000 ]
|2⟩: 0,000000 + 0,000000 i               [ 0,000000 ]
|3⟩: 0,707107 + 0,000000 i == ********** [ 0,500000 ] --- [ 0,00000 rad ]
```

The file `entanglement.txt` from Listing 7-17 shows the qubit states for the two entangled qubits. From this, it is clear that the two qubits are entangled, because there is a 50% chance of them collapsing to |0⟩ or |00⟩ and a 50% chance of them collapsing to |3⟩ or |11⟩.

DumpRegister

Just like the function `DumpMachine`, `DumpRegister` can output to a text file. The only difference is that you can specify which qubits need to be output. One thing to keep in mind is that if you want to isolate a qubit and only want `DumpRegister` to output that specific qubit, it cannot be entangled with another qubit. The state for an entangled qubit cannot be represented by itself, and multiple entangled qubits should always be output as a whole.

To show you the power of the `DumpRegister` function, I will revisit the teleportation circuit from Chapter 4. Figure 7-12 shows you the teleportation circuit one more time.

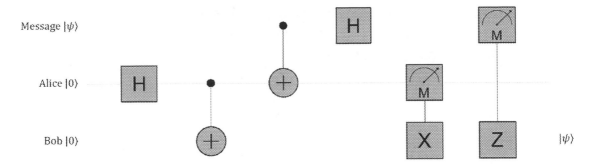

Figure 7-12. *The quantum teleportation circuit which uses entanglement on three qubits*

You are going to translate the teleportation circuit from Figure 7-12 to a Q# standalone console application. With the knowledge you have right now, you can try to figure out how to convert it to valid Q# code. Use the circuit diagram to figure out how many qubits you need and which operations you need to perform on them in which order. You can use Listing 7-18 as a reference or to compare your version with my version. Remember: There can be multiple ways to achieve the same result. The Q# code in Listing 7-18 already contains multiple calls to the DumpRegister function. More on that later.

Listing 7-18. A possible implementation for the teleportation circuit

```
01 namespace _07_18_DumpRegister_QSharp
02 {
03    open Microsoft.Quantum.Canon;
04    open Microsoft.Quantum.Intrinsic;
05    open Microsoft.Quantum.Math;
06    open Microsoft.Quantum.Diagnostics;
07
08    @EntryPoint()
09    operation SayHello() : Unit
10    {
11        use (qMessage, qAlice, qBob)
12            = (Qubit(), Qubit(), Qubit());
13
14        Ry( 2.0 * PI() / 3.0, qMessage );
15
```

```
16        DumpRegister("qMessage-before.txt", [qMessage]);
17        DumpRegister("qAlice-before.txt", [qAlice]);
18        DumpRegister("qBob-before.txt", [qBob]);
19
20        H(qAlice);
21        CNOT(qAlice, qBob);
22
23        CNOT(qMessage, qAlice);
24        H(qMessage);
25
26        let bAlice = M(qAlice);
27        if( bAlice == One )
28        {
29            X(qBob);
30        }
31
32        let bMessage = M(qMessage);
33        if( bMessage == One )
34        {
35            Z(qBob);
36        }
37
38        DumpRegister("qMessage-after.txt", [qMessage]);
39        DumpRegister("qAlice-after.txt", [qAlice]);
40        DumpRegister("qBob-after.txt", [qBob]);
41
42        Reset(qMessage);
43        Reset(qAlice);
44        Reset(qBob);
45    }
46 }
```

The code in Listing 7-18 starts to get interesting on line 11. You should allocate the three qubits necessary and give them appropriate variable names so that the remainder of the code is easy to understand. To prove the teleportation circuit works, the message qubit qMessage has an arbitrary rotation applied to it. Teleporting the $|0\rangle$ or $|1\rangle$ state is boring; teleporting a superposition state is more exciting. Apply your trigonometric and mathematical skill to figure out what probabilities you get for the two computational basis states $|0\rangle$ and $|1\rangle$. The angle with which the qubit is rotated around the y-axis is $2 \cdot \pi/3$. You can calculate the probabilities by using the sine and cosine functions squared, which will lead you to 75% and 25% probabilities.

Tip   Read through Appendix I if you need a refresher on trigonometry or want some more exercise.

Before starting the teleportation circuit, the state for all three qubits is written to a file separately by calling the `DumpRegister` function three times on lines 16, 17, and 18. This will give you a starting point as you can verify the state of all three qubits. The message qubit should be in that complex superposition state, and the qubits for Alice and Bob should be in their initial $|0\rangle$ state. Let's look inside these files. I added them here in Listings 7-19, 7-20, and 7-21.

Listing 7-19. Output qMessage-before.txt

```
# wave function for qubits with ids (least to most significant): 0
|0>: 0,500000 + 0,000000 i == ******            [ 0,250000 ]      ---
[  0,00000 rad ]
|1>: 0,866025 + 0,000000 i == **************    [ 0,750000 ]      ---
[  0,00000 rad ]
```

Listing 7-19 shows you that the superposition state for the message qubit has a 25% probability of collapsing to $|0\rangle$ and a 75% probability of collapsing to $|1\rangle$.

Listing 7-20. Output qAlice-before.txt

```
# wave function for qubits with ids (least to most significant): 1
|0>: 1,000000 + 0,000000 i == ******************* [ 1,000000 ]    ---
[  0,00000 rad ]
|1>: 0,000000 + 0,000000 i ==                     [ 0,000000 ]
```

Listing 7-20 shows you that the qubit for Alice is in its default $|0\rangle$ state.

Listing 7-21. Output qBob-before.txt

```
# wave function for qubits with ids (least to most significant): 2
|0⟩: 1,000000 + 0,000000 i == ******************* [ 1,000000 ]    ---
[ 0,00000 rad ]
|1⟩: 0,000000 + 0,000000 i ==                      [ 0,000000 ]
```

Listing 7-21 shows you that the qubit for Bob is in its default |0⟩ state.

Now that you verified the initial states for out three qubits, you can start executing the actual teleportation circuit. Listing 7-22 repeats the Q# code for your reference.

Listing 7-22. Teleportation circuit in Q#

```
20 H(qAlice);
21 CNOT(qAlice, qBob);
22
23 CNOT(qMessage, qAlice);
24 H(qMessage);
25
26 let bAlice = M(qAlice);
27 if( bAlice == One )
28 {
29     X(qBob);
30 }
31
32 let bMessage = M(qMessage);
33 if( bMessage == One )
34 {
35     Z(qBob);
36 }
```

Lines 20 and 21 from Listing 7-22 perform the entanglement between the qubits from Alice and Bob. Lines 23 and 24 perform the second entanglement between the message qubit and the qubit from Alice. Lines 26 through 30 take care of the measurement of the qubit from Alice and apply the X-operation to the qubit from Bob if that measurement results in |1⟩. Lines 32 through 36 take care of the measurement of the message qubit and apply the Z-operation to the qubit from Bob if that measurement results in |1⟩.

This completes the teleportation circuit. You can now call the DumpRegister function again for all three qubits to compare their states with the initial states, and this would help you to verify if teleportation worked. Listings 7-23, 7-24, and 7-25 show you the output for the three qubits.

Listing 7-23. Output qMessage-after.txt

```
# wave function for qubits with ids (least to most significant): 0
|0⟩: 1,000000 + 0,000000 i == ******************** [ 1,000000 ]        ---
[  0,00000 rad ]
|1⟩: 0,000000 + 0,000000 i ==                       [ 0,000000 ]
```

Listing 7-23 shows you that the initial message qubit has lost its message. This is to be expected since quantum states cannot be copied, only teleported. The initial state is destroyed, and in this specific case, it has been collapsed to |0⟩ by the measurement that you performed on this qubit.

Listing 7-24. Output qAlice-after.txt

```
# wave function for qubits with ids (least to most significant): 1
|0⟩: 1,000000 + 0,000000 i == ******************** [ 1,000000 ]        ---
[  0,00000 rad ]
|1⟩: 0,000000 + 0,000000 i ==                       [ 0,000000 ]
```

Listing 7-24 shows you that the qubit from Alice is not entangled. You measured it to decide what to do with the qubit from Bob, so in this specific case, it has collapsed to |0⟩ by the measurement.

Listing 7-25. Output qBob-after.txt

```
# wave function for qubits with ids (least to most significant): 2
|0⟩: 0,500000 + 0,000000 i == ******                [ 0,250000 ]        ---
[  0,00000 rad ]
|1⟩: 0,866025 + 0,000000 i == **************         [ 0,750000 ]        ---
[  0,00000 rad ]
```

Listing 7-25 shows you the magic of the teleportation circuit. Initially, the qubit from Bob was in the $|0\rangle$ state. You entangled it with the qubit from Alice and optionally executed the X-operation and Z-operation to it. The X-operation and Z-operation are 180° rotations and can never result in the 120° rotation needed to get to the superposition state represented by Listing 7-25. Entanglement is the hero in this teleportation circuit.

The Last Word

In this chapter, you learned about the different tools that are part of the Microsoft Quantum Development Kit which can help you to write your quantum programs. Just like many modern classical programming languages, you can debug and test entire applications and parts of your code.

Take advantage of tools like Visual Studio Code to help you step through your code line by line to learn and investigate the inner workings of your code. Write some unit tests if your code performs complex operations that are hard to follow from the top of your head. And finally, use the diagnostic functions like `DumpMachine` and `DumpRegister` to gain insights in your qubit states.

This chapter conclude the second part of this introductory book on quantum computing and Microsoft Q#. In the next part, you'll be submerged into some existing quantum algorithms to help you gain more understanding into how quantum computing can help us achieve much more than classical computing.

PART III

Quantum Algorithms

## CHAPTER 8

Deutsch's Algorithm

In Part 1 of this book, you learned about some of the theoretical concepts of quantum computing, and in Part 2, you got acquainted with Microsoft Q#, a quantum programming language and simulator. Actual quantum algorithms, and, as an extension on that, quantum programs, are hard to invent and write. Firstly, you need a very specific problem to solve, and secondly, you need to think of a process that can leverage quantum properties to solve your problem.

In this chapter, you will get to know Deutsch's algorithm, named after British physicist David Deutsch. Deutsch's algorithm is based on a paper written by David Deutsch in 1985 and discusses a specific problem that can be solved deterministically on a quantum computer.

Deutsch's algorithm is, in my opinion, one of the easiest algorithms to comprehend. On the following pages, you will learn, step by step, what Deutsch's algorithm is all about and how to recreate it using Microsoft Q#.

The Deutsch Oracle

The problem that Deutsch's algorithm solves is not very useful. It is an artificial problem, specifically designed to prove that a quantum computer can outsmart a classical computer, and it was one of the first solutions to a problem that came to this conclusion with success.

The problem is about a binary function that works on a single bit. If you think about a single bit, there are four classical operations or functions you can execute on that bit:

- **Constant-0**: The output of the function is zero, regardless of the input:

$$f(x) = 0$$

J. Hooyberghs, *Introducing Microsoft Quantum Computing for Developers*,
https://doi.org/10.1007/978-1-4842-7246-6_8

- **Constant-1**: The output of the function is one, regardless of the input:

$$f(x) = 1$$

- **Identity**: The output of the function repeats the input:

$$f(x) = x$$

- **Negation**: The output of the function negates the input:

$$f(x) = \neg x$$

Now, to formulate the problem, you have to ask yourself the question: If one of those four functions is put inside of a black box and you are able to test the input and output values of that black box, are you able to predict what the function actually is? Figure 8-1 shows you a schematic of an input value x and an output value $f(x)$. In between is the black box containing the mystery function.

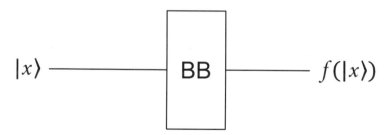

Figure 8-1. *A circuit with input x, a black box containing a binary function, and output f(x)*

To answer the question: it depends. You cannot identify the binary function by just testing with a single input value. If you test with input 0 and the output also equals 0, the binary function can be constant-0 or identity. Think about it yourself, and take some time to test with different input and output values.

The result is that you always need two evaluations to know for sure what binary function is hidden inside of the black box. The point of Deutsch's algorithm is to find an alternative that can run on a quantum computer and only needs a single evaluation to figure out the binary function in the black box. In order to convert this binary function into something that is compatible with the laws of quantum, Deutsch needed a small change.

In the world of quantum physics, a quantum operation needs to be unitary and thus be reversible. If you think about the classical binary function constant-0, it cannot be reversible. You can't reverse the function and return to your input if you start with the output. If constant-0 returns 0, you don't know if the input was 0 or 1. The input was lost.

On a quantum computer, you can rewrite the circuit from Figure 8-1 and use an additional qubit to store the input value. Figure 8-2 shows the same black box as before but extended using two input and two output values. On the left-hand side, there is a constant $|0\rangle$ state on the top and the input $|x\rangle$ state in the bottom. On the right-hand side, there is the output $f(|x\rangle)$ state on the top and the input state $|x\rangle$ repeated in the bottom. Because the output repeats the input, this quantum operation is now reversible, and you can always invert the binary function to get back to the input.

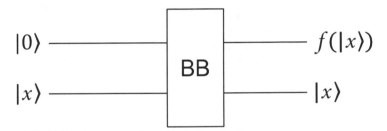

Figure 8-2. *The circuit from Figure 8-1, converted to the quantum world*

Deutsch, however, was in for some frustration. He was not able to figure out a quantum implementation to solve his problem, and he needed to think outside of the box. It seems asking the question "What binary function is inside the black box?" is not the correct question to ask. A quantum algorithm, just like the classical version, needs to run twice to find the solution. Deutsch rephrased his question to "Is the binary function inside the black box constant or variable?" For this specific question, Deutsch was able to figure out a quantum algorithm that only needs to run once, while its classical counterpart still needs two iterations to find a solution.

A Quantum Oracle

In quantum computing, an oracle is a black box operation that can be used as input to another operation.

For Deutsch's algorithm specifically, the algorithm itself can determine whether the binary function is constant or variable by using a specific set of quantum gates. The actual binary function should also be part of the algorithm and acts like an oracle; a black-box operation that will be used as input to another operation. This will become clear when you implement Deutsch's algorithm in Q# at the end of this chapter.

Back to the Deutsch Oracle

By using the power of superposition, Deutsch found a very specific circuit that is able to determine what is inside the black box by running the circuit only once using input state $|0\rangle$ for both qubits. Figure 8-3 shows you the circuit that does exactly this.

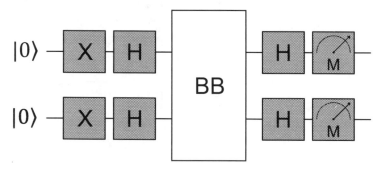

Figure 8-3. *The circuit for Deutsch algorithm*

In order to actually test this circuit, you will need to implement the possible binary functions inside the black box as a quantum oracle. The next part of this chapter will guide you through the quantum versions of those four binary functions and will prove to you that Deutsch's algorithm works by using a mathematical approach.

Constant-0

If you only look at the black box inside Deutsch's circuit, the input is on the left-hand side of the black box, and the output is on the right-hand side of the black box. Figure 8-4 shows you this partial circuit with the actual binary input $|x\rangle$ on the bottom of the left-hand side and the binary function output $|0\rangle$ on the top of the right-hand side. The top input will always be $|0\rangle$ for all binary functions, and the bottom output will always repeat the input $|x\rangle$ to make the function reversible.

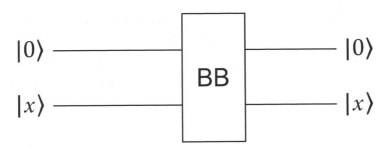

Figure 8-4. *The black box with the input and output for the constant-0 binary function*

With everything you have learned in the previous chapters, you should be able to come up with a circuit that will actually perform the constant-0 binary function. Just remember that the top output on the right-hand side needs to be $|0\rangle$ and the bottom output on the right-hand side needs to repeat the input $|x\rangle$.

Figure 8-5 shows you the necessary operations. Indeed, no operations needed. The constant-0 function has the easiest circuit. You don't need to change anything. The top qubit should always output $|0\rangle$, and it is inputted as $|0\rangle$. The bottom qubit is inputted as $|x\rangle$, and it should keep $|x\rangle$ as the output.

$$|0\rangle \text{———————} |0\rangle$$

$$|x\rangle \text{———————} |x\rangle$$

Figure 8-5. *The quantum circuit representing the binary function constant-0*

A circuit is a collection of operations performed on one or multiple qubits. This collection of operations can be expressed as a mathematical expression, and the resulting states can thus be calculated. The following formula expresses the circuit from Figure 8-5:

$$I_0 I_1 \left(\begin{pmatrix} 1 \\ 0 \end{pmatrix} \otimes \begin{pmatrix} \alpha \\ \beta \end{pmatrix} \right) = \begin{pmatrix} 1 \\ 0 \end{pmatrix} \otimes \begin{pmatrix} \alpha \\ \beta \end{pmatrix}$$

There are no quantum gates used in this circuit, which is represented by the Identity I operation in the mathematical expression. The qubits are represented by their quantum state matrices where the first qubit is represented by the matrix for the $|0\rangle$ state and the second qubit is represented by the matrix for the $\alpha |0\rangle + \beta |1\rangle$ state. Because the circuit describes a combined two-qubit state, the two qubit states should be expressed as a combined state by applying the tensor product ⊗.

So, to recap, we apply the I operation on the first I_0 and second I_1 qubit of a combined qubit state $|0\rangle \otimes \alpha |0\rangle + \beta |1\rangle$ which results in the exact same combined state.

If you incorporate this black-box circuit into Deutsch's circuit, it will look like Figure 8-6.

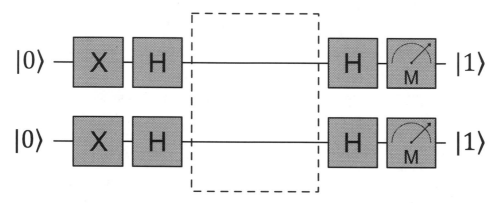

Figure 8-6. *Deutsch's algorithm with the constant-0 binary function integrated*

If you think about the circuit from Figure 8-6 logically, it makes sense. The circuit always starts with two qubits in state $|0\rangle$. Next, you put both qubits through the X-gate to flip them to state $|1\rangle$, and afterward you put both qubits through the H-gate to put them in a superposition state $1/\sqrt{2}|0\rangle + 1/\sqrt{2}|1\rangle$. At this point, you are testing the constant-0 binary function with an input that is in superposition, so you are testing with both 0 and 1 at the same time. After performing the constant-0 function, doing nothing, the qubits are put through the H-gate again to pull them out of superposition. The measured output will always be the expected $|1\rangle \otimes |1\rangle$ state.

Again, you can prove this mathematically by executing the operation using some linear algebra. The calculation is broken down for you in the following paragraphs:

$$H_0 H_1 H_0 H_1 X_0 X_1 \left(\begin{pmatrix} 1 \\ 0 \end{pmatrix} \otimes \begin{pmatrix} 1 \\ 0 \end{pmatrix} \right) = H_0 H_1 H_0 H_1 \left(\begin{pmatrix} 0 & 1 \\ 1 & 0 \end{pmatrix} \begin{pmatrix} 1 \\ 0 \end{pmatrix} \otimes \begin{pmatrix} 0 & 1 \\ 1 & 0 \end{pmatrix} \begin{pmatrix} 1 \\ 0 \end{pmatrix} \right)$$

A range of operations is executed on the combined qubit state $|0\rangle \otimes |0\rangle$ – from right to left, the X-gate on both qubits, the H-gate on both qubits, and finally, the H-gate again on both qubits. You can work out the operations one step at the time and move the X-gate operations to the right-hand side of the equal sign. Multiply each qubit state matrix with the X-gate matrix:

$$H_0 H_1 H_0 H_1 \left(\begin{pmatrix} 0 \\ 1 \end{pmatrix} \otimes \begin{pmatrix} 0 \\ 1 \end{pmatrix} \right) = H_0 H_1 \left(\left(\begin{pmatrix} \frac{1}{\sqrt{2}} & \frac{1}{\sqrt{2}} \\ \frac{1}{\sqrt{2}} & \frac{-1}{\sqrt{2}} \end{pmatrix} \begin{pmatrix} 0 \\ 1 \end{pmatrix} \right) \otimes \left(\begin{pmatrix} \frac{1}{\sqrt{2}} & \frac{1}{\sqrt{2}} \\ \frac{1}{\sqrt{2}} & \frac{-1}{\sqrt{2}} \end{pmatrix} \begin{pmatrix} 0 \\ 1 \end{pmatrix} \right) \right)$$

Next, you can rewrite the expression after multiplying the matrices. Again, you can move the H-gate operations to the right-hand side of the equal sign and multiply each qubit state matrix with the H-gate matrix:

$$H_0 H_1 \left(\begin{pmatrix} \frac{1}{\sqrt{2}} \\ \frac{-1}{\sqrt{2}} \end{pmatrix} \otimes \begin{pmatrix} \frac{1}{\sqrt{2}} \\ \frac{-1}{\sqrt{2}} \end{pmatrix} \right) = \begin{pmatrix} \frac{1}{\sqrt{2}} & \frac{1}{\sqrt{2}} \\ \frac{1}{\sqrt{2}} & \frac{-1}{\sqrt{2}} \end{pmatrix} \begin{pmatrix} \frac{1}{\sqrt{2}} \\ \frac{-1}{\sqrt{2}} \end{pmatrix} \otimes \begin{pmatrix} \frac{1}{\sqrt{2}} & \frac{1}{\sqrt{2}} \\ \frac{1}{\sqrt{2}} & \frac{-1}{\sqrt{2}} \end{pmatrix} \begin{pmatrix} \frac{1}{\sqrt{2}} \\ \frac{-1}{\sqrt{2}} \end{pmatrix}$$

Now, execute those matrix multiplications, and move the final H-gate operations to the right-hand side of the equal sign. Now, there are no operations left, and you can multiply matrices one last time to get to the $|1\rangle \otimes |1\rangle$ state:

$$H_0 H_1 H_0 H_1 X_0 X_1 \left(\begin{pmatrix} 1 \\ 0 \end{pmatrix} \otimes \begin{pmatrix} 1 \\ 0 \end{pmatrix} \right) = \begin{pmatrix} 0 \\ 1 \end{pmatrix} \otimes \begin{pmatrix} 0 \\ 1 \end{pmatrix} = |11\rangle$$

At the start of this chapter, you learned that Deutsch's algorithm always results in $|11\rangle$ for constant functions. The binary function constant-0 is a constant function, so your implementation works. You can think about it in a logical way by looking at the circuit, and you can prove it using some basic linear algebra.

Constant-1

The constant-1 binary function is very similar to the constant-0 binary function with the only difference that the top output qubit on the right-hand side should always output $|1\rangle$. Figure 8-7 shows you the expected inputs and outputs for the constant-1 binary function black box.

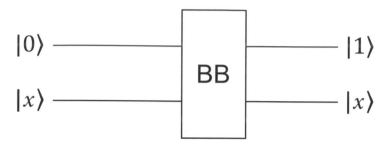

Figure 8-7. *The black box with the input and output for the constant-1 binary function*

Just like before, try to come up with any number of operations to get the desired output qubits using the specified input qubits from Figure 8-7. Figure 8-8 shows you the solution.

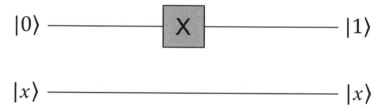

Figure 8-8. *The quantum circuit representing the binary function constant-1*

Because the top input qubit is in state $|0\rangle$, you only need to flip it to $|1\rangle$ using the X-gate. Again, the bottom input qubit doesn't need to be changed to repeat the input as output.

If you incorporate the circuit from Figure 8-8 into the black box of Deutsch's circuit, you will get Figure 8-9.

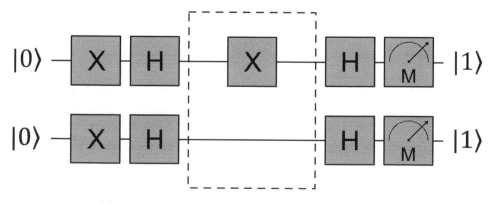

Figure 8-9. *Deutsch's algorithm with the constant-1 binary function integrated*

With the constant-1 binary function incorporated into Deutsch's circuit, you can see that the additional X-gate will not cause the measured output to change. This is because flipping a qubit in superposition doesn't change its probability distribution. If this is not clear to you, think about the Bloch sphere, and imagine the qubit in superposition. The vector is exactly on top of the x-axis; hence, rotating it around that vector will not change the orientation of that vector. Pulling the qubit out of superposition will rotate the vector state back to its original $|0\rangle$.

Again, you can use mathematics to calculate this as proof. Just perform the same steps as before, but add the additional X-gate on the first qubit in the correct order:

$$H_0 H_1 X_0 H_0 H_1 X_0 X_1 \left(\begin{pmatrix} 1 \\ 0 \end{pmatrix} \otimes \begin{pmatrix} 1 \\ 0 \end{pmatrix} \right) = H_0 H_1 H_0 H_1 \left(\begin{pmatrix} 0 & 1 \\ 1 & 0 \end{pmatrix} \begin{pmatrix} 1 \\ 0 \end{pmatrix} \otimes \begin{pmatrix} 0 & 1 \\ 1 & 0 \end{pmatrix} \begin{pmatrix} 1 \\ 0 \end{pmatrix} \right)$$

The first step is the exact same as before. Apply the X-gate to both qubits:

$$H_0 H_1 X_0 H_0 H_1 \left(\begin{pmatrix} 0 \\ 1 \end{pmatrix} \otimes \begin{pmatrix} 0 \\ 1 \end{pmatrix} \right) = H_0 H_1 X_0 \left(\begin{pmatrix} \frac{1}{\sqrt{2}} & \frac{1}{\sqrt{2}} \\ \frac{1}{\sqrt{2}} & \frac{-1}{\sqrt{2}} \end{pmatrix} \begin{pmatrix} 0 \\ 1 \end{pmatrix} \otimes \begin{pmatrix} \frac{1}{\sqrt{2}} & \frac{1}{\sqrt{2}} \\ \frac{1}{\sqrt{2}} & \frac{-1}{\sqrt{2}} \end{pmatrix} \begin{pmatrix} 0 \\ 1 \end{pmatrix} \right)$$

The second step is also the exact same as before. Apply the H-gate to both qubits:

$$H_0 H_1 X_0 \left(\begin{pmatrix} \frac{1}{\sqrt{2}} \\ \frac{-1}{\sqrt{2}} \end{pmatrix} \otimes \begin{pmatrix} \frac{1}{\sqrt{2}} \\ \frac{-1}{\sqrt{2}} \end{pmatrix} \right) = H_0 H_1 \left(\begin{pmatrix} \frac{1}{\sqrt{2}} \\ \frac{-1}{\sqrt{2}} \end{pmatrix} \otimes \begin{pmatrix} 0 & 1 \\ 1 & 0 \end{pmatrix} \begin{pmatrix} \frac{1}{\sqrt{2}} \\ \frac{-1}{\sqrt{2}} \end{pmatrix} \right)$$

In the third step, things get more interesting. You need to apply the X-gate only to the first qubit. That first qubit is in superposition, so the probability distribution is flipped. Because the probability distribution is 50/50, nothing really changes, except for the sign, which moves from the $|1\rangle$ state to the $|0\rangle$ state. When you calculate the probability, you need to take the absolute value squared. $-1/\sqrt{2}$ is a real number, so the absolute value will get rid of that sign, and the result is still 50%:

$$H_0 H_1 \left(\begin{pmatrix} \frac{1}{\sqrt{2}} \\ \frac{-1}{\sqrt{2}} \end{pmatrix} \otimes \begin{pmatrix} \frac{-1}{\sqrt{2}} \\ \frac{1}{\sqrt{2}} \end{pmatrix} \right) = \begin{pmatrix} \frac{1}{\sqrt{2}} & \frac{1}{\sqrt{2}} \\ \frac{1}{\sqrt{2}} & \frac{-1}{\sqrt{2}} \end{pmatrix} \begin{pmatrix} \frac{1}{\sqrt{2}} \\ \frac{-1}{\sqrt{2}} \end{pmatrix} \otimes \begin{pmatrix} \frac{1}{\sqrt{2}} & \frac{1}{\sqrt{2}} \\ \frac{1}{\sqrt{2}} & \frac{-1}{\sqrt{2}} \end{pmatrix} \begin{pmatrix} \frac{-1}{\sqrt{2}} \\ \frac{1}{\sqrt{2}} \end{pmatrix}$$

Finally, you need to apply the H-gate to the two qubits, which is no different than before. The only exception is the sign change. In our final state, we still have the sign for the first qubit. This sign is insignificant after a measurement because of the same reason as before. The absolute value squared of -1 is 100%, so the final state is $|11\rangle$:

$$H_0 H_1 X_0 H_0 H_1 X_0 X_1 \left(\begin{pmatrix} 1 \\ 0 \end{pmatrix} \otimes \begin{pmatrix} 1 \\ 0 \end{pmatrix} \right) = \begin{pmatrix} 0 \\ 1 \end{pmatrix} \otimes \begin{pmatrix} 0 \\ -1 \end{pmatrix} = |11\rangle$$

So, just like the binary function constant-0, constant-1 also results in state $|11\rangle$. Deutsch's algorithm states that constant functions always result in state $|11\rangle$, so you are still on the right track.

Identity

The previous binary functions were child's play. Now you enter the realm of variable functions. The left-hand side stays the same, but the top output qubit should equal the bottom input qubit. Figure 8-10 shows you these expected input and output qubit states.

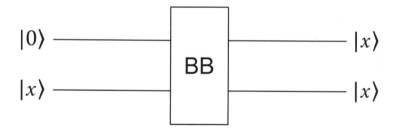

Figure 8-10. *The black box with the input and output for the identity binary function*

Just like before, try to break inside of the black box, and think about which operations you can execute to get the top output qubit to reflect the bottom input qubit. Figure 8-11 shows you the solution.

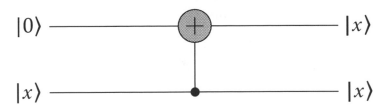

Figure 8-11. *The quantum circuit representing the binary function identity*

Since the first qubit needs to be dependent on the second qubit, you can use the CNOT-gate where the second qubit is the control qubit and the first qubit is the target qubit. The first qubit will be in the $|0\rangle$ state from the start and will be flipped by the CNOT-gate, only if the second qubit is $|1\rangle$.

If you incorporate the circuit from Figure 8-11 into the black box of Deutsch's circuit, you will get Figure 8-12.

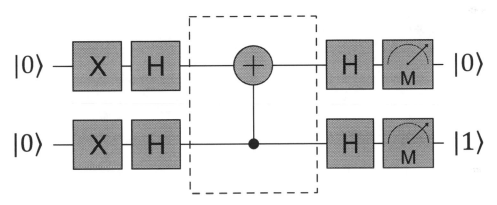

Figure 8-12. *Deutsch's algorithm with the identity binary function integrated*

By looking at the circuit from Figure 8-12, things become much more complicated. It is harder to think about a CNOT-gate if you are dealing with superposition. This is the time that mathematics can really help you, and this is why this book spends so much effort to teach you the basics.

Again, you can go through the calculations by writing down the expressions step by step. Only now, you have to deal with the additional complexity of multi-qubit-gates like the CNOT-gate. The CNOT-gate is expressed using the C_{10} identifier with a double-numbered subscript where the first number is the control qubit index and the second number is the target qubit index:

$$H_0 H_1 C_{10} H_0 H_1 X_0 X_1 \left(\begin{pmatrix} 1 \\ 0 \end{pmatrix} \otimes \begin{pmatrix} 1 \\ 0 \end{pmatrix} \right) = H_0 H_1 C_{10} H_0 H_1 \left(\begin{pmatrix} 0 & 1 \\ 1 & 0 \end{pmatrix} \begin{pmatrix} 1 \\ 0 \end{pmatrix} \otimes \begin{pmatrix} 0 & 1 \\ 1 & 0 \end{pmatrix} \begin{pmatrix} 1 \\ 0 \end{pmatrix} \right)$$

The first step is the exact same as before. Apply the X-gate to both qubits:

$$H_0 H_1 C_{10} H_0 H_1 \left(\begin{pmatrix} 0 \\ 1 \end{pmatrix} \otimes \begin{pmatrix} 0 \\ 1 \end{pmatrix} \right) = H_0 H_1 C_{10} \left(\begin{pmatrix} \frac{1}{\sqrt{2}} & \frac{1}{\sqrt{2}} \\ \frac{1}{\sqrt{2}} & \frac{-1}{\sqrt{2}} \end{pmatrix} \begin{pmatrix} 0 \\ 1 \end{pmatrix} \otimes \begin{pmatrix} \frac{1}{\sqrt{2}} & \frac{1}{\sqrt{2}} \\ \frac{1}{\sqrt{2}} & \frac{-1}{\sqrt{2}} \end{pmatrix} \begin{pmatrix} 0 \\ 1 \end{pmatrix} \right)$$

The second step is also the exact same as before. Apply the H-gate to both qubits:

$$H_0 H_1 C_{10} \left(\begin{pmatrix} \frac{1}{\sqrt{2}} \\ \frac{-1}{\sqrt{2}} \end{pmatrix} \otimes \begin{pmatrix} \frac{1}{\sqrt{2}} \\ \frac{-1}{\sqrt{2}} \end{pmatrix} \right) = H_0 H_1 \left(\begin{pmatrix} 1 & 0 & 0 & 0 \\ 0 & 1 & 0 & 0 \\ 0 & 0 & 0 & 1 \\ 0 & 0 & 1 & 0 \end{pmatrix} \begin{pmatrix} \frac{1}{2} \\ -\frac{1}{2} \\ -\frac{1}{2} \\ \frac{1}{2} \end{pmatrix} \right)$$

Again, in the third step, things become interesting. A CNOT-gate applies to two qubits and is represented by a 4 times 4 operation matrix. If you want to multiply this matrix with a state matrix, you need to combine the qubit states by executing the tensor product:

$$H_0 H_1 \begin{pmatrix} \frac{1}{2} \\ -\frac{1}{2} \\ \frac{1}{2} \\ -\frac{1}{2} \end{pmatrix} = H_0 H_1 \left(\begin{pmatrix} \frac{1}{\sqrt{2}} \\ \frac{1}{\sqrt{2}} \end{pmatrix} \otimes \begin{pmatrix} \frac{1}{\sqrt{2}} \\ \frac{-1}{\sqrt{2}} \end{pmatrix} \right) = \begin{pmatrix} \frac{1}{\sqrt{2}} & \frac{1}{\sqrt{2}} \\ \frac{1}{\sqrt{2}} & \frac{-1}{\sqrt{2}} \end{pmatrix} \begin{pmatrix} \frac{1}{\sqrt{2}} \\ \frac{1}{\sqrt{2}} \end{pmatrix} \otimes \begin{pmatrix} \frac{1}{\sqrt{2}} & \frac{1}{\sqrt{2}} \\ \frac{1}{\sqrt{2}} & \frac{-1}{\sqrt{2}} \end{pmatrix} \begin{pmatrix} \frac{1}{\sqrt{2}} \\ \frac{-1}{\sqrt{2}} \end{pmatrix}$$

Finally, to apply the H-gate to both qubits, you need to try to return to the separated qubit states. Reverse the tensor product, and apply the H-gate operation to each qubit separately:

$$H_0 H_1 C_{10} H_0 H_1 X_0 X_1 \left(\begin{pmatrix} 1 \\ 0 \end{pmatrix} \otimes \begin{pmatrix} 1 \\ 0 \end{pmatrix} \right) = \begin{pmatrix} 1 \\ 0 \end{pmatrix} \otimes \begin{pmatrix} 0 \\ 1 \end{pmatrix} = |01\rangle$$

The result is $|01\rangle$, just like stated by Deutsch's algorithm for variable functions. Identity is a variable binary function because its output is variable, based on its input.

Negation

Just like identity, negation is a variable function because the output is correlated with the input. One final time, the left-hand side stays the same, but the top output qubits should be the inverse value of the bottom input qubit. Figure 8-13 shows you these expected input and output qubit states.

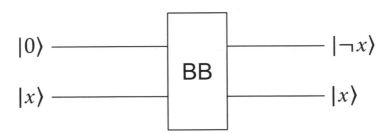

Figure 8-13. *The black box with the input and output for the negation binary function*

For this final binary function, think inside the black box, and figure out the operations to get the top output qubit to be the flipped version of the bottom input qubit. Which operation could you need to add to the identity circuit to invert the output qubit? Figure 8-14 shows you the solution.

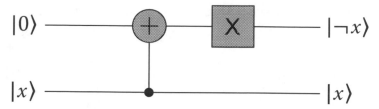

Figure 8-14. *The quantum circuit representing the binary function negation*

Just like the identity circuit, you need the first qubit to be dependent on the second qubit, and you can still do this by using the CNOT-gate. The first qubit will be in the $|0\rangle$ state from the start and will be flipped by the CNOT-gate, only if the second qubit is $|1\rangle$. In this way, the first and the second qubit are correlated. If you put the first qubit through an additional X-gate, the value will be flipped one more time. So, if the second qubit was $|0\rangle$, the first qubit will not be flipped by the CNOT-gate, but it will be flipped by the X-gate, resulting in $|1\rangle$. If the second qubit was $|1\rangle$, the first qubit will be flipped by the CNOT-gate and will be flipped again by the X-gate, resulting in $|0\rangle$.

If you incorporate the circuit from Figure 8-14 into the black box of Deutsch's circuit, you will get Figure 8-15.

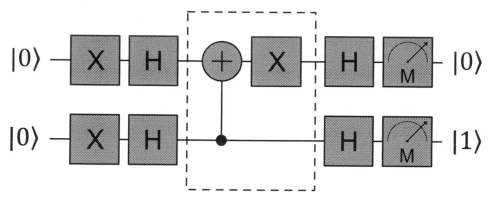

Figure 8-15. *Deutsch's algorithm with the negation binary function integrated*

By looking at the circuit from Figure 8-15, things look very familiar to Deutsch's identity circuit. But just like with constant binary function, the additional X-gate shouldn't really make a lot of difference to a qubit in superposition, so the end result should be very similar.

To verify this gut-feeling, you can go through the calculations by writing down the expressions step by step. Again, the process will be very similar to the identity binary function but with the additional X-gate on the first qubit:

$$H_0 H_1 X_0 C_{10} H_0 H_1 X_0 X_1 \left(\begin{pmatrix} 1 \\ 0 \end{pmatrix} \otimes \begin{pmatrix} 1 \\ 0 \end{pmatrix} \right) = H_0 H_1 X_0 C_{10} H_0 H_1 \left(\begin{pmatrix} 0 & 1 \\ 1 & 0 \end{pmatrix} \begin{pmatrix} 1 \\ 0 \end{pmatrix} \otimes \begin{pmatrix} 0 & 1 \\ 1 & 0 \end{pmatrix} \begin{pmatrix} 1 \\ 0 \end{pmatrix} \right)$$

The first step of the final expression is the exact same as before. Apply the X-gate to both qubits:

$$H_0 H_1 X_0 C_{10} H_0 H_1 \left(\begin{pmatrix} 0 \\ 1 \end{pmatrix} \otimes \begin{pmatrix} 0 \\ 1 \end{pmatrix} \right) = H_0 H_1 X_0 C_{10} \left(\begin{pmatrix} \frac{1}{\sqrt{2}} & \frac{1}{\sqrt{2}} \\ \frac{1}{\sqrt{2}} & \frac{-1}{\sqrt{2}} \end{pmatrix} \begin{pmatrix} 0 \\ 1 \end{pmatrix} \otimes \begin{pmatrix} \frac{1}{\sqrt{2}} & \frac{1}{\sqrt{2}} \\ \frac{1}{\sqrt{2}} & \frac{-1}{\sqrt{2}} \end{pmatrix} \begin{pmatrix} 0 \\ 1 \end{pmatrix} \right)$$

The second step is also the exact same as before. Apply the H-gate to both qubits:

$$H_0 H_1 X_0 C_{10} \left(\begin{pmatrix} \frac{1}{\sqrt{2}} \\ \frac{-1}{\sqrt{2}} \end{pmatrix} \otimes \begin{pmatrix} \frac{1}{\sqrt{2}} \\ \frac{-1}{\sqrt{2}} \end{pmatrix} \right) = H_0 H_1 X_0 \begin{pmatrix} 1 & 0 & 0 & 0 \\ 0 & 1 & 0 & 0 \\ 0 & 0 & 0 & 1 \\ 0 & 0 & 1 & 0 \end{pmatrix} \begin{pmatrix} \frac{1}{2} \\ -\frac{1}{2} \\ -\frac{1}{2} \\ \frac{1}{2} \end{pmatrix}$$

Now, just like with identity, you need to work out the CNOT-gate after calculating the tensor product to work with the combined qubit state:

$$H_0 H_1 X_0 \begin{pmatrix} \frac{1}{2} \\ -\frac{1}{2} \\ \frac{1}{2} \\ -\frac{1}{2} \end{pmatrix} = H_0 H_1 X_0 \left(\begin{pmatrix} \frac{1}{\sqrt{2}} \\ \frac{1}{\sqrt{2}} \end{pmatrix} \otimes \begin{pmatrix} \frac{1}{\sqrt{2}} \\ \frac{-1}{\sqrt{2}} \end{pmatrix} \right) = H_0 H_1 \left(\begin{pmatrix} \frac{1}{\sqrt{2}} \\ \frac{1}{\sqrt{2}} \end{pmatrix} \otimes \begin{pmatrix} 0 & 1 \\ 1 & 0 \end{pmatrix} \begin{pmatrix} \frac{1}{\sqrt{2}} \\ \frac{-1}{\sqrt{2}} \end{pmatrix} \right)$$

Finally, something different is happening. This time, you will execute the additional X-gate on the first qubit by multiplying with the X-gate operation matrix and thus flipping the state matrix:

$$H_0H_1\left(\begin{pmatrix}\dfrac{1}{\sqrt{2}}\\[2mm]\dfrac{1}{\sqrt{2}}\end{pmatrix}\otimes\begin{pmatrix}\dfrac{-1}{\sqrt{2}}\\[2mm]\dfrac{1}{\sqrt{2}}\end{pmatrix}\right)=\begin{pmatrix}\dfrac{1}{\sqrt{2}}&\dfrac{1}{\sqrt{2}}\\[2mm]\dfrac{1}{\sqrt{2}}&\dfrac{-1}{\sqrt{2}}\end{pmatrix}\begin{pmatrix}\dfrac{1}{\sqrt{2}}\\[2mm]\dfrac{1}{\sqrt{2}}\end{pmatrix}\otimes\begin{pmatrix}\dfrac{1}{\sqrt{2}}&\dfrac{1}{\sqrt{2}}\\[2mm]\dfrac{1}{\sqrt{2}}&\dfrac{-1}{\sqrt{2}}\end{pmatrix}\begin{pmatrix}\dfrac{-1}{\sqrt{2}}\\[2mm]\dfrac{1}{\sqrt{2}}\end{pmatrix}$$

Finally, to apply the H-gate to both qubits, you need to try to return to the separated qubit states. Reverse the tensor product, and apply the H-gate operation to each qubit separately.

$$H_0H_1X_0C_{10}H_0H_1X_0X_1\left(\begin{pmatrix}1\\0\end{pmatrix}\otimes\begin{pmatrix}1\\0\end{pmatrix}\right)=\begin{pmatrix}1\\0\end{pmatrix}\otimes\begin{pmatrix}0\\-1\end{pmatrix}=|01\rangle$$

The result is $|01\rangle$, just like stated by Deutsch's algorithm for variable functions. Negation is a variable binary function because its output is variable, based on its input.

So, unlinked to whatever binary function is inside the black box, Deutsch's algorithm can determine that the function inside the black box is constant or variable by only running the algorithm one time. No classical algorithm, except for a simulated quantum version, is known today that can solve this problem in only one iteration. Congratulations to quantum computing!

Deutsch's Algorithm in Q#

Now that you are overwhelmed with all this theory, it is time to finally put all of this into some quantum code! This book is about teaching you the basics of quantum computing with Microsoft Q#, so you should finally get down to some actual Q#.

A Classical Version

Before going into the actual quantum implementation, you should have a look at the classical version. Grab Visual Studio Code, and start a new standalone quantum console application. You can write classical algorithms in Q#, so no qubits need to suffer under the following code. Listing 8-1 shows you a complete listing of the entire classical version of Deutsch's algorithm.

Listing 8-1. Classical version of Deutsch's algorithm

```
01 namespace _08_01_Classical_Deutsch_QSharp
02 {
03   open Microsoft.Quantum.Canon;
04   open Microsoft.Quantum.Intrinsic;
05
06   @EntryPoint()
07   function ClassicalDeutsch() : Unit
08   {
09     let constantZeroResult = Deutsch(ConstantZero);
10     Message($"ConstantZero => {constantZeroResult}");
11
12     let constantOneResult = Deutsch(ConstantOne);
13     Message($"ConstantOne => {constantOneResult}");
14
15     let identityResult = Deutsch(Identity);
16     Message($"Identity => {identityResult}");
17
18     let negationResult = Deutsch(Negation);
19     Message($"Negation => {negationResult}");
20   }
21
22   function ConstantZero(bInput: Bool) : Bool
23   {
24     return false;
25   }
26
27   function ConstantOne(bInput: Bool) : Bool
28   {
29     return true;
30   }
31
```

```
32   function Identity(bInput: Bool) : Bool
33   {
34     return bInput;
35   }
36
37   function Negation(bInput: Bool) : Bool
38   {
39     return not bInput;
40   }
41
42   function Deutsch(oracle: ((Bool) -> Bool)) : String
43   {
44     let output1 = oracle(false);
45     let output2 = oracle(true);
46
47     if( output1 == output2 )
48     {
49       return "CONSTANT";
50     }
51     else
52     {
53       return "VARIABLE";
54     }
55   }
56 }
```

The classical code from Listing 8-1 starts with the `ClassicalDeutsch` entry-point operation. This operation is repeated in Listing 8-2 for your convenience. It calls the `Deutsch` operation a total of four times, on lines 9, 12, 15, and 18, each time with a different oracle. The oracle is represented by each of the four binary functions: `ConstantZero`, `ConstantOne`, `Identity`, and `Negation`. After the `Deutsch` operation is executed, the result is printed to the console output on lines 10, 13, 16, and 19. Passing the binary functions as an oracle to another operation is very comparable to a lambda expression in programming languages like C# or Java. If you are familiar with this concept, it should ring a bell. If you are not familiar with this concept, look at it as if you are passing a shortcut to another operation.

Listing 8-2. The ClassicalDeutsch entry-point operation

```
06 @EntryPoint()
07 function ClassicalDeutsch() : Unit
08 {
09   let constantZeroResult = Deutsch(ConstantZero);
10   Message($"ConstantZero => {constantZeroResult}");
11
12   let constantOneResult = Deutsch(ConstantOne);
13   Message($"ConstantOne => {constantOneResult}");
14
15   let identityResult = Deutsch(Identity);
16   Message($"Identity => {identityResult}");
17
18   let negationResult = Deutsch(Negation);
19   Message($"Negation => {negationResult}");
20 }
```

This Deutsch operation implements the classical version of Deutsch's algorithm, and it is repeated in Listing 8-3. In the signature of the operation on line 42, you can see a parameter with the name oracle, which is of type ((Bool) -> Bool). The arrow represents an oracle which receives a Boolean as input and returns another Boolean as output. As you learned in the beginning of this chapter, the only way to know if the binary function is constant or variable is by executing this black box function twice. Once with zero and once with one. Therefore, the oracle is executed twice, on lines 44 and 45, with false representing zero and true representing one. On lines 47 through 54, output1 and output2 are compared, and if they are equal, the oracle was constant; if they are not equal, the oracle was variable. If the output of the oracle is equal regardless of the input, the binary function must be constant. If the output of the oracle is not equal, the binary function must be constant.

Listing 8-3. The classical Deutsch operation

```
42 function Deutsch(oracle: ((Bool) -> Bool)) : String
43 {
44   let output1 = oracle(false);
45   let output2 = oracle(true);
46
```

```
47   if (output1 == output2)
48   {
49     return "CONSTANT";
50   }
51   else
52   {
53     return "VARIABLE";
54   }
55 }
```

Finally, implementing the four classical binary functions is easy. First, like in Listing 8-4, the ConstantZero function should always return false, which represents zero, regardless of the input.

Listing 8-4. The classical ConstantZero operation

```
22 function ConstantZero(bInput: Bool) : Bool
23 {
24   return false;
25 }
```

Second, the ConstantOne function from Listing 8-5 should always return true, which represents one, regardless of the input.

Listing 8-5. The classical ConstantOne operation

```
27 function ConstantOne(bInput: Bool) : Bool
28 {
29   return true;
30 }
```

Third, the Identity function from Listing 8-6 should always return the unchanged input.

Listing 8-6. The classical Identity operation

```
32 function Identity(bInput: Bool) : Bool
33 {
34   return bInput;
35 }
```

Fourth, the `Negation` function from Listing 8-7 should always return the opposite of the input.

Listing 8-7. The classical Negation function

```
37 function Negation(bInput: Bool) : Bool
38 {
39   return not bInput;
40 }
```

The Quantum Version

Based on the classical version, it should be easy to expand into the quantum version. Based upon the circuits from earlier in this chapter and the knowledge from the classical version, you can try to achieve a working Q# application by yourself. When you are finished, you can verify the result by looking at the console output and by looking at the code from Listing 8-8.

Listing 8-8. Quantum version of Deutsch's algorithm

```
01 namespace _08_02_Quantum_Deutsch_QSharp
02 {
03   open Microsoft.Quantum.Canon;
04   open Microsoft.Quantum.Intrinsic;
05   open Microsoft.Quantum.Measurement;
06
07   @EntryPoint()
08   operation QuantumDeutsch() : Unit
09   {
10     let constantZeroResult = Deutsch(ConstantZero);
11     Message($"ConstantZero => {constantZeroResult}");
12
13     let constantOneResult = Deutsch(ConstantOne);
14     Message($"ConstantOne => {constantOneResult}");
15
```

```
16    let identityResult = Deutsch(Identity);
17    Message($"Identity => {identityResult}");
18
19    let negationResult = Deutsch(Negation);
20    Message($"Negation => {negationResult}");
21  }
22
23  operation ConstantZero(
24    qInput: Qubit, qOutput: Qubit) : Unit
25  {
26    // NOP
27  }
28
29  operation ConstantOne(
30    qInput: Qubit, qOutput: Qubit) : Unit
31  {
32    X(qOutput);
33  }
34
35  operation Identity(
36    qInput: Qubit, qOutput: Qubit) : Unit
37  {
38    CNOT(qInput, qOutput);
39  }
40
41  operation Negation(
42    qInput: Qubit, qOutput: Qubit) : Unit
43  {
44    CNOT(qInput, qOutput);
45    X(qOutput);
46  }
47
```

```
48    operation Deutsch(
49      oracle: ((Qubit, Qubit) => Unit)) : String
50    {
51      use (qInput, qOutput) = (Qubit(), Qubit());
52
53      X(qInput);
54      X(qOutput);
55
56      H(qInput);
57      H(qOutput);
58
59      oracle(qInput, qOutput);
60
61      H(qInput);
62      H(qOutput);
63
64      let bInput = MResetZ(qInput);
65      let bOutput = MResetZ(qOutput);
66
67      if (bInput == bOutput)
68      {
69        return "CONSTANT";
70      }
71      else
72      {
73        return "VARIABLE";
74      }
75    }
76 }
```

The entry-point operation QuantumDeutsch is unchanged and can be reused completely from the classical version. Listing 8-9 repeats this operation for your convenience.

Listing 8-9. The QuantumDeutsch entry-point operation

```
07 @EntryPoint()
08 operation QuantumDeutsch () : Unit
09 {
10   let constantZeroResult = Deutsch(ConstantZero);
11   Message($"ConstantZero => {constantZeroResult}");
12
13   let constantOneResult = Deutsch(ConstantOne);
14   Message($"ConstantOne => {constantOneResult}");
15
16   let identityResult = Deutsch(Identity);
17   Message($"Identity => {identityResult}");
18
19   let negationResult = Deutsch(Negation);
20   Message($"Negation => {negationResult}");
21 }
```

The Deutsch operation needs to implement the quantum algorithm by Deutsch by using two qubits and quantum superposition. The operation signature on lines 48 and 49 still has a parameter oracle. This time the oracle type is different because it will receive two qubits as input, and it will not return a value of any kind. It will rather perform a unitary operation on top of those two qubits. Hence, the type ((Qubit, Qubit) => Unit) is used. On line 51, two qubits are allocated with the names qInput and qOutput. The names may be a little confusing, but qInput represents the bottom qubit in the circuits, and qOutput represents the top qubit in the circuits. Figure 8-16 shows you the circuit with all oracle functions displayed together but this time with the qInput and qOutput labels.

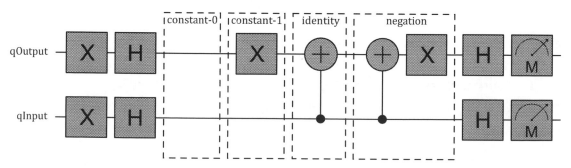

Figure 8-16. *The Deutsch circuit overview with all oracle functions displayed together*

Just like in the circuit, you should put the qubits through the X-gates on lines 53 and 54 form Listing 8-10 to flip their states and then through the H-gates on lines 56 and 57 to put them into superposition. On line 59, the qubits are put through the black box, which is represented by the oracle operation. The final step for Deutsch's algorithm is to put both qubits through the H-gates again on lines 61 and 62 to pull them back out of superposition. On lines 64 and 65, the qubits are measured, and their binary results are compared. If the output is $|11\rangle$, the binary function inside the black box is constant; if the output is $|01\rangle$, the binary function is variable. For simplicity's sake, lines 67 through 74 just compare the two binary values to make the distinction. If both binary output values are equal, the binary function is constant; otherwise, it is variable.

Listing 8-10. The quantum Deutsch operation

```
48  operation Deutsch(
49    oracle: ((Qubit, Qubit) => Unit)) : String
50  {
51    use (qInput, qOutput) = (Qubit(), Qubit());
52
53    X(qInput);
54    X(qOutput);
55
56    H(qInput);
57    H(qOutput);
58
59    oracle(qInput, qOutput);
60
61    H(qInput);
62    H(qOutput);
63
64    let bInput = MResetZ(qInput);
65    let bOutput = MResetZ(qOutput);
66
67    if (bInput == bOutput)
68    {
69      return "CONSTANT";
70    }
```

```
71   else
72   {
73     return "VARIABLE";
74   }
75 }
```

Finally, the four quantum versions of the binary function can be implemented just like the circuits described them. Listing 8-11 shows you the ConstantZero operation that does not do anything. The comment NOP on line 26 stands for "no operation" but is not obligatory.

Listing 8-11. The quantum ConstantZero operation

```
23 operation ConstantZero(
24   qInput: Qubit, qOutput: Qubit) : Unit
25 {
26   // NOP
27 }
```

Listing 8-12 shows you the ConstantOne operation that just flips the qOuput qubit on line 32.

Listing 8-12. The quantum ConstantOne operation

```
29 operation ConstantOne(
30   qInput: Qubit, qOutput: Qubit) : Unit
31 {
32   X(qOutput);
33 }
```

Listing 8-13 shows you the Identity operation that executes a CNOT-gate on line 38 where the qInput qubit is the control qubit and the qOutput qubit is the target qubit.

Listing 8-13. The quantum Identity operation

```
35 operation Identity(
36   qInput: Qubit, qOutput: Qubit) : Unit
37 {
38   CNOT(qInput, qOutput);
39 }
```

Listing 8-14 shows you the Negation operation that executes a CNOT-gate on line 44 where the qInput qubit is the control qubit and the qOutput qubit is the target qubit. Additionally, on line 45, the qOutput qubit needs to be put through the X-gate to flip its state.

Listing 8-14. The quantum Negation operation

```
41 operation Negation(
42    qInput: Qubit, qOutput: Qubit) : Unit
43 {
44    CNOT(qInput, qOutput);
45    X(qOutput);
46 }
```

With this, you have finished Deutsch's algorithm. You can run your quantum console application as many times as you like; it will always have the same result because it is deterministic. Deutsch's algorithm will always be able to determine whether the binary function is constant or variable with you only running it once.

The Last Word

This chapter has introduced you to one of the oldest quantum computing algorithms. It is not very useful by itself; a classical computer only needs to run a classical algorithm twice to know the same thing, and that will not take a long time, but it was one of the first ideas that saw great potential in quantum computing.

Deutsch's algorithm is a good subject to teach you about drawing quantum circuits, calculating quantum state operations using linear algebra, and implementing them in Microsoft Q#. Hopefully, you were able to see the importance of quantum computing, and you are eager to continue the following chapters that will discuss other popular quantum algorithms.

CHAPTER 9

Deutsch-Jozsa Algorithm

In the previous chapter, you learned about Deutsch's algorithm. David Deutsch introduced his paper, discussing this algorithm, in 1985 and made improvements with the help from Richard Jozsa, an Australian mathematician. Together, they proposed the Deutsch-Jozsa algorithm in 1992.

Just like Deutsch's original algorithm, it doesn't solve a real-life problem, but it proves that a quantum algorithm can be more efficient than any possible deterministic classical algorithm.

Deutsch's algorithm solves a problem concerning a single classical bit, whereas the Deutsch-Jozsa algorithm expands this problem to support any number of bits.

The Deutsch-Jozsa Oracle

The artificial problem that the Deutsch-Jozsa algorithm solves is about a function that works on an array of bits and, depending on the outcome of that function, decides if that function is constant or balanced. You probably remember a similar approach from Deutsch's original algorithm where the function on a single bit can be constant or variable.

A constant function on an array of bits always outputs a constant bit value, 0 or 1, regardless of the input. A balanced function outputs 0 for half of the input values and 1 for the other half of the input values.

To design the quantum Deutsch-Jozsa algorithm in Q#, you need to specify several functions on an array of bits that will yield a constant or a balanced result. The following four functions, two constant and two balanced, should get you started:

- **Constant-0**: The output of the function is 0, regardless of the input:

$$f\left(\left\{x_1, x_2, x_3, \ldots\right\}\right) = 0$$

© Johnny Hooyberghs 2022
J. Hooyberghs, *Introducing Microsoft Quantum Computing for Developers*,
https://doi.org/10.1007/978-1-4842-7246-6_9

- **Constant-1**: The output of the function is 1, regardless of the input:

$$f\left(\{x_1, x_2, x_3, \ldots\}\right) = 1$$

- **X mod 2**: The output of the function is 0 if the integer that is represented by the binary array is divisible by 2, or 1 otherwise:

$$f\left(\{x_1, x_2, x_3, \ldots\}\right) = \{0,1\}$$

- **Odd number of ones**: The output of the function is 0 if there are an even number of 1s in the input or 1 if there are an odd number of 1s in the input:

$$f\left(\{x_1, x_2, x_3, \ldots\}\right) = \{0,1\}$$

Next, we create a classical circuit, without using any qubits, where each one of the four functions is put inside of a black box and the output is tested against the input.

The Classical Deutsch-Jozsa Algorithm in Q#

To implement the classical Deutsch-Jozsa algorithm in Q#, you should first find an implementation for the four functions discussed previously.

Constant-0

The constant-0 function, a constant function, should always return 0, regardless of the input. If you know the input is an array of 0s and 1s, the code in Listing 9-1 should make a lot of sense.

Listing 9-1. Classical implmeentation for the constant-0 function

```
function ConstantZero(input: Bool[]) : Bool
{
    return false;
}
```

The Bool data type in Q# can represent false or 0 and true or 1. The input arguments for the ConstantZero function contain a single array of Bool, and the output for the function is a single Bool. The body of the function just returns false, regardless of the input.

Table 9-1 shows you the possible input values and their respective output value for a total of three input bits.

Table 9-1. *Data table to represent all possible classical input and output values for the constant-0 function if the input contains three bits*

Input	Output
0 0 0	0
0 0 1	0
0 1 0	0
0 1 1	0
1 0 0	0
1 0 1	0
1 1 0	0
1 1 1	0

Constant-1

If you look at the classical implementation for the constant-0 function, it should be easy enough to modify it to use for the constant-1 function, also a constant function. Listing 9-2 shows you how to do this.

Listing 9-2. Classical implementaton for the constant-1 function

```
function ConstantOne(input: Bool[]) : Bool
{
    return true;
}
```

The ConstantOne function returns true instead of false, regardless of the input.

Table 9-2 shows you the possible input values and their respective output value for a total of three input bits.

Table 9-2. *Data table to represent all possible classical input and output values for the constant-1 function if the input contains three bits*

Input	Output
0 0 0	1
0 0 1	1
0 1 0	1
0 1 1	1
1 0 0	1
1 0 1	1
1 1 0	1
1 1 1	1

Modulo 2

The X-mod-2 function, or modulo-2 function, a balanced function, takes an array of bits as input and outputs `false` or 0 for half of the inputs and `true` or 1 for the other half of the inputs. One of the possible ways to achieve this behavior is to convert the array of bits to an integer and check if the integer is odd or even. Checking an integer for evenness can be achieved by dividing it by the number two and checking the remainder with the modulo function. The modulo-2 function returns 0 if the integer is even and 1 if the integer is odd.

Table 9-3 shows you the possible input values with their integer representations and their respective output value for a total of three input bits.

Table 9-3. *Data table to represent all possible classical input and output values for the x-mod-2 function if the input contains three bits*

Input	Output
0 0 0 (0)	0
0 0 1 (1)	1
0 1 0 (2)	0
0 1 1 (3)	1
1 0 0 (4)	0
1 0 1 (5)	1
1 1 0 (6)	0
1 1 1 (7)	1

Listing 9-3 shows you a possible implementation in Q#.

Listing 9-3. Classical implementation for the modulo-2 function

```
function Xmod2(input: Bool[]) : Bool
{
    return input[Length(input)-1];
}
```

If you look at Table 9-3, you can see that the binary representation for odd integers always has a 1 at its last index. Because of this, we can just return the last Bool from the array. The result from this function will be truly balanced for all its possible inputs.

Odd Number of Ones

The final function, odd number of ones, also a balanced function, should be different from the x-mod-2 function but still outputs 0 for half of its input and 1 for the other half. If you would count the number of 1s in the input array of bits and only output 1 if there are an odd number of them, that should work.

Table 9-4 shows you what this data would look like.

Table 9-4. *Data table to represent all possible classical input and output values for the odd number of ones function if the input contains three bits*

Input	Output
0 0 0 (even number of ones)	0
0 0 1 (odd number of ones)	1
0 1 0 (odd number of ones)	1
0 1 1 (even number of ones)	0
1 0 0 (odd number of ones)	1
1 0 1 (even number of ones)	0
1 1 0 (even number of ones)	0
1 1 1 (odd number of ones)	1

Listing 9-4. Classical implementation for the odd number of ones function

```
function OddNumberOfOnes(input: Bool[]) : Bool
{
    mutable output = false;

    for bit in input
    {
        if( bit )
        {
            set output = not output;
        }
    }

    return output;
}
```

The code from Listing 9-4 looks the most complex of the four functions but is actually very simple. Basically, you start with an output of 0, and for each 1 bit you encounter in the input array of bits, you flip the output bit from 0 to 1 and vice versa.

The Full Implementation in Q#

If you combine the four implementations into a larger application that can test the classical version of the Deutsch-Jozsa algorithm, it can look something like Listing 9-5.

Listing 9-5. Classical version of the Deutsch-Jozsa algorithm

```
01 namespace _09_01_Classical_Deutsch_Jozsa_QSharp
02 {
03   open Microsoft.Quantum.Canon;
04   open Microsoft.Quantum.Convert;
05   open Microsoft.Quantum.Intrinsic;
06
07   @EntryPoint()
08   function ClassicalDeutschJozsa() : Unit
09   {
10     let constantZeroResult = DeutschJozsa(3, ConstantZero);
11     Message($"ConstantZero => {constantZeroResult}");
12
13     let constantOneResult = DeutschJozsa(3, ConstantOne);
14     Message($"ConstantOne => {constantOneResult}");
15
16     let xmodResult = DeutschJozsa(3, Xmod2);
17     Message($"X mod 2 => {xmodResult}");
18
19     let oddOnesResult = DeutschJozsa(3, OddNumberOfOnes);
20     Message($"Odd number of Ones => {oddOnesResult}");
21   }
22
23   function ConstantZero(input: Bool[]) : Bool
24   {
25     return false;
26   }
27
```

```
28    function ConstantOne(input: Bool[]) : Bool
29    {
30      return true;
31    }
32
33    function Xmod2(input: Bool[]) : Bool
34    {
35      return input[0];
36    }
37
38    function OddNumberOfOnes(input: Bool[]) : Bool
39    {
40      mutable output = false;
41
42      for bit in input
43      {
44        if( bit )
45        {
46          set output = not output;
47        }
48      }
49
50      return output;
51    }
52
53    function DeutchJozsa(
54        n: Int,
55        oracle: Bool[] -> Bool) : String
56      {
57        mutable resultBits = new Int[2 ^ n];
58        mutable zeroCount = 0;
59        mutable oneCount = 0;
60
```

```
61      for input in 0 .. 2 ^ n - 1
62      {
63        let bits = IntAsBoolArray(input, n);
64        let nextValue = oracle(bits);
65        set resultBits w/= input <- nextValue ? 1 | 0;
66
67        if (nextValue == false)
68        {
69          set zeroCount += 1;
70        }
71
72      if (nextValue == true)
73      {
74        set oneCount += 1;
75      }
76    }
77
78    mutable result = "RANDOM";
79
80    if (zeroCount == 0 or oneCount == 0)
81    {
82      set result = "CONSTANT";
83    }
84
85    if (zeroCount == oneCount)
86    {
87      set result = "BALANCED";
88    }
89
90    return $"{result} {resultBits}";
91  }
92 }
```

You can find the four implemented functions from before in Listing 9-5 on lines 23, 28, 33, and 38. There is a small modification for the Xmod2 function, but you will get an answer to that a little further down the line.

The most important part of the algorithm is in the DeutschJozsa function implemented in lines 53 through 76. For your reference, the DeutschJozsa function is repeated in Listing 9-6.

Listing 9-6. The DeutschJozsa function

```
53   function DeutschJozsa(
54       n: Int,
55       oracle: Bool[] -> Bool) : String
56   {
57       mutable resultBits = new Int[2 ^ n];
58       mutable zeroCount = 0;
59       mutable oneCount = 0;
60
61       for input in 0 .. 2 ^ n - 1
62       {
63         let bits = IntAsBoolArray(input, n);
64         let nextValue = oracle(bits);
65         set resultBits w/= input <- nextValue ? 1 | 0;
66
67         if (nextValue == false)
68         {
69           set zeroCount += 1;
70         }
71
72       if (nextValue == true)
73       {
74         set oneCount += 1;
75       }
76     }
77
78     mutable result = "RANDOM";
79
```

```
80      if (zeroCount == 0 or oneCount == 0)
81      {
82        set result = "CONSTANT";
83      }
84
85      if (zeroCount == oneCount)
86      {
87        set result = "BALANCED";
88      }
89
90      return $"{result} {resultBits}";
91    }
92 }
```

The DeutschJozsa function takes a number and an oracle function that takes an array of bits and returns a single bit. The number n represents the number of bits in the array of input bits. The oracle function oracle represents one of our four functions. The DeutschJozsa function returns a string that describes the outcome of the algorithm: Constant or balanced.

On line 57, you start by declaring a mutable array of numbers to store the output values for all inputs. This array will contain 0s and 1s for all the possible inputs. This will help you understand why a function is constant or balanced.

Based on the number n, you will need to generate all possible input arrays. A few pages back, you implemented the four functions and used input arrays containing three bits as an example. This number n represents that number three. The total number of possible input arrays for three bits is eight or two to the power of three. The array on line 57 has exactly that length and will contain the output of the oracle function, 0 or 1, for each of the possible input arrays.

On lines 58 and 59, you declare mutable helper variables to keep track of the number of times the oracle function returned zero or one.

The loop on lines 61 through 76 execute the oracle function on all the possible input arrays for the number n. Line 63 converts the integer number to a binary array acting as the input array for the oracle function on line 64. Depending on the Boolean result from that oracle function, the nth item of the resultBits array will be set to 0 or 1. Lines 67 through 70 and 72 through 75 will increase the zeroCount or oneCount variables depending on that same oracle function output.

If all the outputs were `false`, or all the outputs were `true`, the algorithm concludes, and the oracle function was constant. If the number of zeroes and ones are equal, the oracle function was balanced. In any other case, it was random. These final decisions are made on lines 78 through 88, and the resulting string is returned on line 90. Listing 9-7 shows you what the output should look like.

Listing 9-7. The output after running the classical DeutschJozsa algorithm

```
ConstantZero        => CONSTANT [0,0,0,0,0,0,0,0]
ConstantOne         => CONSTANT [1,1,1,1,1,1,1,1]
X mod 2             => BALANCED [0,1,0,1,0,1,0,1]
Odd number of Ones  => BALANCED [0,1,1,0,1,0,0,1]
```

The output from Listing 9-7 shows you very clearly that the informational array of outputs only contains 0s or 1s for the constant functions and contains a balanced amount of 0s and 1s for the balanced functions.

Finally, you were told earlier that the Xmod2 function was slightly adjusted. Listing 9-8 shows you that you need to return the first bit from the array and not the last bit.

Listing 9-8. The adjusted Xmod2 function

```
33 function Xmod2(input: Bool[]) : Bool
34 {
35   return input[0];
36 }
```

The `IntAsBoolArray` function from Q#, used on lines 60 and 65 from Listing 9-6, creates an array of bits using the Little-Endian representation. This means that the least-significant bit is stored at the smallest index in the resulting array. In the examples from before, the binary notation for integers uses the Big-Endian representation, putting the most-significant bit to the left and the least-significant bit to the right. To know if an integer is divisible by two, or if it is odd or even, you need to check the least-significant bit. Therefore, you need to return the first bit of the input array on line 35 from Listing 9-8.

To be complete, the entry-point function `ClassicalDeutchJozsa` is repeated in Listing 9-9.

Listing 9-9. The ClassicalDeutschJozsa function

```
07 @EntryPoint()
08 function ClassicalDeutschJozsa() : Unit
09 {
10   let constantZeroResult = DeutschJozsa(3, ConstantZero);
11   Message($"ConstantZero => {constantZeroResult}");
12
13   let constantOneResult = DeutschJozsa(3, ConstantOne);
14   Message($"ConstantOne => {constantOneResult}");
15
16   let xmodResult = DeutschJozsa(3, Xmod2);
17   Message($"X mod 2 => {xmodResult}");
18
19   let oddOnesResult = DeutschJozsa(3, OddNumberOfOnes);
20   Message($"Odd number of Ones => {oddOnesResult}");
21 }
```

This operation is very similar to the one from the previous chapter on the Deutsch algorithm. The Deutsch-Jozsa algorithm, implemented by the DeutschJozsa function, is executed for each oracle black-box function, and the output is printed as a message. There is an additional argument n to specify the number of bits in the input array. You can play around with this code and increase the number n to make sure the algorithm also works for larger input arrays.

If you start changing the number n to a higher value, you will see from the informational output array that the oracle function will be called many more times. The number of times the oracle function is called increases exponentially making this an exponential problem.

Back to the Quantum World

To make the same algorithm work in the quantum world, there are several different approaches. In this chapter, you will get acquainted with one of those approaches where you will allocate a qubit for each bit in the input array of bits plus one additional output qubit.

Figure 9-1 shows you the generic circuit for the Deutsch-Jozsa algorithm. The top part of the circuit is repeated for n bits, and the bottom part is one additional qubit that holds the output state.

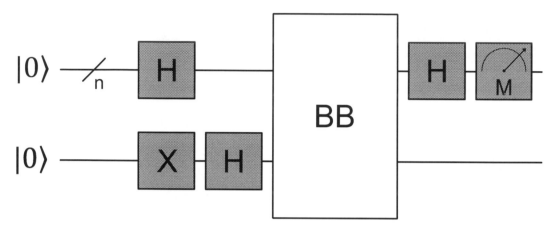

Figure 9-1. *The generic Deutsch-Jozsa algorithm for n number of input bits*

When implementing the four classical functions a few pages back, you used an input array with three bits. For simplicity, the next pages will contain circuits and examples using only an input array with two bits.

Figure 9-2 shows you a quantum implementation for the Deutsch-Jozsa algorithm by encoding the input array of two bits into the top two qubits and adding an additional qubit that contains the output value.

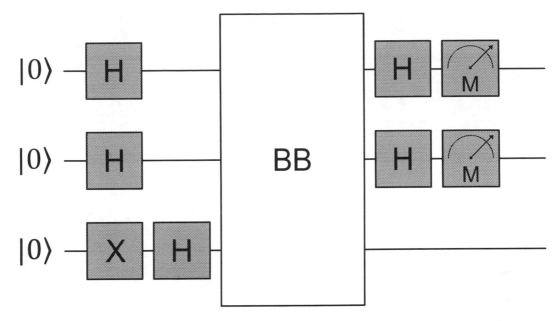

Figure 9-2. *The Deutsch-Jozsa algorithm for two bits around a back-box function*

The Deutsch-Jozsa algorithm works by putting the qubits that represent the input array bits into superposition and additionally also putting the output qubit in superposition after flipping it to the $|1\rangle$ state. After executing one of the four oracle functions, you need to put the input qubits trough the Hadamard gate one more time and measure their result. If the oracle function is constant, the input qubits will not have changed state. If the oracle function is balanced, their state will have changed.

Just like with the Deutsch algorithm, you need to find a quantum representation for the four classical functions.

Constant-0

Again, this one should be simple. Regardless of the input, the output qubit needs to remain in the $|0\rangle$ state. Figure 9-3 shows you the quantum circuit for the constant-0 function. No operators are needed.

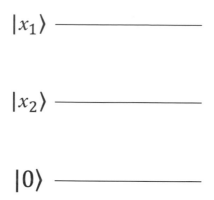

$$|x_1\rangle \ \text{——————}$$

$$|x_2\rangle \ \text{——————}$$

$$|0\rangle \ \text{——————}$$

Figure 9-3. *The quantum circuit for the constant-0 function*

If you introduce the quantum circuit for the constant-0 function into the circuit for the Deutsch-Jozsa algorithm, it will look like Figure 9-4.

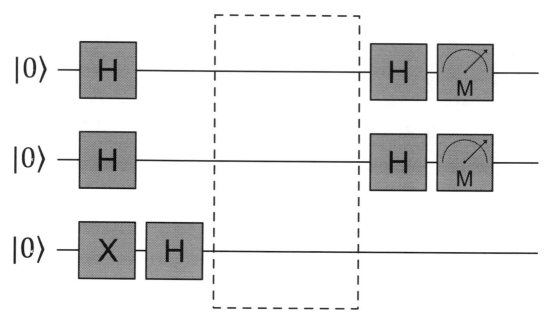

Figure 9-4. *The Deutsch-Jozsa algorithm with the constant-0 binary function integrated*

The Deutsch-Jozsa algorithm tells us that the function inside the black box is constant if the qubits that represent the input bits are unchanged. From the circuit in Figure 9-4, you can probably see that without the need for further verification. The qubits start in state $|0\rangle$, and putting them through the Hadamard gate, which is self-adjoint, keeps them in state $|0\rangle$.

For your reference and as a good exercise, you can do the calculations and arrive at the same conclusion. You start by noting down the sequence of operations, the qubit index for each operation, and the combined quantum state.

$$H_0 H_1 H_2 H_0 H_1 X_2 \left(\begin{pmatrix} 1 \\ 0 \end{pmatrix}_2 \otimes \begin{pmatrix} 1 \\ 0 \end{pmatrix}_1 \otimes \begin{pmatrix} 1 \\ 0 \end{pmatrix}_0 \right)$$

Now, step by step, you execute the operations on the correct qubits. The first step would be to execute the H-gate on the qubit with index 0 and 1 and the X-gate on the qubit with index 2:

$$= H_0 H_1 H_2 \left(\begin{pmatrix} 0 & 1 \\ 1 & 0 \end{pmatrix}_X \begin{pmatrix} 1 \\ 0 \end{pmatrix}_2 \otimes \begin{pmatrix} \frac{1}{\sqrt{2}} & \frac{1}{\sqrt{2}} \\ \frac{1}{\sqrt{2}} & \frac{-1}{\sqrt{2}} \end{pmatrix}_H \begin{pmatrix} 1 \\ 0 \end{pmatrix}_1 \otimes \begin{pmatrix} \frac{1}{\sqrt{2}} & \frac{1}{\sqrt{2}} \\ \frac{1}{\sqrt{2}} & \frac{-1}{\sqrt{2}} \end{pmatrix}_H \begin{pmatrix} 1 \\ 0 \end{pmatrix}_0 \right)$$

You multiply the state matrices for each qubit with the operation matrix and write down the result:

$$= H_0 H_1 H_2 \left(\begin{pmatrix} 0 \\ 1 \end{pmatrix}_2 \otimes \begin{pmatrix} \frac{1}{\sqrt{2}} \\ \frac{1}{\sqrt{2}} \end{pmatrix}_1 \otimes \begin{pmatrix} \frac{1}{\sqrt{2}} \\ \frac{1}{\sqrt{2}} \end{pmatrix}_0 \right)$$

The first two qubits are now in superposition, and the final qubit is flipped to the $|1\rangle$ state. Next, you apply the next step of operations, which is applying the H-gate to the qubit with index 2:

$$= H_0 H_1 \left(\begin{pmatrix} \frac{1}{\sqrt{2}} & \frac{1}{\sqrt{2}} \\ \frac{1}{\sqrt{2}} & \frac{-1}{\sqrt{2}} \end{pmatrix}_H \begin{pmatrix} 0 \\ 1 \end{pmatrix}_2 \otimes \begin{pmatrix} \frac{1}{\sqrt{2}} \\ \frac{1}{\sqrt{2}} \end{pmatrix}_1 \otimes \begin{pmatrix} \frac{1}{\sqrt{2}} \\ \frac{1}{\sqrt{2}} \end{pmatrix}_0 \right)$$

Again, you multiply the state matrix for that qubit with the operation matrix and write down the result:

$$= H_0 H_1 \left(\begin{pmatrix} \frac{1}{\sqrt{2}} \\ \frac{-1}{\sqrt{2}} \end{pmatrix}_2 \otimes \begin{pmatrix} \frac{1}{\sqrt{2}} \\ \frac{1}{\sqrt{2}} \end{pmatrix}_1 \otimes \begin{pmatrix} \frac{1}{\sqrt{2}} \\ \frac{1}{\sqrt{2}} \end{pmatrix}_0 \right)$$

Finally, you introduce the last round of operations, which is executing the H-gate on the qubits with index 0 and 1:

$$
= \left(\begin{pmatrix} \dfrac{1}{\sqrt{2}} \\ \dfrac{-1}{\sqrt{2}} \end{pmatrix}_2 \otimes \begin{pmatrix} \dfrac{1}{\sqrt{2}} & \dfrac{1}{\sqrt{2}} \\ \dfrac{1}{\sqrt{2}} & \dfrac{-1}{\sqrt{2}} \end{pmatrix}_H \begin{pmatrix} \dfrac{1}{\sqrt{2}} \\ \dfrac{1}{\sqrt{2}} \end{pmatrix}_1 \otimes \begin{pmatrix} \dfrac{1}{\sqrt{2}} & \dfrac{1}{\sqrt{2}} \\ \dfrac{1}{\sqrt{2}} & \dfrac{-1}{\sqrt{2}} \end{pmatrix}_H \begin{pmatrix} \dfrac{1}{\sqrt{2}} \\ \dfrac{1}{\sqrt{2}} \end{pmatrix}_0 \right)
$$

These final multiplications will reset the first two qubits to the $|0\rangle$ state and keep the output qubit in a state of superposition. You can write down the states as a linear combination and see that the qubits that represent the input bits remain in the $|0\rangle$ state.

$$
= \begin{pmatrix} \dfrac{1}{\sqrt{2}} \\ \dfrac{-1}{\sqrt{2}} \end{pmatrix}_2 \otimes \begin{pmatrix} 1 \\ 0 \end{pmatrix}_1 \otimes \begin{pmatrix} 1 \\ 0 \end{pmatrix}_0 = \frac{1}{\sqrt{2}}\left(|000\rangle - |100\rangle \right)
$$

Constant-1

The constant-1 function is again very similar to the constant-0 function. The output qubit needs to be flipped to the $|1\rangle$ state for all possible input states. The circuit will, therefore, disregard the input qubits and always flip the output qubit to the $|1\rangle$ state. Figure 9-5 shows you what this circuit looks like.

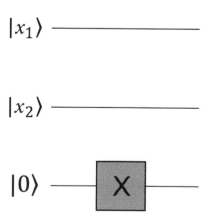

Figure 9-5. *The quantum circuit for the constant-1 function*

If you introduce the quantum circuit for the constant-1 function into the circuit for the Deutsch-Jozsa algorithm, it will look like Figure 9-6.

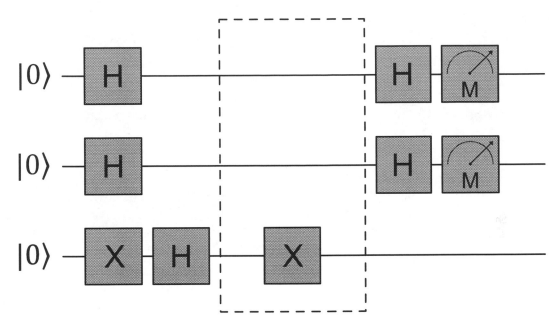

Figure 9-6. *The Deutsch-Jozsa algorithm with the constant-1 binary function integrated*

Because the constant-1 function is also a constant function, the qubits that represent the input bits should also keep their $|0\rangle$ state. Again, you can see the effect clearly. There is no change from the previous constant-0 circuit regarding the first two qubits. Still, doing some mathematics has never hurt anyone.

You start by writing down the sequence of operations and the combined quantum state:

$$H_0 H_1 X_2 H_2 H_0 H_1 X_2 \left(\begin{pmatrix} 1 \\ 0 \end{pmatrix}_2 \otimes \begin{pmatrix} 1 \\ 0 \end{pmatrix}_1 \otimes \begin{pmatrix} 1 \\ 0 \end{pmatrix}_0 \right)$$

You continue by executing the batch of operations by writing down the state matrices and the operation matrices. The first batch of operations is the H-gate for the first two qubits and the X-gate for the final output qubit:

$$= H_0 H_1 X_2 H_2 \left(\begin{pmatrix} 0 & 1 \\ 1 & 0 \end{pmatrix}_X \begin{pmatrix} 1 \\ 0 \end{pmatrix}_2 \otimes \begin{pmatrix} \frac{1}{\sqrt{2}} & \frac{1}{\sqrt{2}} \\ \frac{1}{\sqrt{2}} & \frac{-1}{\sqrt{2}} \end{pmatrix}_H \begin{pmatrix} 1 \\ 0 \end{pmatrix}_1 \otimes \begin{pmatrix} \frac{1}{\sqrt{2}} & \frac{1}{\sqrt{2}} \\ \frac{1}{\sqrt{2}} & \frac{-1}{\sqrt{2}} \end{pmatrix}_H \begin{pmatrix} 1 \\ 0 \end{pmatrix}_0 \right)$$

251

You multiply the state matrices and the operation matrices and write down the result:

$$= H_0 H_1 X_2 H_2 \left(\begin{pmatrix} 0 \\ 1 \end{pmatrix}_2 \otimes \begin{pmatrix} \frac{1}{\sqrt{2}} \\ \frac{1}{\sqrt{2}} \end{pmatrix}_1 \otimes \begin{pmatrix} \frac{1}{\sqrt{2}} \\ \frac{1}{\sqrt{2}} \end{pmatrix}_0 \right)$$

You continue with the next batch, which is the H-gate for the final output qubit:

$$= H_0 H_1 X_2 \left(\begin{pmatrix} \frac{1}{\sqrt{2}} & \frac{1}{\sqrt{2}} \\ \frac{1}{\sqrt{2}} & \frac{-1}{\sqrt{2}} \end{pmatrix}_H \begin{pmatrix} 0 \\ 1 \end{pmatrix}_2 \otimes \begin{pmatrix} \frac{1}{\sqrt{2}} \\ \frac{1}{\sqrt{2}} \end{pmatrix}_1 \otimes \begin{pmatrix} \frac{1}{\sqrt{2}} \\ \frac{1}{\sqrt{2}} \end{pmatrix}_0 \right)$$

Again, you multiply the state matrix and the operation matrix for that final output qubit and write down the result:

$$= H_0 H_1 X_2 \left(\begin{pmatrix} \frac{1}{\sqrt{2}} \\ \frac{-1}{\sqrt{2}} \end{pmatrix}_2 \otimes \begin{pmatrix} \frac{1}{\sqrt{2}} \\ \frac{1}{\sqrt{2}} \end{pmatrix}_1 \otimes \begin{pmatrix} \frac{1}{\sqrt{2}} \\ \frac{1}{\sqrt{2}} \end{pmatrix}_0 \right)$$

Now, you apply the X-gate, which is part of the constant-1 circuit, to the final output qubit:

$$= H_0 H_1 \left(\begin{pmatrix} 0 & 1 \\ 1 & 0 \end{pmatrix}_X \begin{pmatrix} \frac{1}{\sqrt{2}} \\ \frac{-1}{\sqrt{2}} \end{pmatrix}_2 \otimes \begin{pmatrix} \frac{1}{\sqrt{2}} \\ \frac{1}{\sqrt{2}} \end{pmatrix}_1 \otimes \begin{pmatrix} \frac{1}{\sqrt{2}} \\ \frac{1}{\sqrt{2}} \end{pmatrix}_0 \right)$$

And again, you perform the multiplication and write down the result:

$$= H_0 H_1 \left(\begin{pmatrix} \frac{-1}{\sqrt{2}} \\ \frac{1}{\sqrt{2}} \end{pmatrix}_2 \otimes \begin{pmatrix} \frac{1}{\sqrt{2}} \\ \frac{1}{\sqrt{2}} \end{pmatrix}_1 \otimes \begin{pmatrix} \frac{1}{\sqrt{2}} \\ \frac{1}{\sqrt{2}} \end{pmatrix}_0 \right)$$

You apply the final batch of operations, the H-gate on the first two input qubits and write down the multiplications.

$$= \left(\left(\begin{pmatrix} \dfrac{-1}{\sqrt{2}} \\ \dfrac{1}{\sqrt{2}} \end{pmatrix}_2 \otimes \begin{pmatrix} \dfrac{1}{\sqrt{2}} & \dfrac{1}{\sqrt{2}} \\ \dfrac{1}{\sqrt{2}} & \dfrac{-1}{\sqrt{2}} \end{pmatrix}_H \begin{pmatrix} \dfrac{1}{\sqrt{2}} \\ \dfrac{1}{\sqrt{2}} \end{pmatrix}_1 \otimes \begin{pmatrix} \dfrac{1}{\sqrt{2}} & \dfrac{1}{\sqrt{2}} \\ \dfrac{1}{\sqrt{2}} & \dfrac{-1}{\sqrt{2}} \end{pmatrix}_H \begin{pmatrix} \dfrac{1}{\sqrt{2}} \\ \dfrac{1}{\sqrt{2}} \end{pmatrix}_0 \right) \right)$$

Finally, you calculate these multiplications and write down the result. Again, the first two input qubits have been reset to their $|0\rangle$ state, and the final output qubit is in a superposition state:

$$= \begin{pmatrix} \dfrac{-1}{\sqrt{2}} \\ \dfrac{1}{\sqrt{2}} \end{pmatrix}_2 \otimes \begin{pmatrix} 1 \\ 0 \end{pmatrix}_1 \otimes \begin{pmatrix} 1 \\ 0 \end{pmatrix}_0 = \dfrac{-1}{\sqrt{2}} \left(|000\rangle - |100\rangle \right)$$

Modulo 2

The x-mod-2 function is more interesting and is a balanced function. Just like with the classical implementation, the output qubit needs to be flipped to the $|1\rangle$ state, only if the least-significant input qubit is in the $|1\rangle$ state. Luckily, the CNOT-gate is exactly the right operation to do this.

Figure 9-7 shows you what the circuit for the x-mod-2 function looks like.

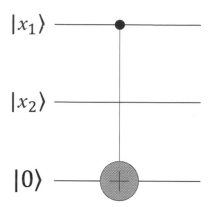

Figure 9-7. *The quantum circuit for the x-mod-2 function*

If you introduce the quantum circuit for the x-mod-2 function into the circuit for the Deutsch-Jozsa algorithm, it will look like Figure 9-8.

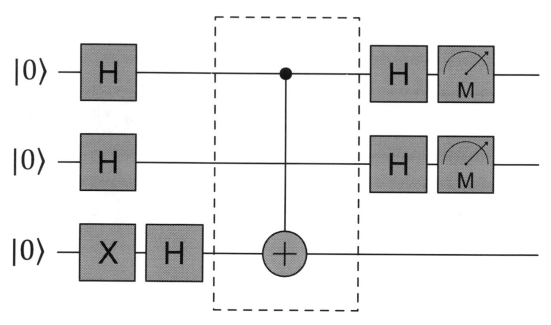

Figure 9-8. *The Deutsch-Jozsa algorithm with the x-mod-2 function integrated*

From this circuit, you can clearly see that there is something going on for the first qubits, and this will probably have an influence on the qubits that represent the input bits. You should perform some calculations to make sure. Just like with the previous calculations, write down the sequence of operations and the combined quantum state:

$$H_0 H_1 CNOT_{02} H_2 H_0 H_1 X_2 \left(\begin{pmatrix} 1 \\ 0 \end{pmatrix}_2 \otimes \begin{pmatrix} 1 \\ 0 \end{pmatrix}_1 \otimes \begin{pmatrix} 1 \\ 0 \end{pmatrix}_0 \right)$$

Apply the first batch of operations, just like before. That would be the H-gate for the input qubits and the X-gate for the output qubit:

$$= H_0 H_1 CNOT_{02} H_2 \left(\begin{pmatrix} 0 & 1 \\ 1 & 0 \end{pmatrix}_X \begin{pmatrix} 1 \\ 0 \end{pmatrix}_2 \otimes \begin{pmatrix} \frac{1}{\sqrt{2}} & \frac{1}{\sqrt{2}} \\ \frac{1}{\sqrt{2}} & \frac{-1}{\sqrt{2}} \end{pmatrix}_H \begin{pmatrix} 1 \\ 0 \end{pmatrix}_1 \otimes \begin{pmatrix} \frac{1}{\sqrt{2}} & \frac{1}{\sqrt{2}} \\ \frac{1}{\sqrt{2}} & \frac{-1}{\sqrt{2}} \end{pmatrix}_H \begin{pmatrix} 1 \\ 0 \end{pmatrix}_0 \right)$$

Execute the multiplications and write down the result:

$$= H_0 H_1 CNOT_{02} H_2 \left(\begin{pmatrix} 0 \\ 1 \end{pmatrix}_2 \otimes \begin{pmatrix} \frac{1}{\sqrt{2}} \\ \frac{1}{\sqrt{2}} \end{pmatrix}_1 \otimes \begin{pmatrix} \frac{1}{\sqrt{2}} \\ \frac{1}{\sqrt{2}} \end{pmatrix}_0 \right)$$

Perform the next operation, which is the H-gate on the output qubit:

$$= H_0 H_1 CNOT_{02} \left(\begin{pmatrix} \frac{1}{\sqrt{2}} & \frac{1}{\sqrt{2}} \\ \frac{1}{\sqrt{2}} & \frac{-1}{\sqrt{2}} \end{pmatrix}_H \begin{pmatrix} 0 \\ 1 \end{pmatrix}_2 \otimes \begin{pmatrix} \frac{1}{\sqrt{2}} \\ \frac{1}{\sqrt{2}} \end{pmatrix}_1 \otimes \begin{pmatrix} \frac{1}{\sqrt{2}} \\ \frac{1}{\sqrt{2}} \end{pmatrix}_0 \right)$$

Calculate the multiplication and write down the result:

$$= H_0 H_1 CNOT_{02} \left(\begin{pmatrix} \frac{1}{\sqrt{2}} \\ \frac{-1}{\sqrt{2}} \end{pmatrix}_2 \otimes \begin{pmatrix} \frac{1}{\sqrt{2}} \\ \frac{1}{\sqrt{2}} \end{pmatrix}_1 \otimes \begin{pmatrix} \frac{1}{\sqrt{2}} \\ \frac{1}{\sqrt{2}} \end{pmatrix}_0 \right)$$

The next batch of operations, the operations inside the x-mod-2 function, apply the CNOT-gate with the first input qubit as the control qubit and the output qubit as the target qubit. To apply the CNOT-operation matrix, you need to write down the combined state matrix for the first and the last qubit. You can do this by calculating the tensor product. Be careful, and use the correct order; the first input qubit is the control qubit, and the output qubit is the target qubit:

$$\begin{pmatrix} \dfrac{1}{\sqrt{2}} \\ \dfrac{1}{\sqrt{2}} \end{pmatrix}_0 \otimes \begin{pmatrix} \dfrac{1}{\sqrt{2}} \\ \dfrac{-1}{\sqrt{2}} \end{pmatrix}_2 = \begin{pmatrix} \dfrac{1}{2} \\ \dfrac{-1}{2} \\ \dfrac{1}{2} \\ \dfrac{-1}{2} \end{pmatrix}_{02}$$

Now, integrate this combined qubit state back into the original sequence of operations:

$$H_0 H_1 CNOT_{02} \left(\begin{pmatrix} \dfrac{1}{\sqrt{2}} \\ \dfrac{-1}{\sqrt{2}} \end{pmatrix}_2 \otimes \begin{pmatrix} \dfrac{1}{\sqrt{2}} \\ \dfrac{1}{\sqrt{2}} \end{pmatrix}_1 \otimes \begin{pmatrix} \dfrac{1}{\sqrt{2}} \\ \dfrac{1}{\sqrt{2}} \end{pmatrix}_0 \right) = H_0 H_1 CNOT_{02} \left(\begin{pmatrix} \dfrac{1}{2} \\ \dfrac{-1}{2} \\ \dfrac{1}{2} \\ \dfrac{-1}{2} \end{pmatrix}_{02} \otimes \begin{pmatrix} \dfrac{1}{\sqrt{2}} \\ \dfrac{1}{\sqrt{2}} \end{pmatrix}_1 \right)$$

Perform the CNOT-gate on the new combined quantum state. Look at the dimensions: The CNOT-gate matrix has a larger dimension which is applicable on the combined state matrix for the first and last qubits:

$$= H_0 H_1 \left(\begin{pmatrix} 1 & 0 & 0 & 0 \\ 0 & 1 & 0 & 0 \\ 0 & 0 & 0 & 1 \\ 0 & 0 & 1 & 0 \end{pmatrix}_{CNOT} \begin{pmatrix} \dfrac{1}{2} \\ \dfrac{-1}{2} \\ \dfrac{1}{2} \\ \dfrac{-1}{2} \end{pmatrix}_{02} \otimes \begin{pmatrix} \dfrac{1}{\sqrt{2}} \\ \dfrac{1}{\sqrt{2}} \end{pmatrix}_1 \right)$$

Now, multiply the CNOT-gate matrix and the combined state matrix. The CNOT-gate matrix is actually very simple and swaps the last two entries. Next, factorize the combined state matrix into its separate qubit states, and go back to the original three qubit states:

$$= H_0 H_1 \left(\begin{pmatrix} \frac{1}{2} \\ \frac{-1}{2} \\ \frac{-1}{2} \\ \frac{1}{2} \end{pmatrix}_{02} \otimes \begin{pmatrix} \frac{1}{\sqrt{2}} \\ \frac{1}{\sqrt{2}} \end{pmatrix}_1 \right) = H_0 H_1 \left(\begin{pmatrix} \frac{1}{\sqrt{2}} \\ \frac{-1}{\sqrt{2}} \end{pmatrix}_2 \otimes \begin{pmatrix} \frac{1}{\sqrt{2}} \\ \frac{1}{\sqrt{2}} \end{pmatrix}_1 \otimes \begin{pmatrix} \frac{1}{\sqrt{2}} \\ \frac{-1}{\sqrt{2}} \end{pmatrix}_0 \right)$$

Finally, apply the last of operations – H-gate on both the input qubits:

$$= \left(\begin{pmatrix} \frac{1}{\sqrt{2}} \\ \frac{-1}{\sqrt{2}} \end{pmatrix}_2 \otimes \begin{pmatrix} \frac{1}{\sqrt{2}} & \frac{1}{\sqrt{2}} \\ \frac{1}{\sqrt{2}} & \frac{-1}{\sqrt{2}} \end{pmatrix}_H \begin{pmatrix} \frac{1}{\sqrt{2}} \\ \frac{1}{\sqrt{2}} \end{pmatrix}_1 \otimes \begin{pmatrix} \frac{1}{\sqrt{2}} & \frac{1}{\sqrt{2}} \\ \frac{1}{\sqrt{2}} & \frac{-1}{\sqrt{2}} \end{pmatrix}_H \begin{pmatrix} \frac{1}{\sqrt{2}} \\ \frac{-1}{\sqrt{2}} \end{pmatrix}_0 \right)$$

Calculate the multiplications and look at the result. The final output qubit is still in a superposition state, but one of the input qubits is in the $|1\rangle$ state, and the other is in the $|0\rangle$ state:

$$= \begin{pmatrix} \frac{1}{\sqrt{2}} \\ \frac{-1}{\sqrt{2}} \end{pmatrix}_2 \otimes \begin{pmatrix} 1 \\ 0 \end{pmatrix}_1 \otimes \begin{pmatrix} 0 \\ 1 \end{pmatrix}_0 = \frac{1}{\sqrt{2}} \left(|001\rangle - |101\rangle \right)$$

The Deutsch-Jozsa algorithm will yield all $|0\rangle$ states on the input qubits if the black-box function is constant and will yield some other state if the black-box function is balanced. In this case, the x-mod-2 function is balanced.

Odd Number of Ones

The odd-number-of-ones function is even more interesting and is also a balanced function. Just like with the classical implementation, the output qubit needs to be flipped to from the $|0\rangle$ to the $|1\rangle$ state and vice versa, for each input qubit in the $|1\rangle$ state. Again, the CNOT-gate is exactly the right operation to do this multiple times for all input qubits.

Figure 9-9 shows you what the circuit for the odd-number-of-ones function looks like.

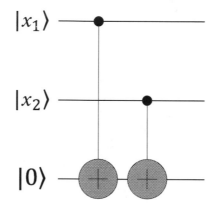

Figure 9-9. *The quantum circuit for the odd-number-of-ones function*

If you introduce the quantum circuit for the odd-number-of-ones function into the circuit for the Deutsch-Jozsa algorithm, it will look like Figure 9-10.

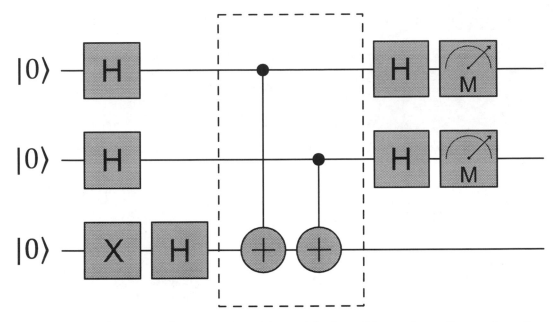

Figure 9-10. *The Deutsch-Jozsa algorithm with the odd-number-of-ones function integrated*

From this circuit, which is very similar to the previous one, you can clearly see that there is also something going on for all the input qubits, and this will probably have an influence on the qubits that represent the input bits. You should perform a final set of calculations to verify. Just like with the previous calculations, write down the sequence of operations and the combined quantum state one last time:

$$H_0 H_1 CNOT_{12} CNOT_{02} H_2 H_0 H_1 X_2 \left(\begin{pmatrix} 1 \\ 0 \end{pmatrix}_2 \otimes \begin{pmatrix} 1 \\ 0 \end{pmatrix}_1 \otimes \begin{pmatrix} 1 \\ 0 \end{pmatrix}_0 \right)$$

Apply the first batch of operations, just like before. That would be the H-gate for the input qubits and the X-gate for the output qubit:

$$= H_0 H_1 CNOT_{12} CNOT_{02} H_2 \left(\begin{pmatrix} 0 & 1 \\ 1 & 0 \end{pmatrix}_X \begin{pmatrix} 1 \\ 0 \end{pmatrix}_2 \otimes \begin{pmatrix} \frac{1}{\sqrt{2}} & \frac{1}{\sqrt{2}} \\ \frac{1}{\sqrt{2}} & \frac{-1}{\sqrt{2}} \end{pmatrix}_H \begin{pmatrix} 1 \\ 0 \end{pmatrix}_1 \otimes \begin{pmatrix} \frac{1}{\sqrt{2}} & \frac{1}{\sqrt{2}} \\ \frac{1}{\sqrt{2}} & \frac{-1}{\sqrt{2}} \end{pmatrix}_H \begin{pmatrix} 1 \\ 0 \end{pmatrix}_0 \right)$$

Calculate the matrix-multiplication and write down the results:

$$= H_0 H_1 CNOT_{12} CNOT_{02} H_2 \left(\begin{pmatrix} 0 \\ 1 \end{pmatrix}_2 \otimes \begin{pmatrix} \dfrac{1}{\sqrt{2}} \\ \dfrac{1}{\sqrt{2}} \end{pmatrix}_1 \otimes \begin{pmatrix} \dfrac{1}{\sqrt{2}} \\ \dfrac{1}{\sqrt{2}} \end{pmatrix}_0 \right)$$

Perform the next batch of operations, which is only the H-gate on the output qubit:

$$= H_0 H_1 CNOT_{12} CNOT_{02} \left(\begin{pmatrix} \dfrac{1}{\sqrt{2}} & \dfrac{1}{\sqrt{2}} \\ \dfrac{1}{\sqrt{2}} & \dfrac{-1}{\sqrt{2}} \end{pmatrix}_H \begin{pmatrix} 0 \\ 1 \end{pmatrix}_2 \otimes \begin{pmatrix} \dfrac{1}{\sqrt{2}} \\ \dfrac{1}{\sqrt{2}} \end{pmatrix}_1 \otimes \begin{pmatrix} \dfrac{1}{\sqrt{2}} \\ \dfrac{1}{\sqrt{2}} \end{pmatrix}_0 \right)$$

Calculate the matrix-multiplications and write down the result:

$$= H_0 H_1 CNOT_{12} CNOT_{02} \left(\begin{pmatrix} \dfrac{1}{\sqrt{2}} \\ \dfrac{-1}{\sqrt{2}} \end{pmatrix}_2 \otimes \begin{pmatrix} \dfrac{1}{\sqrt{2}} \\ \dfrac{1}{\sqrt{2}} \end{pmatrix}_1 \otimes \begin{pmatrix} \dfrac{1}{\sqrt{2}} \\ \dfrac{1}{\sqrt{2}} \end{pmatrix}_0 \right)$$

The next batch of operations, the operations inside the odd-number-of-ones function, apply the CNOT-gate using the first input qubit as the control qubit and the output qubit as the target qubit. To apply the CNOT-operation matrix, you need to write down the combined state matrix for the first and the last qubit. You can do this by calculating the tensor product. Be careful, and use the correct order; the first input qubit is the control qubit, and the output qubit is the target qubit:

$$\begin{pmatrix} \dfrac{1}{\sqrt{2}} \\ \dfrac{1}{\sqrt{2}} \end{pmatrix}_0 \otimes \begin{pmatrix} \dfrac{1}{\sqrt{2}} \\ \dfrac{-1}{\sqrt{2}} \end{pmatrix}_2 = \begin{pmatrix} \dfrac{1}{2} \\ \dfrac{-1}{2} \\ \dfrac{1}{2} \\ \dfrac{-1}{2} \end{pmatrix}_{02}$$

Now, integrate this combined qubit state back into the original sequence of operations:

$$= H_0 H_1 CNOT_{12} CNOT_{02} \left(\begin{pmatrix} \dfrac{1}{2} \\ \dfrac{-1}{2} \\ \dfrac{1}{2} \\ \dfrac{-1}{2} \end{pmatrix}_{02} \otimes \begin{pmatrix} \dfrac{1}{\sqrt{2}} \\ \dfrac{1}{\sqrt{2}} \end{pmatrix}_1 \right)$$

Perform the CNOT-gate on the new combined quantum state:

$$= H_0 H_1 CNOT_{12} \left(\begin{pmatrix} 1 & 0 & 0 & 0 \\ 0 & 1 & 0 & 0 \\ 0 & 0 & 0 & 1 \\ 0 & 0 & 1 & 0 \end{pmatrix}_{CNOT} \begin{pmatrix} \dfrac{1}{2} \\ \dfrac{-1}{2} \\ \dfrac{1}{2} \\ \dfrac{-1}{2} \end{pmatrix}_{02} \otimes \begin{pmatrix} \dfrac{1}{\sqrt{2}} \\ \dfrac{1}{\sqrt{2}} \end{pmatrix}_1 \right)$$

Perform the matrix-multiplication and write down the result:

$$= H_0 H_1 CNOT_{12} \left(\begin{pmatrix} \dfrac{1}{2} \\ \dfrac{-1}{2} \\ \dfrac{-1}{2} \\ \dfrac{1}{2} \end{pmatrix}_{02} \otimes \begin{pmatrix} \dfrac{1}{\sqrt{2}} \\ \dfrac{1}{\sqrt{2}} \end{pmatrix}_1 \right)$$

Next, factorize the combined state matrix into its separate qubit states, and go back to the original three qubit states:

$$= H_0 H_1 CNOT_{12} \left(\begin{pmatrix} \dfrac{1}{\sqrt{2}} \\ \dfrac{-1}{\sqrt{2}} \end{pmatrix}_2 \otimes \begin{pmatrix} \dfrac{1}{\sqrt{2}} \\ \dfrac{1}{\sqrt{2}} \end{pmatrix}_1 \otimes \begin{pmatrix} \dfrac{1}{\sqrt{2}} \\ \dfrac{-1}{\sqrt{2}} \end{pmatrix}_0 \right)$$

For the next CNOT-gate, you should perform the same steps as before, but using the second input qubit as the control qubit and the output qubit as the target qubit. Again, make sure to use the correct order:

$$\begin{pmatrix} \dfrac{1}{\sqrt{2}} \\ \dfrac{1}{\sqrt{2}} \end{pmatrix}_1 \otimes \begin{pmatrix} \dfrac{1}{\sqrt{2}} \\ \dfrac{-1}{\sqrt{2}} \end{pmatrix}_2 = \begin{pmatrix} \dfrac{1}{2} \\ \dfrac{-1}{2} \\ \dfrac{1}{2} \\ \dfrac{-1}{2} \end{pmatrix}_{12}$$

Integrate this combined qubit state back into the original sequence of operations.

$$= H_0 H_1 CNOT_{12} \left(\begin{pmatrix} \dfrac{1}{2} \\ \dfrac{-1}{2} \\ \dfrac{1}{2} \\ \dfrac{-1}{2} \end{pmatrix}_{12} \otimes \begin{pmatrix} \dfrac{1}{\sqrt{2}} \\ \dfrac{-1}{\sqrt{2}} \end{pmatrix}_0 \right)$$

Perform the next CNOT-gate on the combined quantum state for the second input qubit and the output qubit:

$$= H_0 H_1 \left(\begin{pmatrix} 1 & 0 & 0 & 0 \\ 0 & 1 & 0 & 0 \\ 0 & 0 & 0 & 1 \\ 0 & 0 & 1 & 0 \end{pmatrix}_{CNOT} \begin{pmatrix} \dfrac{1}{2} \\ \dfrac{-1}{2} \\ \dfrac{1}{2} \\ \dfrac{-1}{2} \end{pmatrix}_{12} \otimes \begin{pmatrix} \dfrac{1}{\sqrt{2}} \\ \dfrac{-1}{\sqrt{2}} \end{pmatrix}_0 \right)$$

Perform the matrix-multiplication, and factorize the combined quantum state into its original three qubit states:

$$
= H_0 H_1 \left(\begin{pmatrix} \frac{1}{2} \\ \frac{-1}{2} \\ \frac{-1}{2} \\ \frac{1}{2} \end{pmatrix}_{12} \otimes \begin{pmatrix} \frac{1}{\sqrt{2}} \\ \frac{-1}{\sqrt{2}} \end{pmatrix}_0 \right) = H_0 H_1 \left(\begin{pmatrix} \frac{1}{\sqrt{2}} \\ \frac{-1}{\sqrt{2}} \end{pmatrix}_2 \otimes \begin{pmatrix} \frac{1}{\sqrt{2}} \\ \frac{-1}{\sqrt{2}} \end{pmatrix}_1 \otimes \begin{pmatrix} \frac{1}{\sqrt{2}} \\ \frac{-1}{\sqrt{2}} \end{pmatrix}_0 \right)
$$

Apply the final set of operations, which executes the H-gate on both input qubits:

$$
= \left(\begin{pmatrix} \frac{1}{\sqrt{2}} \\ \frac{-1}{\sqrt{2}} \end{pmatrix}_2 \otimes \begin{pmatrix} \frac{1}{\sqrt{2}} & \frac{1}{\sqrt{2}} \\ \frac{1}{\sqrt{2}} & \frac{-1}{\sqrt{2}} \end{pmatrix}_H \begin{pmatrix} \frac{1}{\sqrt{2}} \\ \frac{-1}{\sqrt{2}} \end{pmatrix}_1 \otimes \begin{pmatrix} \frac{1}{\sqrt{2}} & \frac{1}{\sqrt{2}} \\ \frac{1}{\sqrt{2}} & \frac{-1}{\sqrt{2}} \end{pmatrix}_H \begin{pmatrix} \frac{1}{\sqrt{2}} \\ \frac{-1}{\sqrt{2}} \end{pmatrix}_0 \right)
$$

Calculate the multiplications and look at the result. The final output qubit is still in a superposition state, but all the input qubits are in the $|1\rangle$ state:

$$
= \begin{pmatrix} \frac{1}{\sqrt{2}} \\ \frac{-1}{\sqrt{2}} \end{pmatrix}_2 \otimes \begin{pmatrix} 0 \\ 1 \end{pmatrix}_1 \otimes \begin{pmatrix} 0 \\ 1 \end{pmatrix}_0 = \frac{1}{\sqrt{2}} \left(|011\rangle - |111\rangle \right)
$$

The Deutsch-Jozsa algorithm will yield all $|0\rangle$ states on the input qubits if the black-box function is constant and will yield some other state if the black-box function is balanced. In this case, the x-mod-2 function is balanced.

The Full Quantum Implementation in Q#

If you want to translate the previous quantum circuit diagrams to an actual implementation in Q#, you can start with the classical version in Q#. Listing 9-10 contains the full implementation.

Listing 9-10. Quantum version of Deutsch's algorithm

```
01  namespace _09_02_Quantum_Deutsch_Jozsa_QSharp
02  {
03    open Microsoft.Quantum.Canon;
04    open Microsoft.Quantum.Intrinsic;
05    open Microsoft.Quantum.Math;
06    open Microsoft.Quantum.Measurement;
07    open Microsoft.Quantum.Diagnostics;
08
09    @EntryPoint()
10    operation QuantumDeutschJozsa() : Unit
11    {
12      let constantZeroResult = DeutschJozsa(3, ConstantZero);
13      Message($"ConstantZero => {constantZeroResult}");
14
15      let constantOneResult = DeutschJozsa(1, ConstantOne);
16      Message($"ConstantOne => {constantOneResult}");
17
18      let identityResult = DeutschJozsa(1, Xmod2);
19      Message($"X mod 2 => {identityResult}");
20
21      let negationResult = DeutschJozsa(1, OddNumberOfOnes);
22      Message($"Odd number of Ones => {negationResult}");
23    }
24
25    operation ConstantZero(
26      qInputs: Qubit[], qOutput: Qubit) : Unit
27    {
28      // NOP
29    }
30
31    operation ConstantOne(
32      qInputs: Qubit[], qOutput: Qubit) : Unit
```

```
33   {
34     X(qOutput);
35   }
36
37   operation Xmod2(
38     qInputs: Qubit[], qOutput: Qubit) : Unit
39   {
40     CNOT(qInputs[0], qOutput);
41   }
42
43   operation OddNumberOfOnes(
44     qInputs: Qubit[], qOutput: Qubit) : Unit
45   {
46     for q in qInputs
47     {
48       CNOT(q, qOutput);
49     }
50   }
51
52   operation DeutschJozsa(
53     n: Int,
54     oracle: (Qubit[], Qubit) => Unit) : String
55   {
56     mutable isConstant = true;
57
58     use (qInput, qOutput) = (Qubit[n], Qubit());
59
60     ApplyToEachA(H, qInput);
61     X(qOutput);
62     H(qOutput);
63
64     oracle(qInput, qOutput);
65
66     ApplyToEachA(H, qInput);
67
```

```
68      for q in qInput
69      {
70        if (M(q) == One)
71        {
72          set isConstant = false;
73        }
74      }
75
76      ResetAll(qInput);
77      Reset(qOutput);
78
79      return isConstant ? "CONSTANT" | "BALANCED";
80    }
81 }
```

First, there is no change in the entry-point operation QuantumDeutschJozsa. It still calls the DeutschJozsa operation for a total of four times using three input bits.

Next, the four functions, two constant and two balanced, have been slightly adjusted for the quantum world. In the classical version, these functions were actual functions, but now, they have become operations. Listing 9-11 shows you the ConstantZero operation, the quantum version of the constant-0 function.

Listing 9-11. The quantum implementation of the constant-0 function

```
25 operation ConstantZero(
26   qInputs: Qubit[], qOutput: Qubit) : Unit
27 {
28   // NOP
29 }
```

The major difference here is the signature of the operation. The input bits are encoded in qubit states, represented by qInputs, and the output is not returned, but encoded in an additional qubit, represented by qOutput.

Listing 9-12 shows you the ConstantOne operation, the quantum version of the constant-1 function.

Listing 9-12. The quantum implementation of the constant-1 function

```
31 operation ConstantOne(
32   qInputs: Qubit[], qOutput: Qubit) : Unit
33 {
34   X(qOutput);
35 }
```

Line 34 from Listing 9-12 calls the X-operation on the output qubit regardless of the input qubits.

Listing 9-13 shows you the Xmod2 operation, the quantum version of the x-mod-2 function.

Listing 9-13. The quantum implementation of the x-mod-2 function

```
37 operation Xmod2(
38   qInputs: Qubit[], qOutput: Qubit) : Unit
39 {
40   CNOT(qInputs[0], qOutput);
41 }
```

Line 40 from Listing 9-13 calls the CNOT-operation, using the first qubit from the input qubits as the control qubit and the output qubit as the target qubit. The first qubit from the input qubits will represent the least-significant bit from the array of input bits and can, therefore, be used to decide if the input integer is divisible by two.

Listing 9-14 shows you the OddNumberOfOnes operation, the quantum version of the odd-number-of-ones function.

Listing 9-14. The quantum implementation of the odd-number-of-ones function

```
43 operation OddNumberOfOnes(
44   qInputs: Qubit[], qOutput: Qubit) : Unit
45 {
46   for q in qInputs
47   {
48     CNOT(q, qOutput);
49   }
50 }
```

267

Lines 46 through 49 from Listing 9-14 will visit every input qubit and will call the CNOT-operation with that qubit as control qubit on the output qubit as target qubit. This will flip the output qubit from $|0\rangle$ to $|1\rangle$ and vice versa for each 1 bit inside the input array.

Finally, the DeutschJozsa operation is completely different. It contains the most important part of the Deutsch-Jozsa algorithm. Listing 9-15 repeats this operation for your reference.

Listing 9-15. The quantum implementation for the DeutschJozsa operation

```
52 operation DeutschJozsa(
53   n: Int,
54   oracle: (Qubit[], Qubit) => Unit) : String
55 {
56   mutable isConstant = true;
57
58   use (qInput, qOutput) = (Qubit[n], Qubit());
59
60   ApplyToEachA(H, qInput);
61   X(qOutput);
62   H(qOutput);
63
64   oracle(qInput, qOutput);
65
66   ApplyToEachA(H, qInput);
67
68   for q in qInput
69   {
70     if (M(q) == One)
71     {
72       set isConstant = false;
73     }
74   }
75
```

```
76    ResetAll(qInput);
77    Reset(qOutput);
78
79    return isConstant ? "CONSTANT" | "BALANCED";
80 }
```

Line 56 from Listing 9-15 declares a mutable variable to keep as a flag to determine if the oracle function is constant or balanced. The same variable is used to return the "CONSTANT" or "BALANCED" string on line 79.

Line 58 allocates several qubits to represent all possible input bits, based on the argument n plus one additional output qubit.

Line 60 applies the H operation on each of the input qubits. Q# provides the ApplyToEachA operation to make your life easier. Now, you don't have to write a loop and apply the H operation yourself.

Lines 61 and 62 apply the X-operation and H operation on the output qubit. With this, the first part of the Deutsch-Jozsa algorithm is complete. The next step is to apply the black-box function, represented by the oracle on line 64.

After applying the black-box function, all the input qubits are put through the H-gate one final time on line 66, again using the Q# operation ApplyToEachA.

To determine if the black-box function is constant or balanced, you need to check the states of all the input qubits. If they are unchanged, the black-box function is constant; if at least one of them has changed, the black-box function is balanced. Lines 68 through 74 loop through all the input qubits and perform a measurement. If one of the measurements results in the $|1\rangle$ state, the isConstant flag is changed to false on line 72.

Finally, lines 76 and 77 will reset the input and output qubits so they can be released in a clean state.

The Last Word

If you compare the classical version with the quantum version, you can clearly see that the quantum version only needs to call the oracle once, while the classical version needs to call the oracle for each input combination. The power of superposition helps us to encode all the possible scenarios in the array of input qubits and call the black-box function only once to know the effects of that function.

Again, the Deutsch-Jozsa algorithm is not very useful in our day-to-day life, but it is a good example of the possibilities of quantum computing. For this book specifically, it was a good exercise on quantum circuits, their underlying mathematical representation, and the implementation in Q#. Go ahead and play around with the Q# source code. Make some changes; try increasing the number of input bits from 3 to a higher number. Try adding some `DumpMachine` or `DumpRegister` calls to see the qubit states at different locations in the algorithm. Use the debugger to navigate through the code, step by step. Have some fun and learn while you're at it!

CHAPTER 10

The CHSH Game

In this chapter, you will learn about quantum entanglement and how you can use it to your advantage when playing silly games. Thanks to the additional possibilities of quantum theory, there are whole new ways of optimizing your winning strategies.

Measuring Qubits

In Part 1 of this book, you learned that measuring a quantum state forces it to collapse to one of its basis states. For quantum computers and qubits, measuring a qubit in superposition will collapse it to $|0\rangle$ or $|1\rangle$ depending on the wave function probabilities.

If a qubit is measured and the result is $|0\rangle$ or $|1\rangle$, you are measuring in the computational basis. The computational basis is, however, not the only basis you can use for your measurements; there is also the sign basis. For ultimate flexibility, you can even define whatever basis you want for your measurements.

Computational Basis

If you graphically express a qubit state using the unit circle and put the basis states $|0\rangle$ and $|1\rangle$ as vectors on the x-axis and y-axis you will get something like Figure 10-1.

Tip To graphically represent the basis states, you can use the unit circle. To calculate the probabilities for a given state, you can use the trigonometric ratios. Refer to Appendix I to refresh your knowledge on these mathematical concepts.

© Johnny Hooyberghs 2022
J. Hooyberghs, *Introducing Microsoft Quantum Computing for Developers*,
https://doi.org/10.1007/978-1-4842-7246-6_10

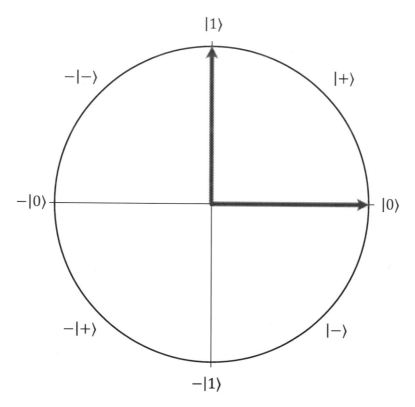

Figure 10-1. *A graphical representation of the computational basis on the unit circle*

A qubit state, reflected by a vector on the unit circle, will collapse to one of its basis states if you measure it using that basis. Collapsing to one of its basis states will be decided by the alignment of the state vector, and the probabilities can be calculated using the trigonometric ratios. Figure 10-2 shows you an arbitrary state vector and the calculation for the probabilities when measured using the computational basis.

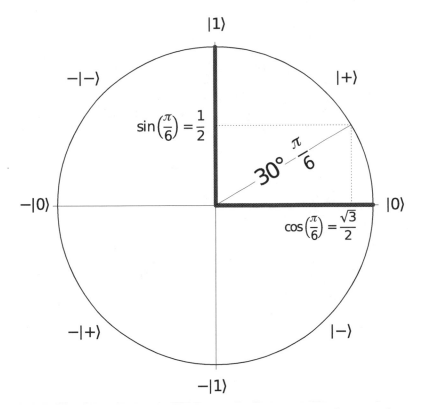

Figure 10-2. *State vector with probabilities when measured using the computational basis*

Sign Basis

Another popular basis for measuring qubit states is the sign basis. Just like the two computational basis states $|0\rangle$ and $|1\rangle$, there are two sign basis states $|+\rangle$ and $|-\rangle$. These sign basis states are just shorthand notations for the two superposition states:

$$|+\rangle = \frac{1}{\sqrt{2}}|0\rangle + \frac{1}{\sqrt{2}}|1\rangle$$

$$|-\rangle = \frac{1}{\sqrt{2}}|0\rangle - \frac{1}{\sqrt{2}}|1\rangle$$

The graphical representation on the unit circle for the sign basis is displayed in Figure 10-3.

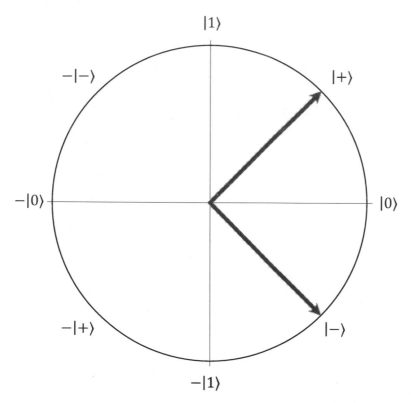

Figure 10-3. *A graphical representation of the sign basis on the unit circle*

Calculating the probabilities when you measure a qubit state using the sign basis is the same as with the computational basis. You only use the sign basis vectors as a reference this time. Figure 10-4 shows you an arbitrary state vector and the calculation for the probabilities when measured using the sign basis.

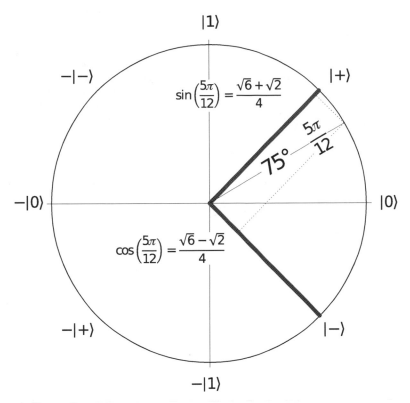

Figure 10-4. *State vector with probabilities when measured using the sign basis*

Measuring in Any Basis

Like the computational basis and the sign basis, you can define a custom basis. Just pick a set of orthogonal vectors that originate from the center of the unit circle. Figure 10-5 shows you two custom defined bases. The one on the left-hand side is defined by rotating the computational basis $\pi/8$ radians counterclockwise, and the one on the right-hand side is defined by rotating the computational basis $\pi/8$ radians clockwise.

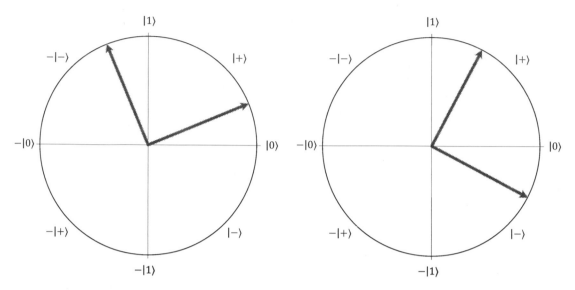

Figure 10-5. *Two custom bases defined by rotating the computational basis by π/8 radians clockwise and counterclockwise*

The CHSH Game

The CHSH game is a hypothetical game designed by John Clauser, Michael Horne, Abner Shimony, and Richard Holt, which is described in their paper "Proposed Experiment to Test Local Hidden-Variable Theories" from 1969. This chapter will not discuss this paper, but it will use the hypothetical CHSH game as an interesting and fun example to describe the power of quantum computing.

You will start to learn about the CHSH game in the classical world, and after you understand the goal and the way to play it, quantum entanglement will be introduced to increase your chances of winning the game more often.

Playing the Classic CHSH Game

The CHSH game is played by two people; let us call them Alice and Bob for the sake of habit. The setup of this game is illustrated in Figure 10-6. A very important aspect of this game is that Alice and Bob cannot communicate while playing the game, and this is illustrated in Figure 10-6 by the barrier in between Alice and Bob.

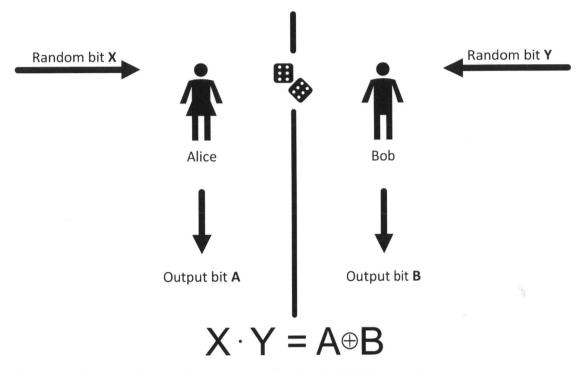

Figure 10-6. *An illustration on how the classic CHSH game is set up*

When the game starts, Alice is given a random bit X, and Bob is given a random bit called Y. If Alice and Bob wish to continue the game, they need to output another bit: A for Alice and B for Bob. Without communication, Alice and bob need to try to satisfy the following logical formula:

$$X \cdot Y = A \oplus B$$

This formula states that X multiplied by Y should equal A exclusive OR B; so, the input for Alice and Bob combined should be related to the output from Alice and Bob combined, but Alice and Bob cannot communicate.

If you remember that X and Y are given to Alice and Bob at random, you can predict that the game cannot always be won. Players Alice and Bob can never predict what value the other player has received and can, therefore, not know if they should return a zero or one to make the formula work. However, if Alice and Bob decide to always return a zero, they have a 75% chance of the formula working to their advantage and thus have a 75% chance of winning the game. Figure 10-7 illustrated the setup for the game, including the binary truth tables for both sides of the target expression.

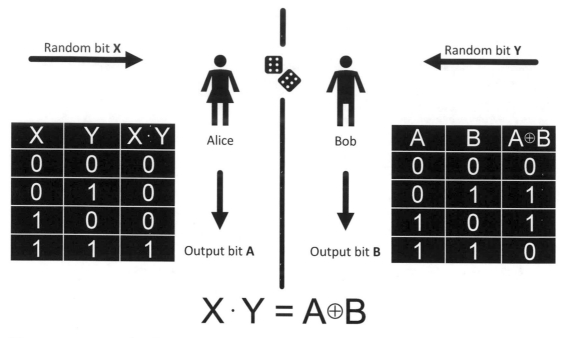

Figure 10-7. *Truth tables for the left-hand side and the right-hand side of the expression*

Based on the input, you can see that the left-hand side of the expression results in 0 in three out of four cases. The result in the remaining case is 1. If this game is played at random and the input is, therefore, random, chances of the left-hand side of the expression being 0 is 75%.

Since the left-hand side of the expression and the right-hand side of the expression need to be equal, Alice and Bob can try to outsmart the game and always return 0 for their output values A and B. This will give them a 75% chance of winning the game, which is not bad. Figure 10-8 lights up these values in the truth tables for your convenience.

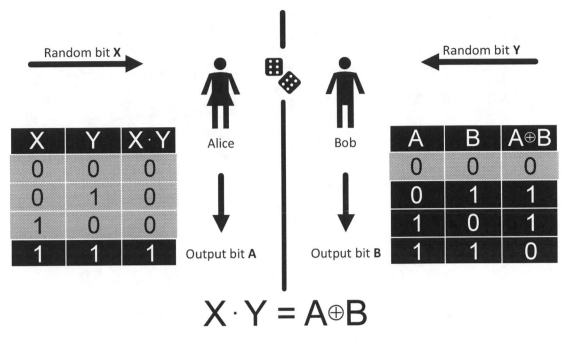

Figure 10-8. *A possible outcome that wins the CHSH game*

Implementing the Classic CHSH Game

Before looking into a possible quantum improvement of this 75% chance of winning the game, you should get familiar with Microsoft Q# some more and try to implement this classical version of the CHSH game. Take Visual Studio Code, and start to write some code! Listing 10-1 shows you a possible version of the code that you can use as a reference.

Listing 10-1. The classical CHSH game, implemented in Q#

```
01 namespace _10_01_Classical_CHSH_QSharp
02 {
03    open Microsoft.Quantum.Canon;
04    open Microsoft.Quantum.Intrinsic;
05    open Microsoft.Quantum.Convert;
06    open Microsoft.Quantum.Math;
07    open Microsoft.Quantum.Measurement;
08
```

```
09    @EntryPoint()
10    operation ClassicalCHSH() : Unit
11    {
12      let numberOfGames = 10000;
13      mutable winCount = 0;
14
15      for playCount in 1 .. numberOfGames
16      {
17        let boolForAlice = GetRandomBit();
18        let boolForBob = GetRandomBit();
19
20        let (classicalXorA, classicalXorB) =
21          PlayClassic(boolForAlice, boolForBob);
22
23        let bitForAlice = BoolArrayAsInt([boolForAlice]);
24        let bitForBob = BoolArrayAsInt([boolForBob]);
25        let bitProduct = bitForAlice * bitForBob;
26        let bitXorClassic =
27          ModulusI(classicalXorA + classicalXorB, 2);
28
29        if( bitProduct == bitXorClassic )
30        {
31          set winCount += 1;
32        }
33      }
34
35      let winPercentage =
36        IntAsDouble(winCount) / IntAsDouble(numberOfGames)
37          * 100.0;
38      Message($"Win percentage: {Round(winPercentage)}%");
39    }
40
41    operation GetRandomBit() : Bool
42    {
43      use q = Qubit();
```

```
44    H(q);
45    let bit = MResetZ(q);
46    return bit == One;
47  }
48
49  function PlayClassic(
50    bitForAlice : Bool, bitForBob : Bool ) : (Int, Int)
51  {
52    return (0, 0);
53  }
54 }
```

Again, the code is separated into multiple operations to improve readability and reusability. Just like many times before, there is one operation that acts as the entry-point, and this time, that operation is called ClassicalCHSH. Listing 10-2 shows you the most boring part of that operation.

Listing 10-2. The ClassicalCHSH entry-point operation without the interesting part

```
09 @EntryPoint()
10 operation ClassicalCHSH() : Unit
11 {
12   let numberOfGames = 10000;
13   mutable winCount = 0;
14
15   for playCount in 1 .. numberOfGames
16   {
..     ...
33   }
34
35   let winPercentage =
36     IntAsDouble(winCount) / IntAsDouble(numberOfGames)
37       * 100.0;
38   Message($"Win percentage: {Round(winPercentage)}%");
39 }
```

This part of the CHSH operation contains the code to simulate running the game many times to get a reliable win percentage. On line 12, the total number of games to play is set at 10,000, and on line 13, the number of games won is initialized at 0. Lines 15 through 33 will loop through the main game logic which will be discussed later. On lines 35 through 37, the actual win percentage is calculated by converting the prepared variables from integer to double and dividing them. Finally, on line 38, the win percentage is written to the console and rounded to the nearest integer.

To be able to write the main game logic, you will need to generate random bits. Luckily, you have access to quantum randomness. Listing 10-3 shows you the GetRandomBit operation that will be able to provide you with random bits.

Listing 10-3. The GetRandomBit operation

```
41 operation GetRandomBit() : Bool
42 {
43   use q = Qubit();
44   H(q);
45   let bit = MResetZ(q);
46   return bit == One;
47 }
```

Qubits are the perfect tool to achieve true randomness. You just need to allocate a single qubit on line 43 from Listing 10-3, put it through the H-gate to put it in superposition on line 44, and measure it on line 45. The result of this operation should be a Boolean, so we will use a binary expression to compare the measured result one line 46.

The function, PlayClassic, will play the classic CHSH game for a given input. Listing 10-4 shows you this operation.

Listing 10-4. The PlayClassic function

```
49 function PlayClassic(
50   bitForAlice : Bool, bitForBob : Bool ) : (Int, Int)
51 {
52   return (0, 0);
53 }
```

Regardless of the input, Alice and Bob should output 0 to maximize their winning chances. Line 52 from Listing 10-4 returns a tuple containing two 0 integers.

Finally, Listing 10-5 shows you the part of the entry-point CHSH operation which was omitted in Listing 10-2.

Listing 10-5. The main game loop which was ommitted in Listing 10-2

```
17 let boolForAlice = GetRandomBit();
18 let boolForBob = GetRandomBit();
19
20 let (classicalXorA, classicalXorB) =
21   PlayClassic(boolForAlice, boolForBob);
22
23 let bitForAlice = BoolArrayAsInt([boolForAlice]);
24 let bitForBob = BoolArrayAsInt([boolForBob]);
25 let bitProduct = bitForAlice * bitForBob;
26 let bitXorClassic =
27   ModulusI(classicalXorA + classicalXorB, 2);
28
29 if( bitProduct == bitXorClassic )
30 {
31   set winCount += 1;
32 }
```

Lines 17 and 18 from Listing 10-5 will generate the random input bits X and Y for Alice and Bob by using your GetRandomBit operation from Listing 10-3. Line 20 gets the output tuple A and B from your PlayClassic function from Listing 10-4. Lines 23 through 25 calculate the left-hand side of the target expression by converting the input bits X and Y to integers so they can be multiplied. Lines 26 and 27 calculate the right-hand side of the target expression by adding the output values A and B and getting the modulus when divided by two. An exclusive OR for two one-bit numbers can be substituted by their sum modulo two. Finally, on lines 29 through 32, the number of wins is increased only when the left-hand side of the target expression, the bitProduct, equals the right-hand side, the bitXorClassic.

There you go: this classical version of the CHSH hopefully gave you some understanding of what this hypothetical game is all about. You practiced writing some Q# logic and are now ready to dive deep into the quantum version of this game and how it can increase your chances of winning!

Playing the quantum CHSH game

Playing the CHSH game using quantum techniques will help Alice and Bob to increase their winning chances. Alice and Bob are not allowed to communicate, but they can share an entangled qubit-pair. Before starting the game, both Alice and Bob receive half of a pre-entangled qubit-pair. From that moment on, they play the game as before using the same set of rules, but now, they can use their half of the entangled qubit-pair without communicating with each other.

Figure 10-9 illustrates the same game setup from before, but now, the barrier separating Alice and Bob shows the entangled qubit-pair.

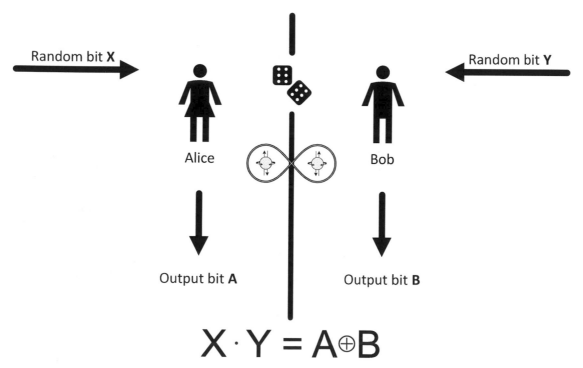

Figure 10-9. *An illustration of how the CHSH game is set up using an entangled qubit-pair*

You have learned about measuring qubits using different sets of basis states in the beginning of this chapter. Remember that measuring a qubit that is entangled with another qubit will cause both qubits to collapse simultaneously, and in the world of quantum computing, these qubits will collapse to the same basis state.

Figure 10-10 illustrates the game setup, but with some quantum magic added to it. The setup includes the input bits X and Y for Alice and Bob, and it illustrates four basis vectors, two for Alice and two for Bob.

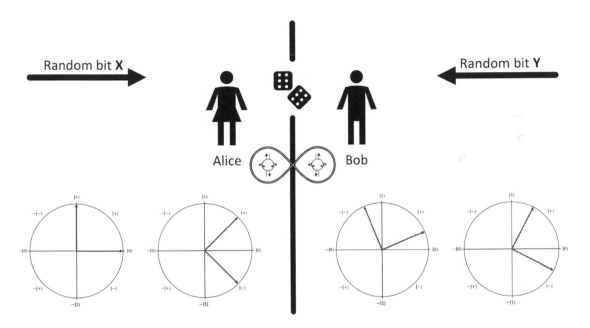

Figure 10-10. *An illustration of the different bases that will be used for measurement*

If you take a closer look at the basis vectors from Figure 10-10, you can see that Alice will need to know about measuring in both the computational basis and the sign basis. Bob needs to know about measuring using two other basis vectors. You learned about these basis vectors in the beginning of this chapter. Both basis state vectors from Bob are rotated $\pi/8$ radians relative to the computational basis vectors and the sign basis vectors from Alice.

The main idea is that if you are very clever with these basis state vectors, you can increase the probability to win based on the input bits and the measured state of the entangled qubit-pair. On the following pages, you will learn about all the different scenarios that will help Alice and Bob to increase their winning chances.

Figure 10-11 shows the specific scenario where both Alice and Bob receive 0 for their input bits X and Y.

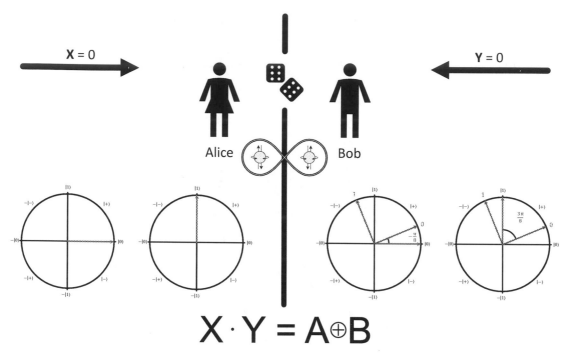

$$X \cdot Y = A \oplus B$$

Figure 10-11. *Measurements in the case where x equals 0 and y equals 0*

Look carefully at Figure 10-11 and remember the following: If Alice receives 0 as her input bit X, she will measure her half of the entangled qubit-pair using the computational basis. The outcome of this measurement will result in either $|0\rangle$ or $|1\rangle$, and depending on these outcomes, Alice will output 0 or 1 for A.

Alice and Bob cannot communicate, but Alice has just measured her half of the entangled qubit-pair. This means that Bob's other half has also collapsed to the same basis state. The smart thing to do is that Bob does not measure this state using the computational basis, but he measures using a pair of basis vectors that is rotated $-\pi/8$ radians relative to the computational basis. Bob makes this decision based on his input, Y = 0, and not on whatever is happening to Alice. Figure 10-11 shows these basis vectors relative to the collapsed state. Because Bob measures using another basis, the state of his half of the entangled qubit-pair will measure with a probability relative to that basis. Using some trigonometry, you should be able to figure out what these probabilities are.

Table 10-1 shows you an overview of the different cases for the scenario where Alice and Bob receive 0 as input X and y.

Table 10-1. *Measurement probabilities for inputs 0 and 0*

Alice measures and outputs using the computational basis	Bob's qubit after Alice has measured	Bob will output 0 with probability	Bob will output 1 with probability
0	$|0\rangle$	$cos^2\left(-\dfrac{\pi}{8}\right) \approx 0.85$	$sin^2\left(-\dfrac{\pi}{8}\right) \approx 0.15$
1	$|1\rangle$	$cos^2\left(\dfrac{3\pi}{8}\right) \approx 0.15$	$sin^2\left(\dfrac{3\pi}{8}\right) \approx 0.85$

If you compare Figure 10-11 and Table 10-1, you notice that if Alice outputs 0, Bob will output 0 with a higher probability than he would 1. If Alice outputs 1, Bob will output 1 with a higher probability than he would 0. The exact probabilities can be calculated using the trigonometric ratios based on the angles relative to the basis vectors.

Figure 10-12 shows you the truth tables. On the left-hand side, you can see the inputs X and Y being 0 with the product of X and Y also being 0. On the right-hand side, you can see that if Alice outputs 0 for A, Bob will also output 0 for B, and if Alice outputs 1 for A, Bob will also output 1 for B. The exclusive OR for A and B will be 0 in both cases. For this specific case of inputs, Alice and Bob will win the game. Don't forget that the probabilities based on the measurements are 85%. So, Alice and Bob have an 85% chance of winning the game, which is higher than the 75% chance if they were playing the game classically.

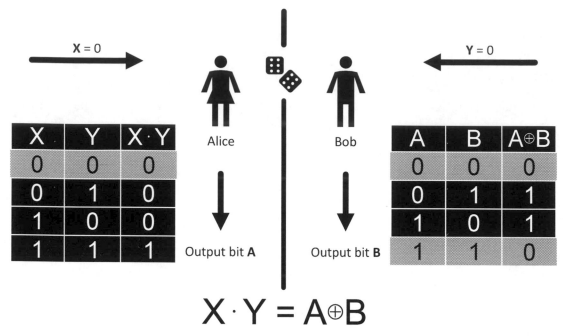

Figure 10-12. *Thruth tables in the case where x equals 0 and y equals 0*

To be thorough, you need to figure out the measurement basis vectors for all possible scenarios. Figure 10-13 shows you the scenario where Alice still receives 0 for her input bit X, but Bob receives 1 for his input bit Y.

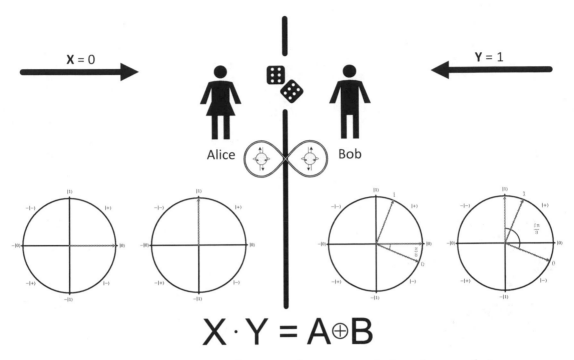

Figure 10-13. *Measurements in the case where x equals 0 and y equals 1*

As you can see in Figure 10-13, there is no change for Alice. She still receives 0 for her bit X, so she measures using the computational basis. Bob receives 1 for his input Y, so he measures using a pair of basis vectors that is rotated $\pi/8$ radians relative to the computational basis. This is the opposite direction from before, so maybe something different will happen? If you look closely at Figure 10-13, you can see that this rotation still looks like the probabilities are equal, and Table 10-2 also forms this conclusion.

Table 10-2. *Measurement probabilities for inputs 0 and 1*

Alice measures and outputs using the computational basis	Bob's qubit after Alice has measured	Bob will output 0 with probability	Bob will output 1 with probability
0	$|0\rangle$	$cos^2\left(\dfrac{\pi}{8}\right) \approx 0.85$	$sin^2\left(\dfrac{\pi}{8}\right) \approx 0.15$
1	$|1\rangle$	$cos^2\left(\dfrac{5\pi}{8}\right) \approx 0.15$	$sin^2\left(\dfrac{5\pi}{8}\right) \approx 0.85$

The truth tables in Figure 10-14 will make it clear that this specific scenario still needs Alice and Bob to output 0 or 1 for both A and B to win the game. Again, Alice and Bob have an 85% chance of winning the game by using the same logic.

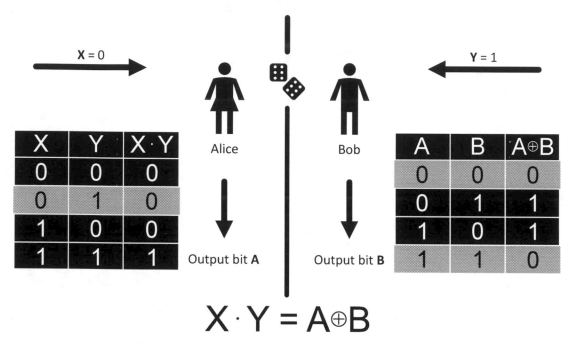

$$X \cdot Y = A \oplus B$$

Figure 10-14. *Thruth tables in the case where x equals 0 and y equals 1*

In the third scenario, Alice receives 1 for her bit X and Bob receives 0 for his bit Y. Figure 10-15 shows the setup for this third scenario. Because Alice receives 1 for her bit X, she will now measure her half of the entangled qubit-pair using the sign basis instead of the computation basis. Bob receives a 0 for his bit Y, so he reverts to measuring using a pair of basis vectors that is rotated $-\pi/8$ radians relative to the computational basis, just like with the first scenario.

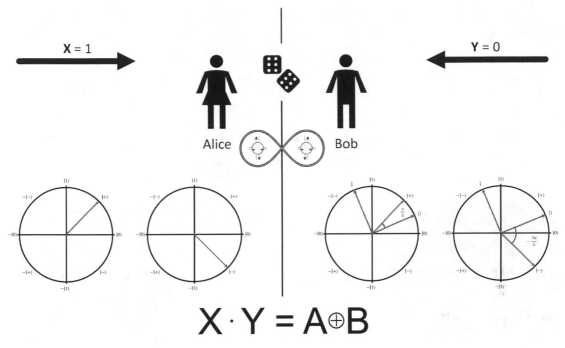

$$X \cdot Y = A \oplus B$$

Figure 10-15. *Measurements in the case where x equals 1 and y equals 0*

Again, based on the unit circles from Figure 10-15, you can calculate the values for Table 10-3. Alice will output 0 if the qubit measures $|+\rangle$ and 1 if the qubit measures $|-\rangle$. Bob measures using a pair of basis vectors that is rotated $-\pi/8$ radians, and thanks to the entangled states $|+\rangle$ and $|-\rangle$, he still measures the same outputs.

Table 10-3. *Measurement probabilities for inputs 1 and 0*

Alice measures and outputs using the sign basis	Bob's qubit after Alice has measured	Bob will output 0 with probability	Bob will output 1 with probability
0	$|+\rangle$	$cos^2\left(\dfrac{\pi}{8}\right) \approx 0.85$	$sin^2\left(\dfrac{\pi}{8}\right) \approx 0.15$
1	$|-\rangle$	$cos^2\left(-\dfrac{3\pi}{8}\right) \approx 0.15$	$sin^2\left(-\dfrac{3\pi}{8}\right) \approx 0.85$

For the third scenario, Figure 10-16 shows you the truth tables. Alice and Bob still output 0 or 1 for both A and B with a probability of 85%. That is 85% chance of winning the game for three scenarios. Only one scenario is left to investigate.

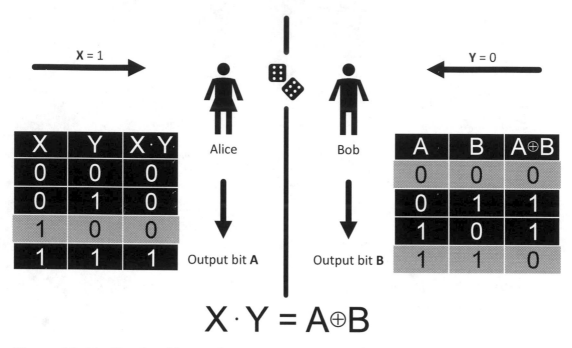

$$X \cdot Y = A \oplus B$$

Figure 10-16. *Truth tables in the case where x equals 1 and y equals 0*

For the final scenario, both Alice and Bob receive 1 for their bits X and Y. Figure 10-17 shows you the game setup. Because Alice receives 1 for her input bit X, she measures using the sign basis, and because Bob receives 1 for his input bit Y, he measures using the $\pi/8$ basis.

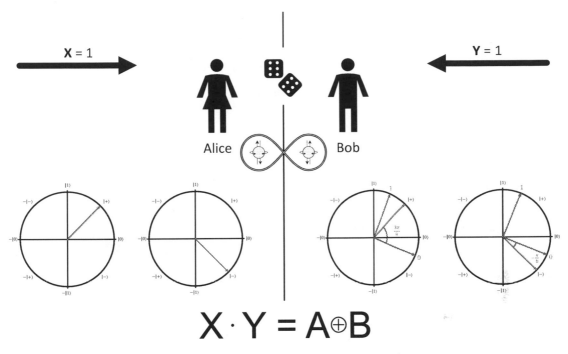

$$X \cdot Y = A \oplus B$$

Figure 10-17. *Measurements in the case where x equals 1 and y equals 1*

In Figure 10-17 and Table 10-4, it becomes clear why the basis vectors for Bob are what they are. The $-\pi/8$ radians and $\pi/8$ radians were carefully chosen to help us toward these results. In this specific scenario, the outcome has a higher chance of resulting in Alice and Bob outputting opposite values. If Alice measures $|+\rangle$ and outputs 0, Bob has an 85% probability of outputting 1. If Alice measures $|-\rangle$ and outputs 1, Bob has an 85% probability of outputting 0.

Table 10-4. *Measurement probabilities for inputs 1 and 1*

Alice measures and outputs using the sign basis	Bob's qubit after Alice has measured	Bob will output 0 with probability	Bob will output 1 with probability
0	$|+\rangle$	$cos^2\left(\dfrac{3\pi}{8}\right) \approx 0.15$	$sin^2\left(\dfrac{3\pi}{8}\right) \approx 0.85$
1	$|-\rangle$	$cos^2\left(-\dfrac{\pi}{8}\right) \approx 0.85$	$sin^2\left(-\dfrac{\pi}{8}\right) \approx 0.15$

The final truth table in Figure 10-18 shows this fourth scenario. The product of inputs X and Y results in 1, and the exclusive OR for the outputs of Alice and Bob results in 1 if their outputs are opposite values.

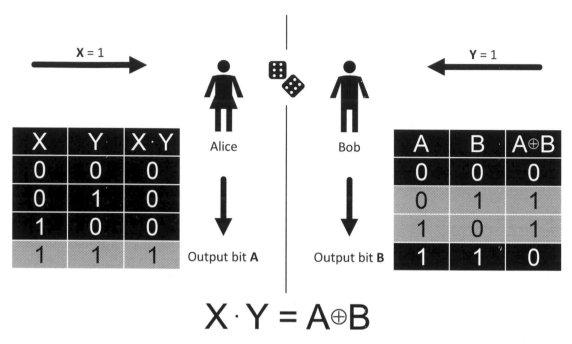

Figure 10-18. *Truth tables in the case where x equals 1 and y equals 1*

You had some fun with the power of mathematics. The CHSH game is a hypothetical game but it shows you a clear advantage in the quantum world. Finally, you are ready to translate the knowledge from the previous pages to actual Q# code.

Implementing the Quantum CHSH Game

Once more, use Visual Studio or Visual Studio Code to create a Q# standalone console application. You can start from the classical version of the CHSH game and try to convert it to the quantum version you learned about just now, or you can use Listing 10-6 as a reference.

Listing 10-6. The quantum CHSH game, implemented in Q#

```
001 namespace _10_02_Quantum_CHSH_QSharp
002 {
003    open Microsoft.Quantum.Canon;
004    open Microsoft.Quantum.Intrinsic;
005    open Microsoft.Quantum.Convert;
006    open Microsoft.Quantum.Math;
007    open Microsoft.Quantum.Measurement;
008
009    @EntryPoint()
010    operation SayHello() : Unit
011    {
012      let numberOfGames = 10000;
013      mutable winCount = 0;
014
015      for playCount in 1 .. numberOfGames
016      {
017        let boolForAlice = GetRandomBit();
018        let boolForBob = GetRandomBit();
019
020        let (quantumXorA, quantumXorB) =
021          PlayQuantum(boolForBob, boolForAlice);
022
023        let bitForAlice = BoolArrayAsInt([boolForAlice]);
024        let bitForBob = BoolArrayAsInt([boolForBob]);
025        let bitProduct = bitForAlice * bitForBob;
026
027        let bitXorQuantum =
028          ModulusI(quantumXorA + quantumXorB, 2);
029        if( bitProduct == bitXorQuantum )
030        {
031          set winCount += 1;
032        }
033      }
034
```

```
035    let winPercentage =
036      IntAsDouble(winCount) / IntAsDouble(numberOfGames)
037        * 100.0;
038    Message($"Win percentage: {Round(winPercentage)}%");
039  }
040
041  operation GetRandomBit() : Bool
042  {
043    use q = Qubit();
044    H(q);
045    let bit = MResetZ(q);
046    return bit == One;
047  }
048
049  operation PlayQuantum(
050    boolForAlice : Bool, boolForBob : Bool ) : (Int, Int)
051  {
052    use (qubitForAlice, qubitForBob) = (Qubit(), Qubit());
053
054    H(qubitForAlice);
055    CNOT(qubitForAlice, qubitForBob);
056
057    if( GetRandomBit() )
058    {
059      let resultForAlice =
060        MeasureForAlice(boolForAlice, qubitForAlice);
061      let bitForAlice = resultForAlice == One ? 1 | 0;
062
063      let resultForBob =
064        MeasureForBob(boolForBob, qubitForBob);
065      let bitForBob = resultForBob == One ? 1 | 0;
066
067      return (bitForAlice, bitForBob);
068    }
```

```
069     else
070     {
071       let resultForBob =
072         MeasureForBob(boolForBob, qubitForBob);
073       let bitForBob = resultForBob == One ? 1 | 0;
074
075       let resultForAlice =
076         MeasureForAlice(boolForAlice, qubitForAlice);
077       let bitForAlice = resultForAlice == One ? 1 | 0;
078
079       return (bitForAlice, bitForBob);
080     }
081   }
082
083   operation MeasureForAlice(
084     bit : Bool, qubit : Qubit) : Result
085   {
086     if( bit )
087     {
088       return MResetX(qubit);
089     }
090     else
091     {
092       return MResetZ(qubit);
093     }
094   }
095
096   operation MeasureForBob(
097     bit : Bool, qubit : Qubit) : Result
098   {
099     if( bit )
100     {
101       Ry(2.0 * PI() / 8.0, qubit);
102     }
```

```
103    else
104    {
105       Ry(-2.0 * PI() / 8.0, qubit);
106    }
107
108    return MResetZ(qubit);
109  }
110 }
```

Lines 9 through 39 from Listing 10-6 contain the same entry-point operation. This time, the operation is called QuantumCHSH, and it contains the quantum version of the CHSH game. Since a large part of the body for operation QuantumCHSH is very similar to the classical version, it will not be repeated here. Lines 17 through 32 from Listing 10-6 are different and are repeated in Listing 10-7 for your reference.

Listing 10-7. The main game loop, taken from the QuantumCHSH entry-point operation

```
017 let boolForAlice = GetRandomBit();
018 let boolForBob = GetRandomBit();
019
020 let (quantumXorA, quantumXorB) =
021   PlayQuantum(boolForBob, boolForAlice);
022
023 let bitForAlice = BoolArrayAsInt([boolForAlice]);
024 let bitForBob = BoolArrayAsInt([boolForBob]);
025 let bitProduct = bitForAlice * bitForBob;
026
027 let bitXorQuantum =
028   ModulusI(quantumXorA + quantumXorB, 2);
029 if( bitProduct == bitXorQuantum )
030 {
031   set winCount += 1;
032 }
```

Lines 17 and 18 from Listing 10-7 generate the random input bit for Alice and Bob. There is no change needed from the classical implementation, so the GetRandomBit operation will not be explained this time.

Lines 20 and 21 from Listing 10-7 will play the game in a quantum way, and the PlayQuantum operation will return the outputs A and B from Alice and Bob. The PlayQuantum operation will be explained a little further in Listing 10-8.

The input bits X and Y from Alice and Bob are returned by the GetRandomBit operation as Boolean-typed variables. To calculate with these values, you need to convert them to decimal numbers. Lines 23 and 24 from Listing 10-7 use a Q# function BoolArrayAsInt to convert a bit-array or Boolean-array to its base-10 counterpart. In this case, a Boolean false becomes 0 and a Boolean true becomes 1.

Line 25 from Listing 10-7 calculates the product of the input values X and Y from Alice and Bob. Lines 27 and 28 calculate the exclusive OR with the output values A and B from Alice and Bob. The exclusive OR can be calculated by adding the two binary bits and taking the remainder after division by two.

Lines 29 through 32 from Listing 10-7 check if the two parts of the mathematical expression match to decide whether the game has been won or not. If the product and the exclusive OR are equal, the variable winCount is increased.

Playing the CHSH game classically was easy. Alice and Bob should just output 0 for their output bits A and B. Playing the CHSH game in a quantum way is a bit more complicated. Depending on the input bits X and Y, Alice and Bob need to measure their half of the entangled qubit-pair using different bases. Listing 10-8 repeats the code for the PlayQuantum operation.

Listing 10-8. The PlayQuantum operation

```
049 operation PlayQuantum(
050    boolForAlice : Bool, boolForBob : Bool ) : (Int, Int)
051 {
052    use (qubitForAlice, qubitForBob) = (Qubit(), Qubit());
053
054    H(qubitForAlice);
055    CNOT(qubitForAlice, qubitForBob);
056
```

```
057   if( GetRandomBit() )
058   {
059     let resultForAlice =
060       MeasureForAlice(boolForAlice, qubitForAlice);
061     let bitForAlice = resultForAlice == One ? 1 | 0;
062
063     let resultForBob =
064       MeasureForBob(boolForBob, qubitForBob);
065     let bitForBob = resultForBob == One ? 1 | 0;
066
067     return (bitForAlice, bitForBob);
068   }
069   else
070   {
071     let resultForBob =
072       MeasureForBob(boolForBob, qubitForBob);
073     let bitForBob = resultForBob == One ? 1 | 0;
074
075     let resultForAlice =
076       MeasureForAlice(boolForAlice, qubitForAlice);
077     let bitForAlice = resultForAlice == One ? 1 | 0;
078
079     return (bitForAlice, bitForBob);
080   }
081 }
```

Line 52 from Listing 10-8 allocates the two qubits needed for entanglement and playing the CHSH game in a quantum way. Lines 54 and 55 entangle the qubits allocated before by using the H-gate and CNOT-gate.

Lines 57 through 80 contain a large decision based on a random bit to play the game in two possible ways. In the theoretical approach for the quantum CHSH game on the previous pages, you always looked at the game from the perspective of Alice. Alice always measures her qubit first, collapsing the entangled qubits for Bob to measure second. In this Q# implementation, the order in which Alice or Bob measures their half of the qubit-pair is randomized to prove that this is not a factor in gaining a higher winning chance.

Lines 59 through 61 from Listing 10-8 use the MeasureForAlice operation to decide on the correct measurement basis for Alice and return the result of that measurement. Lines 63 through 65 use the MeasureForBob operation to decide on the correct measurement basis for Bob and return the result of that measurement. Finally, line 67 returns a tuple containing both outputs A and B from Alice and Bob. The MeasureForAlice and MeasureForBob are explained in Listings 10-9 and 10-10, respectively.

Lines 71 through 77 will execute the exact same code as lines 59 through 67 but in the reverse order.

Listing 10-9. The MeasureForAlice operation

```
083 operation MeasureForAlice(
084   bit : Bool, qubit : Qubit) : Result
085 {
086   if( bit )
087   {
088     return MResetX(qubit);
089   }
090   else
091   {
092     return MResetZ(qubit);
093   }
094 }
```

Depending on the input bit X for Alice, she needs to measure using the computational basis or the sign basis. This decision is made on line 86 from Listing 10-9.

Measuring using the sign basis can be performed in Q# by measuring using the Pauli X basis. Think about the Bloch sphere from Chapter 2 to visualize a measurement using the x-axis. Line 88 from Listing 10-9 shows this measurement and will reset the qubit afterward.

Measuring using the computational basis can be performed in Q# by measuring using the Pauli Z basis. Think about the Bloch sphere from Chapter 2 to visualize a measurement using the z-axis. Line 92 from Listing 10-9 performs this measurement and will reset the qubit afterward.

Listing 10-10. The MeasureForBob operation

```
096 operation MeasureForBob(
097   bit : Bool, qubit : Qubit) : Result
098 {
099   if( bit )
100   {
101     Ry(2.0 * PI() / 8.0, qubit);
102   }
103   else
104   {
105     Ry(-2.0 * PI() / 8.0, qubit);
106   }
107
108   return MResetZ(qubit);
109 }
```

Depending on the input bit Y for Bob, he needs to measure using the $-\pi/8$ basis or the $\pi/8$ basis. This decision is made on line 99 from Listing 10-10.

Measuring using a custom basis is not possible out of the box in Q#. You can only measure using the Pauli X, Pauli Y, and Pauli Z bases. Fortunately, a custom measurement is possible by first rotating the state vector and then measuring using one of these three bases. In this case, you can rotate the state vector $-\pi/8$ radians or $\pi/8$ radians on the unit circle and then measure using the computational basis with the built-in MResetZ operation. For arbitrary rotations, Q# offers the R operations with specialized Rx, Ry, and Rz versions for rotating around one of these axes on the Bloch sphere. Q# does not use the unit circle for its internal representation of qubit state vector rotations but uses the Bloch sphere vector representation. Remember that the opposite basis vectors for the computational basis are aligned on the z-axis of the Bloch sphere, and the opposite basis vectors for the sign basis are aligned on the x-axis of the Bloch sphere. Check out Figure 2-3 if you need a refresher.

Line 101 from Listing 10-10 rotates the qubit vector state $2 \cdot \pi/8$ radians around the y-axis using the Ry operation. Multiplying the $\pi/8$ rotation with two is needed to convert from our unit circle representation to the internal Q# Bloch sphere representation. Rotating around the y-axis is needed to rotate the state vector on the plane that is shared with the x-axis and the z-axis. This will make sure the rotation is always in accordance with the computational basis or sign basis from Alice.

Line 105 from Listing 10-10 rotates the qubit vector state $2 \cdot - \pi/8$ radians around the y-axis using the Ry operation. Line 108 return a measurement using the computational basis, which represents a measurement using the custom $-\pi/8$ and $\pi/8$ bases as discussed in the previous paragraphs.

The Last Word

It is possible that you need to read this chapter multiple times to exactly understand what is going on. This is, in my opinion, however, one of the more fun algorithms out there that show you the ingenuity of some of the quantum algorithms. Quantum algorithms are hard. They need a different way of thinking than classical algorithms, and the only way to train your brain is to read and learn from existing algorithms. The quantum computing community is alive and kicking for several decades already, and a large amount of quantum algorithms are already out there. Have fun and explore!

The CHSH game is the third and last algorithm discussed in this book and concludes Part 3. The next part, Part 4, will discuss the future of quantum computing and will touch on Azure Quantum public preview, at the time of writing, the very new quantum cloud offering from Microsoft.

PART IV

What to Do Next?

CHAPTER 11

Azure Quantum

Microsoft offers a hugely popular cloud platform that listens to the name Azure or Microsoft Azure. Over the past decade, Azure has grown to one of the most popular cloud platforms and offers a wide range of IaaS (Infrastructure as a Service), PaaS (Platform as a Service), and SaaS (Software as a Service) offerings.

Because quantum computing is just in its early stages, running a quantum computer from within your own home is not easy or cheap, especially for educational purposes. Today, quantum computers are very sensitive devices that need to be nurtured and monitored from high-tech laboratories. To create the best possible environment for the quantum particles to behave stable, the quantum processing unit needs to be cooled as close to 0 Kelvin as possible. Thanks to cloud platforms like Azure, companies like Microsoft and their hardware partners can bring these high-tech devices closer to users by developing a service that can bridge the gap between your software and the physical quantum computer.

Azure Quantum is still in public preview. That means that Azure Quantum is available for the public and you have access to physical quantum hardware from external vendors via the Azure Marketplace, but Azure Quantum will still undergo changes and can quickly introduce new features and new partnerships with external vendors.

Note Because Azure Quantum is still in public preview while writing this book, it is possible that not all information in this chapter is up to date. Please refer to the official online documentation if something has changed since this chapter was written.

© Johnny Hooyberghs 2022
J. Hooyberghs, *Introducing Microsoft Quantum Computing for Developers*,
https://doi.org/10.1007/978-1-4842-7246-6_11

Quantum Computing

Azure Quantum provides a workspace that allows you to access different physical quantum computers and simulated quantum environments from different hardware vendors. You can run your Q# quantum programs on physical hardware for a monthly fee or for a pay-as-you-go fee based on your actual usage. You are also able to use simulated cloud-scale quantum computers for free.

The previous chapters in this book have mostly covered the quantum computing part of Azure Quantum, and you should be able to run some of the examples from this book on actual quantum hardware thanks to Azure Quantum.

Azure Quantum

Azure Quantum is the name of an Azure cloud resource that you can create using the Azure Portal. If you visit the Microsoft Azure web page and create a new account and subscription, you will be able to experiment with Azure Quantum in only 15 minutes.

Note   This book will not guide you with the creation of an Azure user account and subscription. You will find the most up-to-date information online, and creating an Azure account and subscription is an easy and straightforward process. You will need a valid credit card to register a subscription, but you can start a free trial and not have anything charged on your credit card. You don't have to pay subscription costs. You only pay what you use, and during your trial period, many services can be used for free for a limited time.

If you have an active Azure subscription, you can open the Azure portal and have a look at your home page. Figure 11-1 shows you an empty home page that contains no active cloud services.

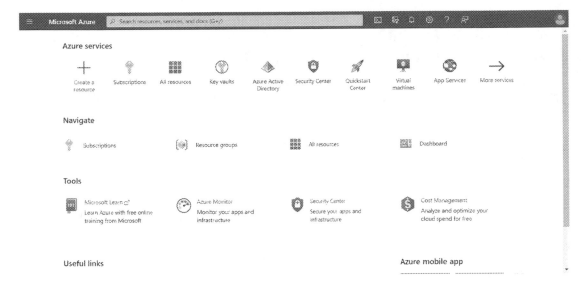

Figure 11-1. *The Azure home page for your Azure cloud account*

Between all the links and buttons, you can find a big "Create a resource" button. Cloud services on Azure are called resources, and this button allows you to create new services from a marketplace containing different kinds of services. Figure 11-2 shows you how to search for the "Azure Quantum" resource in the resource marketplace.

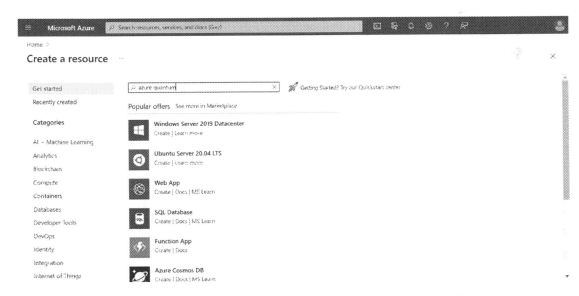

Figure 11-2. *Search for "azure quantum" in the resource marketplace*

If you press the Enter key after typing the "azure quantum" search keywords, you should get a list which contains the Azure Quantum service. Figure 11-3 shows you several results, where the fourth result is the one that you need to select.

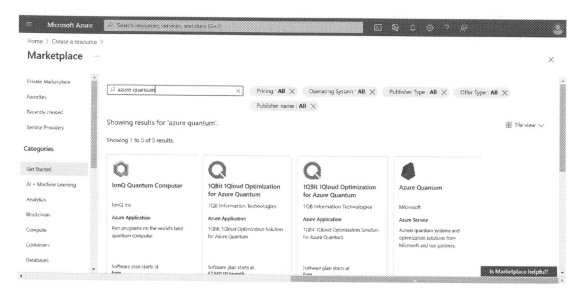

Figure 11-3. *Azure quantum search results*

If you select the "Azure Quantum" service, you will get a detailed overview for this service. Figure 11-4 shows you what this overview looks like.

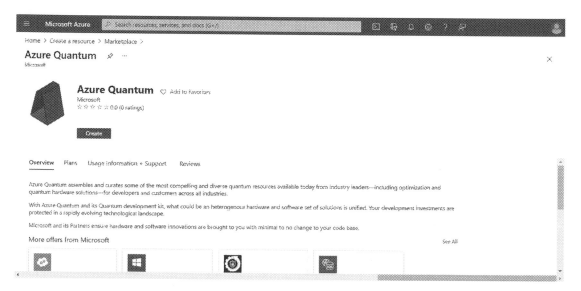

Figure 11-4. *Detailed overview for the "Azure Quantum" resource*

310

Click the "Create" button to start a wizard that will help you to create your first Azure Quantum workspace.

Quantum Workspace

Most of the complexity that goes with running your quantum programs on quantum hardware is hidden from you. You just write Q# source code and upload that code to the Azure Quantum cloud service. Azure Quantum will do most of the heavy lifting to make sure your code runs on a physical quantum computer.

Azure Quantum provides a single point of entry for all your quantum-related computing solutions, a quantum workspace. The Azure Quantum workspace is your front door to the quantum world and provides you with a dashboard and some tools to keep track of your work.

The wizard that will help you to create this workspace will ask you for some data and configuration. Figure 11-5 gives you an idea of what the first page of this wizard looks like.

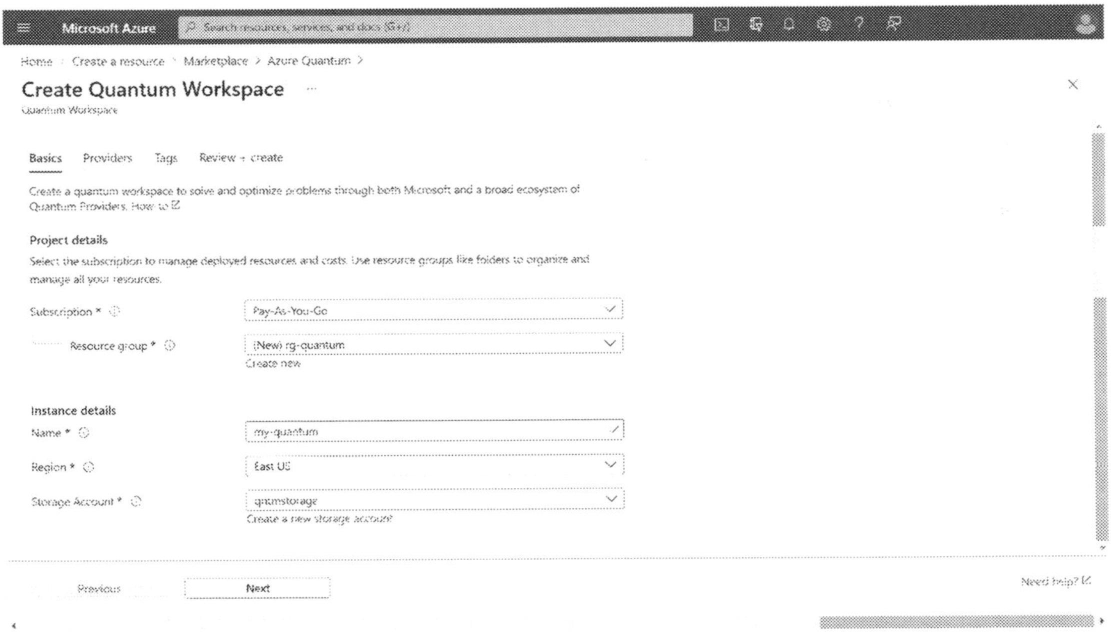

Figure 11-5. *The first wizard page to create a quantum workspace*

Note   The Azure portal is always evolving. It is possible that the figures in this chapter are not up to date when you are reading this book. If this is the case, don't hesitate to look through the Azure portal documentation or explore for yourself.

Tip   You can always perform these actions using a command-line tool and the Azure CLI with the az quantum extension. You can find documentation on the az quantum extension online by searching it using your favorite search engine. Closer to the end of this chapter, you will be guided to use the Azure CLI for running quantum programs.

Azure cloud services are called resources, and these resources are managed in a hierarchical way. The top level of this hierarchy is the subscription you have created with your user account and credit card. Within a subscription, you can create resource groups to manage your resources the way you want. Every resource needs a parent resource group, so your Azure Quantum workspace also needs a resource group. You can select an existing one or create a new one just as easily.

Every Azure resource needs a name, so you can name your resource whatever you want. Some resources that you create should have a unique name in the whole wide world, and some need to be unique in your subscription. The Azure Quantum workspace name needs to be unique for your subscription.

Almost every Azure resource needs a region. This is the physical region where the underlying hardware is running. You can select the default East US region.

Finally, for this first page, you need to select a storage account. A storage account is a specific Azure resource that can store data. Your Azure Quantum workspace needs a location to store its input and output data, so you need to link it to a storage account. You can select an existing one or create a new one. Your best option is to select the same region for your Azure Quantum workspace and your Storage Account so that these resources are physically hosted close together.

Providers and Targets

If you are finished with configuring the basics, you can move ahead to the next page which allows you to configure your providers and targets. Figure 11-6 shows you an overview of this next page.

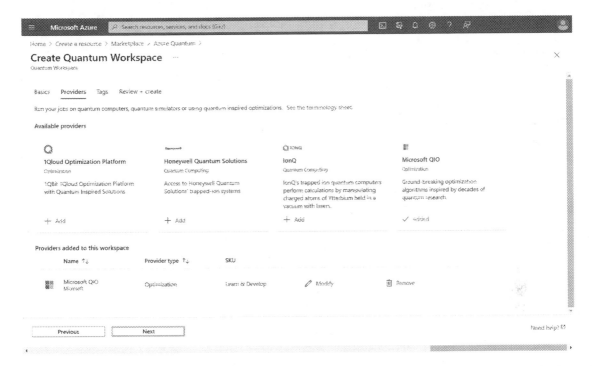

Figure 11-6. *The second page for the Azure Quantum worspace creation wizard*

On this page, you should select all providers you want to use. A provider is a plug-and-play target you can use from your quantum workspace. By default, the Microsoft Quantum Inspired Optimization provider is added to your workspace. With this provider, you can run your optimization programs. If you want to also run your actual quantum programs, you need to add a provider that supports quantum hardware. For now, you can select the IonQ provider and go for the "Pay as you Go" offering. Figure 11-7 shows you the IonQ provider page.

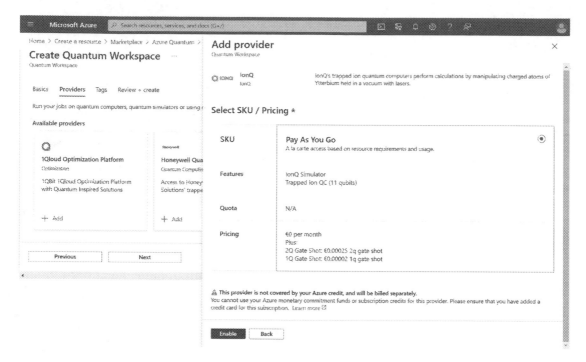

***Figure 11-7.** Adding a provider to your quantum workspace*

The IonQ provider for Azure Quantum offers targets that can run your Q# quantum programs on physical quantum hardware and on simulated classical hardware. You don't need to pay any subscription costs for now, and running on their simulated hardware is free. Running Q# programs on their quantum hardware will cost you a very small fee and is charged based on your usage. In Figure 11-7, you can see the cost per execution of a quantum gate for one-qubit-gates and two-qubit-gates. Running simple quantum programs will be cheap. Running more complex quantum programs will be more expensive.

Note   If you are using the free Microsoft Azure trial or have access to a Microsoft Azure subscription with available credits, the IonQ provider will still be charged using your credit card. Be careful, and always double-check the programs that you are sending to the IonQ quantum target.

After you have added the IonQ provider, this change should be reflected in your overview. Figure 11-8 shows you the updated page.

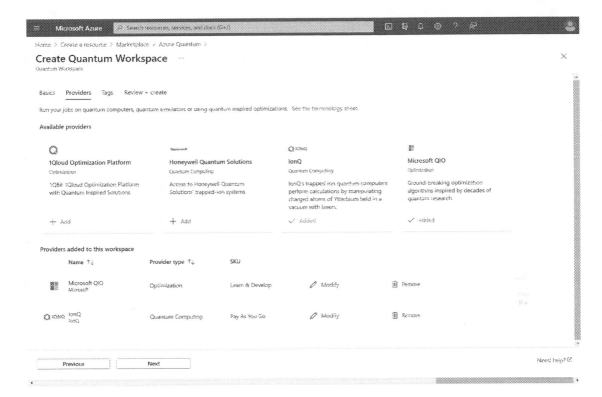

Figure 11-8. *The list of providers with the Microsoft QIO and IonQ providers added*

If you are happy with your configuration and list of providers, you can skip the "Tags" page and move straight to the "Review + create" page. This page asks you to accept the terms and conditions for your selected targets. Figures 11-9 and 11-10 show you how to read and accept these conditions and create the Azure Quantum workspace resource.

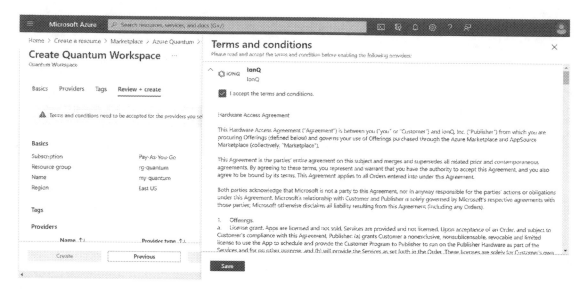

Figure 11-9. *First, accept the terms and conditions*

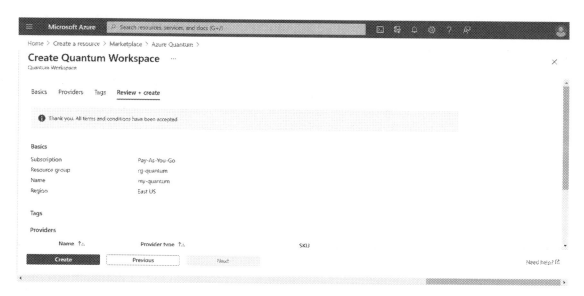

Figure 11-10. *Create the Azure Quantum workspace by clicking the "Create" button*

Jobs

After finishing the create an "Azure Quantum Workspace" wizard, you need to wait for Microsoft Azure to create all your requested resources. You are getting a deployment status page that will keep you updated on the deployment progress and status. Figures 11-11 and 11-12 show you the ongoing deployment and, after a while, the finished deployment.

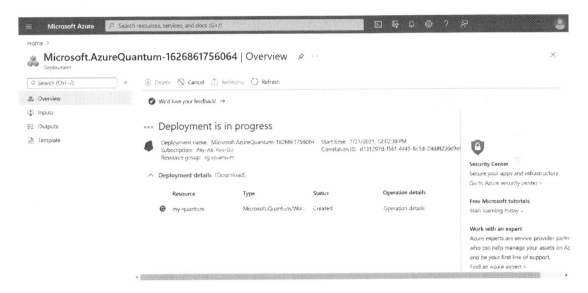

Figure 11-11. *The deployment is in progress*

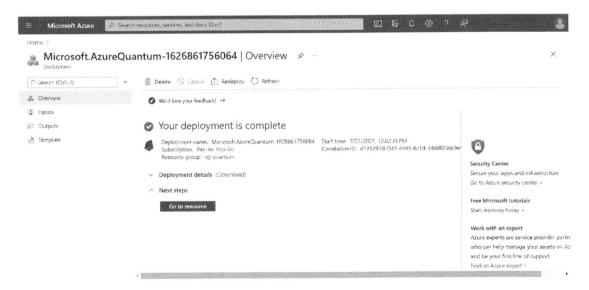

Figure 11-12. *The deployment is complete*

You can click the "Go to resource" button to open your resource and see its dashboard. You can also find your resource from your account home page by looking at the correct icon and the unique name you have provided during the creation process. Figure 11-13 shows you how to identify your resource from the home page.

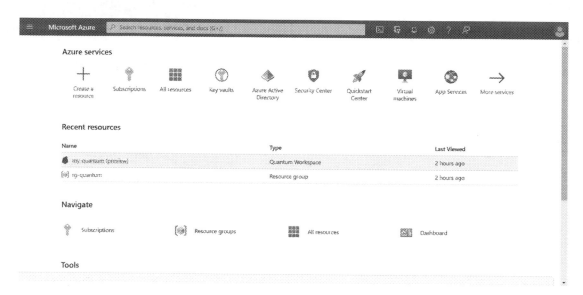

Figure 11-13. *Find your Azure Quantum workspace resource from the Microsoft Azure home page*

The Azure Quantum workspace dashboard gives you an overview of your quantum workspace. Figure 11-14 shows you the overview page for the Azure Quantum workspace resource.

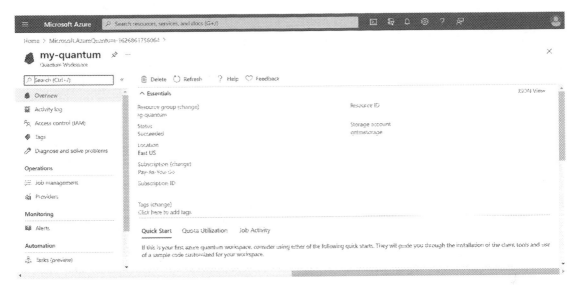

Figure 11-14. *The dashboard for your Azure Quantum workspace*

Even after creating your Azure Quantum workspace, you are still able to add and remove providers and targets. Find the "Providers" link on the left-hand side, and open the corresponding page. Figure 11-15 shows you the "Providers" page.

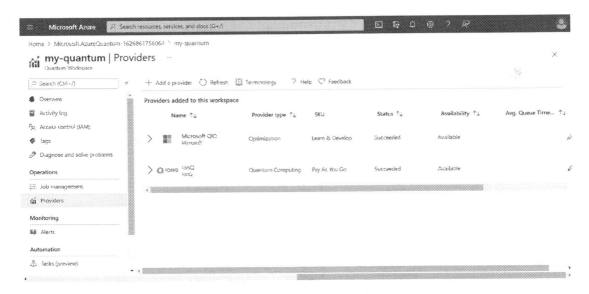

Figure 11-15. *Configure additional providers or remove existing ones from your workspace*

If you start developing Q# programs or optimization programs and run them from your Azure Quantum workspace, they will become available as jobs. A job is a piece of quantum software that has an input and an output. The input can be the program itself and some arguments. The output can be the result or solution that your program has found. The input and output data are stored within your Azure Storage account, and the jobs themselves are shown on the "Job management" page. You can open this page by finding the "Job management" link on the left-hand side. Figure 11-16 shows you the empty "Job management" page, because you have not added any jobs.

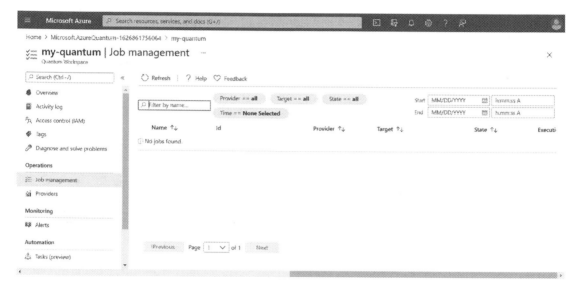

Figure 11-16. *Empty "Job management" page*

To create new jobs, you must go back to Visual Studio Code or Microsoft Visual Studio and start to develop some programs that can be executed on Azure Quantum.

Quantum Computing Jobs

If you create a new Q# project, the Microsoft Quantum Development Kit provides you with the option to select an execution target. Figures 11-17 and 11-18 show you how to select the IonQ project template from Visual Studio Code. Figure 11-19 shows you how to select the IonQ project template from Microsoft Visual Studio.

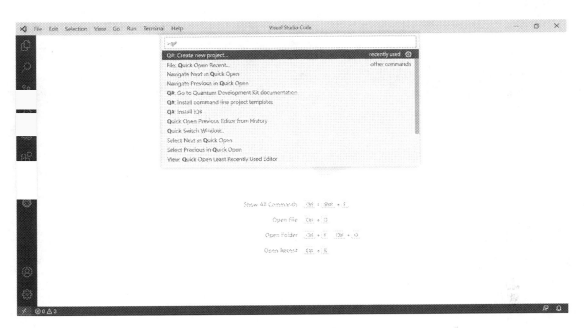

Figure 11-17. *Create a new Q# project from Visual Studio Code*

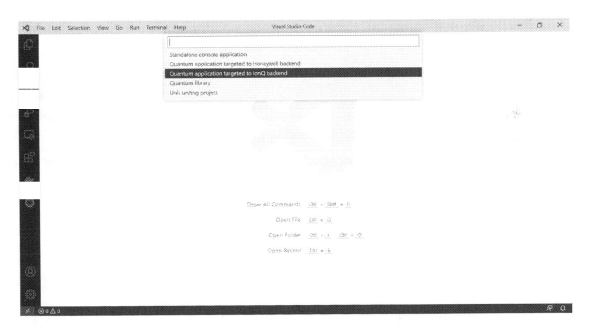

Figure 11-18. *Select the IonQ project template from Visual Studio Code*

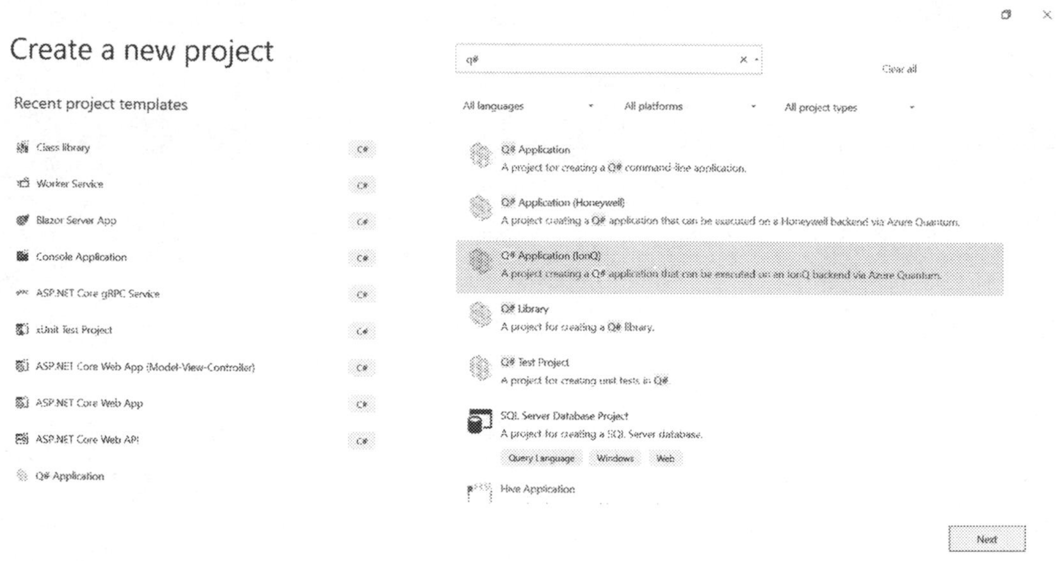

Figure 11-19. *Create a new Q# project targetting IonQ from Microsoft Visual Studio*

If you compare the Q# project file to the ones you have created earlier, you should see a small difference. There is an additional XML property `ExecutionTarget` that specifies the IonQ quantum processing unit or QPU. Creating Q# projects that have this additional information helps you during your development process because not all quantum hardware is the same. Some providers and their targets have limitations, and not the whole Q# feature set is available for these QPUs. The Q# compiler will warn you about these limitations and will show you an error if a Q# feature is not supported on your selected quantum target.

Listing 11-1 shows you the contents for a Q# project file that targets the IonQ QPU. Line 6 contains the additional `ExecutionTarget` property.

Listing 11-1. A Q# project file that targets the IonQ QPU

```
01 <Project Sdk="Microsoft.Quantum.Sdk/0.21.2111177148">
02
03  <PropertyGroup>
04     <OutputType>Exe</OutputType>
05     <TargetFramework>netcoreapp3.1</TargetFramework>
```

```
06      <ExecutionTarget>ionq.qpu</ExecutionTarget>
07    </PropertyGroup>
08
09 </Project>
```

You can go ahead and create a new Q# project, targeting the IonQ QPU, and implement the entanglement circuit. To make things a little more interesting, you could use a custom rotation around the y-axis to create custom superposition probabilities. Listing 11-2 shows you the complete source code.

Listing 11-2. The superposition circuit for IonQ

```
01 namespace _11_01_Quantum_Entanglement_QSharp_IonQ
02 {
03   open Microsoft.Quantum.Canon;
04   open Microsoft.Quantum.Intrinsic;
05   open Microsoft.Quantum.Math;
06
07   @EntryPoint()
08   operation EntangleQubits() : (Result, Result)
09   {
10     use (q1, q2) = (Qubit(), Qubit());
11
12     Ry(2.0 * PI() / 3.0, q1);
13     CNOT(q1,q2);
14
15     return (M(q1), M(q2));
16   }
17 }
```

The entry-point for this quantum program on line 8 returns a tuple of two `Result` typed values on line 15. This will be the output data if we push this Q# program to our Azure Quantum workspace. The input data will be the compiled Q# source code. The IonQ provider is responsible for running our compiled Q# code on their runtime. They most likely need to do some additional compilation to make our code compatible with the instructions their quantum hardware needs.

To push your code to Azure Quantum, you need the Azure Command-Line Interface or CLI. You can download the Azure CLI for Windows, MacOS, or Linux from https://docs.microsoft.com/en-us/cli/azure/install-azure-cli. Figures 11-20, 11-21, and 11-22 show you what you can expect from the installation wizard.

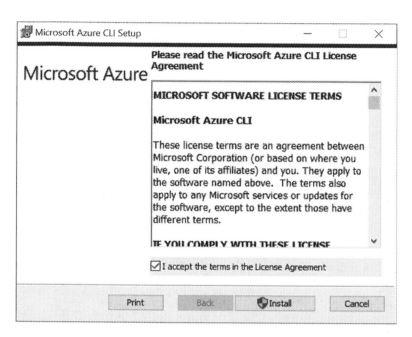

Figure 11-20.   *The Azure CLI Setup welcome screen*

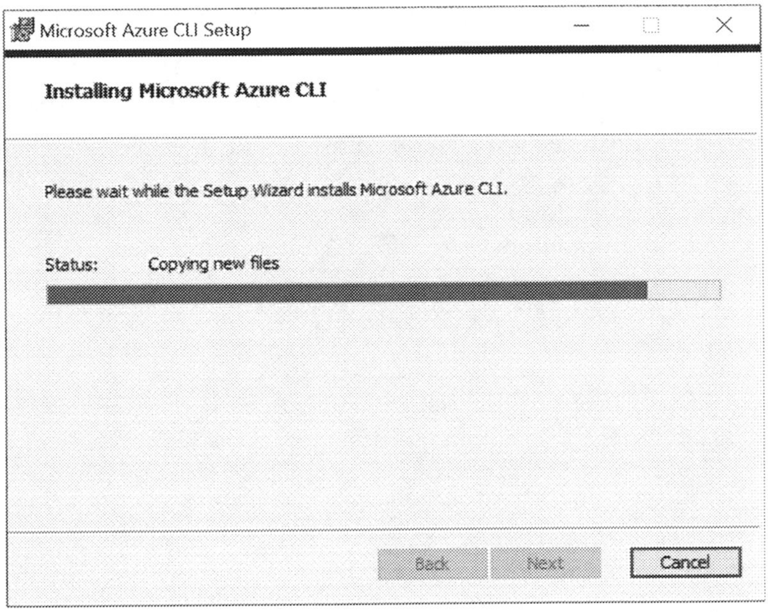

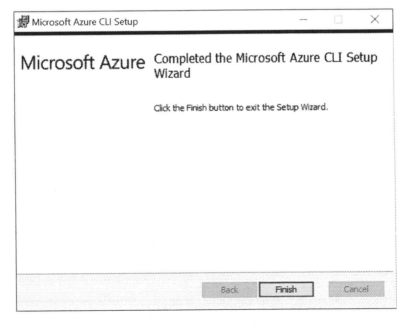

Figure 11-21. *The Azure CLI Setup progress*

Figure 11-22. *The Azure CLI Setup finished page*

The Azure CLI contains several commands that you can use to interface with Microsoft Azure from your command-line tools. The Azure CLI has many extensions, and support for Azure Quantum is available through an Azure CLI extension. Open a terminal or command-line tool, and use the following command to install the Azure Quantum Azure CLI extension:

```
$> az extension add -n quantum
```

This should install the support for Azure Quantum or let you know that the extension is already installed.

Next, you can use the Azure CLI to log into your Azure account by using the following command:

```
$> az login
```

The `az login` command should open your browser and ask for your Microsoft Azure credentials. If your login is successful, you can close your browser and return to your terminal or command-line tool. The `az login` command should have returned some JSON data listing your Azure subscriptions.

Because an Azure account can contain multiple subscriptions, you need to select the current active subscription. Use the following command to select the correct subscription. You can find the subscription ID from the JSON data, outputted by the `az login` command, or from the Microsoft Azure website and your Azure Quantum workspace Overview page.

```
$> az account set --subscription <subscription-id>
```

Because your Azure subscription can contain multiple Azure Quantum workspaces, you need to assign a current active workspace. You need to know the name of the resource group, the name of your Azure Quantum workspace, and the region or location for the following command to work. If you forget, you can find all this information on the Azure Quantum workspace overview page.

```
$> az quantum workspace set --resource-group <resource-group>
      --workspace <quantum-workspace> --location eastus
```

CHAPTER 11   AZURE QUANTUM

You have added a few providers and targets to your Azure Quantum workspace. All these targets have a unique identifier or target ID. Use the following command to get a list of available targets for your Azure Quantum workspace:

```
$> az quantum target list --output table
```

The following table is a possible output from the previous command, containing all possible quantum targets for you to choose from:

```
Provider    Target-id                                          Average Queue Time
------------------------------------------------------------------------
Microsoft   microsoft.simulatedannealing.                                0
Microsoft   microsoft.simulatedannealing-parameterfree.fpga              0
Microsoft   microsoft.paralleltempering-parameterfree.cpu                0
Microsoft   microsoft.paralleltempering.cpu                              0
Microsoft   microsoft.simulatedannealing-parameterfree.cpu               0
Microsoft   microsoft.simulatedannealing.cpu                             0
Microsoft   microsoft.tabu-parameterfree.cpu                             0
Microsoft   microsoft.tabu.cpu                                           0
Microsoft   microsoft.qmc.cpu                                            0
Microsoft   microsoft.populationannealing.cpu                           0
Microsoft   microsoft.populationannealing-parameterfree.cpu             0
ionq        ionq.qpu                                                    79
ionq        ionq.simulator                                               1
```

At this stage, you have all the information to send your Q# program to you Azure Quantum workspace. Execute the following command to run your quantum program on the IonQ simulator. The IonQ simulator is very similar to the IonQ quantum computer, but it typically has no queue time, and it is free to use. You need to assign a job name to your execution. You can use Async-Entanglement to describe your job:

```
$> az quantum job submit --target-id ionq.simulator
    --job-name Async-Entanglement --output table
```

You should get the following output, which represents a table with your job entry and its status:

```
Name                       Id
------------------------------------------------------------------
Async-Entanglement         c845b8b6-436f-48fa-8c08-aab1c83e6c9c

Status     Target          Submission time
------------------------------------------------------------------
Waiting    ionq.simulator    2021-09-30T11:48:33.609276+00:00
```

Submitting a job like this is asynchronous. The output from this command does not contain the result for the computation but the status of the job itself. Running jobs on physical quantum hardware can take some time, and there can be queue times. Regularly check your job statuses on the Azure Quantum workspace Job management web page, or use the following command. The job ID is the unique identifier you got from the output earlier.

```
$> az quantum job show --output table --job-id <job-id>
```

The output from the previous command is very similar to the previous. If your job has a "Succeeded" status, you will see an additional completion time, and you can use the following command to retrieve the output data. You still need your job unique identifier.

```
$> az quantum job output -o table --job-id <job-id>
```

The output should look something like this:

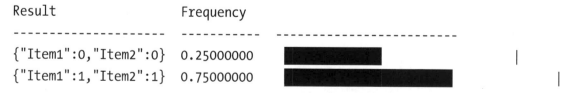

```
Result                  Frequency
--------------------    -----------    -------------------------
{"Item1":0,"Item2":0}   0.25000000                                      |
{"Item1":1,"Item2":1}   0.75000000                                      |
```

So, what has happened? The IonQ quantum simulator has run your quantum program many times, which can be configured, and sent us a histogram of the frequencies or probabilities. You have entangled two qubits after putting one in a custom superposition state. The histogram shows us that the output from our Q# program was (0, 0) 25% of the time and (1, 1) 75% of the time. The qubits are indeed entangled because the (Result, Result) tuple output always produces equal values, and the probabilities are 25% and 75% because we rotated $2\pi/3$ around the y-axis.

The physical quantum computer from IonQ will output the exact same result, but you will need to be patient and spend around $1 to make that happen.

If you visit your Azure Quantum workspace job management page, you can review your past jobs and even get to its input and output data. See Figures 11-23 and 11-24 for your reference.

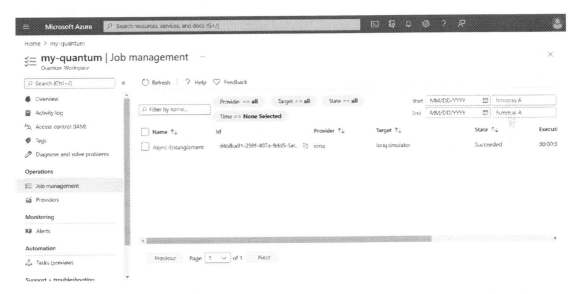

Figure 11-23. *The Azure Quantum workspace job management page showing your quantum computing job*

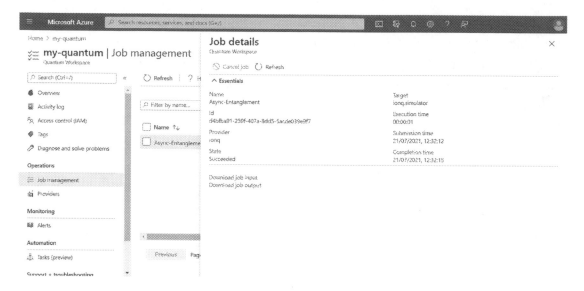

Figure 11-24. *The quantum computing job details where you can download input and output data*

Optimization

Azure Quantum not only provides access to physical quantum computing hardware and simulators but also adds optimization algorithms that can be used as a service for your optimization problems. Quantum inspired optimization is often referred to as QIO and uses algorithms based on quantum principles for increased speed and accuracy. Different optimization algorithms are available on different classical computing architectures like CPUs, FPGAs, or GPUs for extra performance based on your specific problem space.

Optimization problems are not specific to the quantum world and are, therefore, not expressed using Q#. Q# is a purely quantum programming language. If you want to learn about optimization and QIO, you'll need to learn some Python. Azure Quantum allows you to express your optimization problems and possible algorithms to solve them using Python, supported by the Microsoft Quantum Development Kit.

Note   Quantum Inspired Optimization is not the focus of this book. This part of the chapter provides you only with a very high-level overview.

Quantum Inspired Optimization

An optimization problem is often a very complicated problem where many variables can influence a possible solution to the problem. The more variables, the more different configurations of the problem you can have to start with. What is the best solution? What is the cheapest solution? What is the fastest solution? If your question sounds something like that, you can probably benefit from a specific optimization algorithm.

One of the most popular basic optimization problems is the one where you need to build a rectangular fence to maximize the area or to minimize the cost of fencing. Figure 11-25 shows you a very basic representation of a rectangular fenced area.

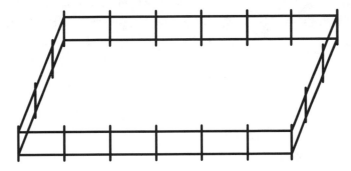

Figure 11-25. *A rectangular fenced area*

Let's say that a 1-meter fence will cost you $100, and you have $2,400 to spend on fences. Some quick math teaches you that you can buy a total of 24 1m fences. You need to build a rectangular area that is completely closed off with fences, and you want to optimize the area based on the width and height of the fenced area.

Because this problem is small and only has a limited number of variables, you can solve it quickly by doing some manual calculations. If you build a fenced area that is only 1 fence wide and 11 fences deep, you need a total of 24 fences. Two times a single fence for the short sides and two times 11 fences for the long side. If one fence is 1 meter wide the total area equals $1 \times 11 = 11$ square meters. If you build a fenced area that is less narrow and decide to split your 24 fences and go for 4 fences wide and 8 fences deep $(4 \times 2 + 8 \times 2 = 24)$, your total area equals $4 \times 8 = 32$ square meters. You can already see that the same number of fences, but used differently, can severely alter your available space. Figure 11-26 shows you an overview for these two calculations.

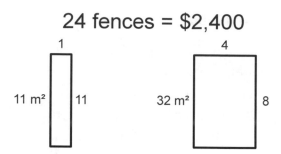

Figure 11-26. *Two fenced areas that need 24 fences but provide a different amount of space*

This optimization problem can be expressed with a function, where the total cost for the number of fences can be expressed in function of the width and the height of the fenced area:

$$\$2,400 = \$100 \cdot (2x + 2y)$$

We need to double the x and y because we need to double the number of fences, because we are building a rectangle. If you work out this expression and bring the $100 within the brackets, you get

$$\$2,400 = 200x + 200y$$

This expression can be simplified even further by dividing each term by 200:

$$12 = x + y$$

You can minimize the cost by maximizing the available area for a given number of fences. To do this, you need to come up with a mathematical function. To maximize that function, you need to take the derivative and set it equal to zero. The function we need to maximize is the space within the fenced area. The expression to calculate the area is easy:

$$Area = x \cdot y$$

To take the derivative of this function, we need to get rid of the y variable and substitute it with x. From the previous formula, we know that $12 = x + y$.

$$12 = x + y \text{ makes } y = 12 - x$$

Now, substitute y with $12 - x$:

$$Area = x \cdot (12 - x)$$

Work out:

$$Area = 12x - x^2$$

Take derivative:

$$0 = 12 - 2x \text{ or } x = 6$$

This calculation concludes that the available space in our fenced area is optimal if both sides are built out of 6 fences which makes 36 square meters.

This kind of calculation makes sense if you plot the function on a graph, which you can see in Figure 11-27:

$$y = 12x - x^2$$

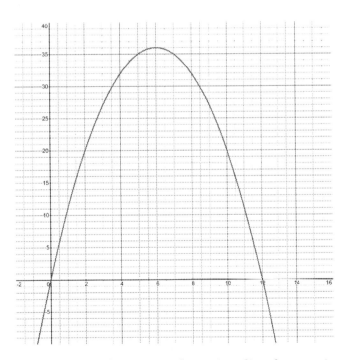

Figure 11-27. *Function plotted on a graph to visualize the maximum area at width of 6*

This graph clearly plots the area for our already calculated examples. If one of your sides, represented by x, equals 1, the area will be 11 m². If one of your sides equals 4, your area equals 32 m². If one of your sides equals 6, the area is maximized and equals 36 m².

This is only a very basic example of optimization problem-solving, and Microsoft QIO can solve more complex optimization problems. The hard part is to define the cost function that needs to be minimized or maximized and to have a solvable search space. Together, the cost function and search space define the optimization landscape, and with the previous basic example, that landscape and its maximum were very clear on the plotted graph.

Optimization Jobs

In Chapter 4, you installed Python and you added it to your PATH environment variable. To build and push Python optimization algorithms to your Azure Quantum workspace, you will need Python and the Azure Quantum Python extension installed.

Python uses the PIP tool to install extra packages to your Python environment. Open your terminal or command-line tool, and use the following command to install the Azure Quantum Python package:

```
$> pip install --upgrade azure-quantum
```

After this is finished, you can create a new *cargo-loading-optimization.py* Python file and copy the code from Listing 11-3.

Listing 11-3. A quantum optimization algorithm to optimize cargo loading

```
01 from azure.quantum import Workspace
02
03 workspace = Workspace(
04   resource_id = "<quantum-workspace-resource-id>"
05 )
06
07 workspace.login()
08
09 from typing import List
10 from azure.quantum.optimization import Problem
11 from azure.quantum.optimization import ProblemType
12 from azure.quantum.optimization import Term
```

```
13
14 def buildTermsForCargoWeights(
15   containerWeights: List[int] ) -> List[Term]:
16
17   terms: List[Term] = []
18
19   for i in range(len(containerWeights)):
20     for j in range(len(containerWeights)):
21       if i == j:
22         continue
23
24       terms.append(
25         Term(
26           w = containerWeights[i] * containerWeights[j],
27           indices = [i, j]
28         )
29       )
30
31   return terms
32
33 cargoWeights = [
34     1, 5, 9, 21, 35, 5, 3, 5, 10, 11,
35     86, 2, 23, 44, 1, 17, 33, 8, 66,
36     24, 16, 5, 102, 2, 39, 16, 12, 26]
37
38 terms = buildTermsForCargoWeights( cargoWeights )
39
40 problem = Pro    blem(
41   name = "Load my ships",
42   problem_type = ProblemType.ising,
43   terms = terms
44 )
45
46 from azure.quantum.optimization import ParallelTempering
47
```

```
48 solver = ParallelTempering( workspace, timeout = 100 )
49 result = solver.optimize( problem )
50
51 def outputResult( result ):
52
53   totalWeightForShip1 = 0
54   totalWeightForShip2 = 0
55
56   for cargo in result['configuration']:
57
58     cargoAssignment = result['configuration'][cargo]
59     cargoWeight = cargoWeights[int(cargo)]
60     ship = ''
61
62     if cargoAssignment == 1:
63       ship = "First"
64       totalWeightForShip1 += cargoWeight
65     else:
66       ship = "Second"
67       totalWeightForShip2 += cargoWeight
68
69     print(f'Cargo: [{cargoWeight} tonnes] -> {ship} ship')
70
71   print(f'\nTotal assigned weights:')
72   print(f'\tShip 1: {totalWeightForShip1} tonnes')
73   print(f'\tShip 2: {totalWeightForShip2} tonnes')
74
75 outputResult(result)
```

This example code specifies your Azure Quantum workspace on lines 3 through 5. You still need to replace the placeholder with your own Azure Quantum workspace resource identifier which you can find on the overview page on Microsoft Azure. Since this book is not focusing on optimization problems, you can just run this piece of code by calling into the Python interpreter by executing the following command:

```
$> py ship-loading-optimization.py
```

If all goes well, you should get the output from Listing 11-4.

Listing 11-4. The output for the cargo loading optimization algorithm

```
...
Cargo: [   5 tonnes] -> Second ship
Cargo: [   9 tonnes] -> First ship
Cargo: [  21 tonnes] -> Second ship
Cargo: [  35 tonnes] -> Second ship
Cargo: [   5 tonnes] -> First ship
Cargo: [   3 tonnes] -> Second ship
Cargo: [   5 tonnes] -> Second ship
Cargo: [  10 tonnes] -> Second ship
Cargo: [  11 tonnes] -> Second ship
Cargo: [  86 tonnes] -> First ship
Cargo: [   2 tonnes] -> Second ship
Cargo: [  23 tonnes] -> Second ship
Cargo: [  44 tonnes] -> First ship
Cargo: [   1 tonnes] -> Second ship
Cargo: [  17 tonnes] -> First ship
Cargo: [  33 tonnes] -> Second ship
Cargo: [   8 tonnes] -> Second ship
Cargo: [  66 tonnes] -> First ship
Cargo: [  24 tonnes] -> First ship
Cargo: [  16 tonnes] -> Second ship
Cargo: [   5 tonnes] -> First ship
Cargo: [102 tonnes] -> Second ship
Cargo: [   2 tonnes] -> First ship
Cargo: [  39 tonnes] -> First ship
Cargo: [  16 tonnes] -> First ship
Cargo: [  12 tonnes] -> Second ship
Cargo: [  26 tonnes] -> Second ship

Total assigned weights:
        Ship 1: 313 tonnes
        Ship 2: 314 tonnes
```

If that worked, and you take look at your Azure Quantum workspace job management page, you should be able to see that your optimization job was run, and you can retrieve the input and output from there. See Figures 11-28 and 11-29 for your reference.

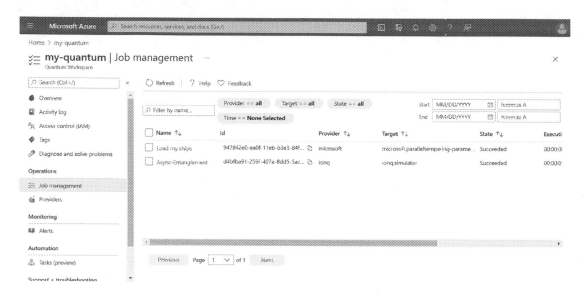

Figure 11-28. *The Azure Quantum workspace job management page showing your optimization job*

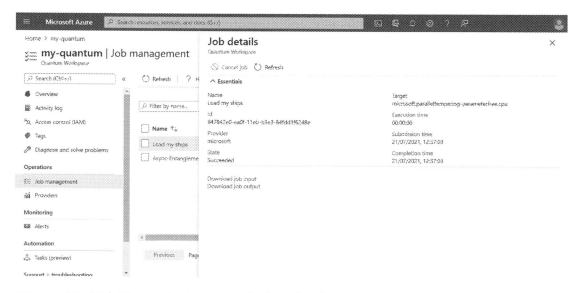

Figure 11-29. *The optimization job details where you can download input and output data*

The Last Word

The goal of this chapter is to introduce you to Azure Quantum, the quantum cloud solution by Microsoft. Microsoft Azure is one of many respected cloud computing providers and offers a wide variety of cloud services. Since early 2021, quantum computing and quantum inspired optimization are part of those cloud services.

It is still early, and Azure Quantum is still in public preview. Microsoft uses these public preview services to obtain user feedback and improve their services before releasing them with a general availability status. The Azure Quantum public preview allows you to learn and test your quantum applications or optimization algorithms on real quantum hardware or cloud-scaled optimization hardware that you otherwise won't have access to.

## CHAPTER 12

What's Next?

Congratulations! You made it to the final chapter of this introductory book on quantum computing and the Microsoft Quantum Development kit.

The future of quantum computing is still very uncertain but exciting, nevertheless. There are still many unknowns, and many concepts are evolving almost every day. Most of the information in this book regarding quantum computing, the underlying math, and the theoretical approach will stay relevant, but the Microsoft Development Kit and the Q# language will evolve rapidly. Always use online resources to gather the most up-to-date information.

Quantum Supremacy

Theoretical work on quantum computing is already going on for many decades. It is only in the last decade that quantum hardware has been successfully built and people are trying to prove that quantum computing can outperform classical computing for specific classes of problems.

Quantum supremacy is a term that is used often to describe the goal of demonstrating that programmable quantum hardware can solve a problem that classical hardware cannot solve in a respectable time frame. Because of this, quantum supremacy is not about the usefulness of the solution to a problem but to solving any problem on quantum hardware, outperforming classical hardware significantly.

Quantum supremacy involves both hardware innovation and software innovation. Engineers and scientists must create the physical hardware that is able to perform quantum operations fast and still be stable enough to be trustworthy. Software engineers must create a programming language and a quantum algorithm that can solve a problem that cannot be solved by classical hardware and software.

© Johnny Hooyberghs 2022
J. Hooyberghs, *Introducing Microsoft Quantum Computing for Developers*,
https://doi.org/10.1007/978-1-4842-7246-6_12

Nobody knows when quantum supremacy will be achieved and if it will stay intact. It is possible that someone discovers a very specific problem that can only be solved by a quantum computer, but someone else eventually finds a workable classical solution for it also.

Quantum supremacy should not be a goal in itself. The goal should be to keep innovating and finding new ways to create stable quantum computers that can provide a large enough number of stable qubits to outperform classical hardware. Another goal should be to develop new quantum algorithms that can solve problems that don't have solutions today.

Quantum Error Correction

Quantum particles that are used to encode qubit state are subject to quantum noise and suffer from decoherence. It is very difficult to keep qubits entangled or even in superposition for long periods of time. Quantum error correction is an important part of building physical quantum computers and poses one of the biggest challenges out there.

To make sure your qubits and their states are trustworthy, you can store your state information multiple times using multiple qubits. All the quantum operations need to be executed on all the redundant qubits simultaneously, and, in the end, the majority vote wins. If you have used 100 physical qubits to represent 1 single logical qubit, the measurements that yield the most equal values will probably represent the correct value. Quantum theory adds another complexity to the problem of error correction because quantum states cannot be copied from one qubit to another. Once a qubit has been measured, it cannot be "unmeasured."

Quantum error correction is one of the most important research areas in quantum computing. It can help us create more reliable quantum computers and achieve a higher qubit density.

Quantum Intermediate Representation

Modern classical programming languages have adopted the concept of intermediate representation and runtimes. Languages and platforms like, for example, Java and .NET leverage the concept of compiling source code to a lower-level language instead of machine code. For Java, this lower-level language is called Java Byte Code, and for .NET, it is called Intermediate Language. This concept has become increasingly popular, even for programming languages that exist for a long time, like C++ (Clang).

Compiling to an intermediate language offers you the flexibility to run your code on different kinds of hardware without the need to recompile your programs multiple times on release. Most programming languages that use this intermediate language use a runtime that can be preinstalled on different kinds of hardware, and this runtime will compile the intermediate language to machine code "just-in-time." JIT compiling happens at runtime, which can have a small performance impact on your programs, but modern runtimes are well-optimized and use advanced techniques to make sure the performance impact is minimal or even unnoticeable. One of these techniques is "ahead-of-time" or AOT compiling to mitigate startup performance costs.

For quantum computing specifically, the same concepts are being introduced right now. Because quantum hardware is still very experimental, many different hardware configurations and implementations exist out in the world. Software vendors, like Microsoft, are designing the languages and tools to write quantum programs, but quantum hardware changes often. This makes it very hard for a software vendor to support compiling to quantum hardware machine code for all hardware available.

In 2021, Microsoft started work on their intermediate language for quantum programs which they are calling Quantum Intermediate Representation, or QIR. Higher-lever quantum operations in Q# will be compiled into lower-level intrinsic quantum operations. Figure 12-1 shows you how multiple quantum programming languages can be compiled into a common intermediate, lower-level, language and can then be compiled to specific machine code for quantum hardware or quantum simulators by a runtime.

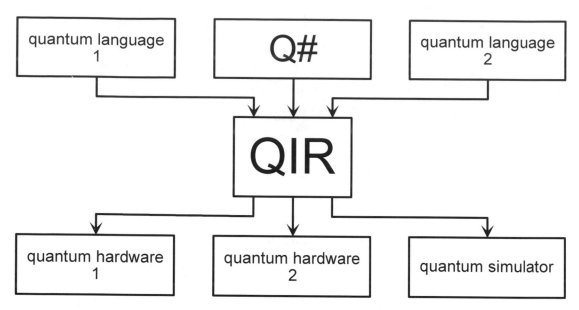

Figure 12-1. *Quantum programming languages compiled into QIR and into machine code*

The ultimate goal is for multiple high-level programming languages to compile into QIR or some other quantum intermediate representational language so that hardware vendors only need to understand that intermediate representation. If a new hardware vendor, or a new kind of quantum hardware configuration, needs to run quantum programs, it only needs a runtime that compiles the quantum intermediate representation into machine code targeting that specific machine.

Quantum hardware only needs to know what intrinsic operations it needs to perform on its qubits. Quantum programming languages like Q# offer many higher-level operations which are built out of these basic quantum operations. Just like many classical programming languages today, quantum programming languages like Q# will grow and evolve into higher-level languages that hide the machine intrinsic operations and encapsulate them with easier-to-understand operations and functions.

Note Decompiling Q# programs today using tools like ILSpy already shows you how more advanced Q# features like conjugations and functors are compiled into more verbose, automatically generated, lower-level code.

Additional Resources

Microsoft offers a lot of additional resources for you to learn about quantum computing and the Microsoft Quantum Development Kit specifically.

The following link provides you with the resources to get started with the Microsoft Quantum Development Kit and Q#:

https://joho.me/39JVjov

If you would like to get started with Azure Quantum and run your quantum programs on actual quantum hardware, you can visit the following link and learn more about that:

https://joho.me/3kNG43V

You can create a free Microsoft Azure Cloud account using the following link:

https://joho.me/3ohShjO

Writing quantum programs can be easy by using the tools provided by Microsoft. Microsoft Visual Studio or Visual Studio Code have support for Q# development through a Microsoft Quantum Development Kit plugin or extension. You can download either Microsoft Visual Studio or Visual Studio Code through the following links:

https://joho.me/3CT9EeG

https://joho.me/3CZLz65

https://joho.me/3CPsMtY

Microsoft also provides comprehensive documentation on quantum computing. Check out the following link for high-level information on quantum computing:

https://joho.me/2Y6VuYF

The following link provides some more information on quantum-inspired optimization:

https://joho.me/3upuUWj

The following links give you an overview of the Q# language and the API reference:

`https://joho.me/39NFUDC`

`https://joho.me/3ujecrE`

The following documentation link provides you with some learning resources specifically targeting Azure Quantum development:

https://joho.me/3AWfATC

Microsoft also built a library of examples and step-by-step learning paths to enrich your quantum knowledge. Check out the following links:

https://joho.me/39OpKJW

https://joho.me/3ibKDDF

https://joho.me/3ogzODX

If you would like to learn more about existing algorithms, the following link will probably keep you busy for a long time. The quantum algorithm zoo is a website that is maintained by Stephen Jordan, a member of the Microsoft quantum team, and contains theoretical explanations for existing quantum algorithms.

https://joho.me/3CUwSkx

If you are searching for like-minded people that are also eager to learn about quantum computing and Microsoft Quantum, the Q# community is your place to be.

https://joho.me/3mccViz

Finally, if you would like to learn and experiment with how the Q# compiler compiles and optimizes your code, you can use the ILSpy .NET decompiler on your compiled DLL files and browse the decompiled source code.

https://joho.me/2XX9S5g

PART V

Appendixes

APPENDIX I

Trigonometry

When you are trying to visualize the quantum state for a qubit, you should have a basic understanding of trigonometry. Trigonometry is a branch of mathematics that explores the relationship between angles and lengths of sides of triangles. The word trigonometry comes from the Greek "trigonon," which translates to "triangle," and "metron," which translates to "measure." Trigonometry has many real-world applications like triangulation in astronomy and Global Positioning System (GPS), optics and acoustics that describe sound and light waves, computer game development, and many more.

This final appendix teaches you some of the basics of trigonometry. You will start with the concept of right-angled triangles, the relationship between degrees and radians and trigonometric ratios, followed by the unit circle and common trigonometric values. This knowledge will help you visualize and calculate some of the probabilities for quantum superposition states.

Right-Angled Triangle

A right-angled triangle, or right triangle, is a two-dimensional geometrical figure or polygon with three edges and three vertices, where the angle of one of the three vertices is a 90° angle, also referred to as a right angle. Figure I-1 displays one of many possible right-angled triangles. Because a triangle is a closed geometrical figure with three vertices, the total sum of the three angles should equal 180°. Right-angled triangles are the basis for trigonometry.

© Johnny Hooyberghs 2022
J. Hooyberghs, *Introducing Microsoft Quantum Computing for Developers*,
https://doi.org/10.1007/978-1-4842-7246-6_13

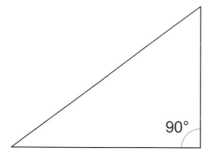

Figure I-1. *A right-angled triangle*

Finally, you should understand that the length of the longest edge, also referred to as the hypotenuse, can be calculated using Pythagoras' theorem. The formal definition of Pythagoras' theorem reads as follows:

> *In a right-angled triangle: the square of the hypotenuse is equal to the sum of the squares of the other two sides.*

A very straightforward example that illustrates Pythagoras' theorem is visualized in Figure I-2. If you draw a right-angled triangle with one edge of length 3 and another edge of length 4, the hypotenuse will have a length of 5 because the sum of the square of length 3 and the square of length 4 equals the square of length 5:

$$3^2 + 4^2 = 5^2 \ or \ 9 + 16 = 25$$

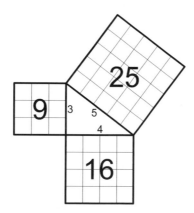

Figure I-2. *A visualization of Pythagoras' theorem*

EXERCISE I-1

Keeping Pythagoras' theorem in mind, find the lengths of the edges of a right-angled triangle that has a hypotenuse of length 10. Try to get whole-numbered lengths; there are multiple possibilities to choose from.

Degrees and Radians

In your everyday life, you are probably used to using degrees when you need to specify an angle. In mathematics, however, you will notice an abundance of angles expressed in radians. The radian is a measure related to the radius of the circle. If you take the radius of a circle and wrap it around the circumference of the circle, you will get to about 57°. The effect of wrapping the radius around the circumference of a circle is visualized in Figure I-3.

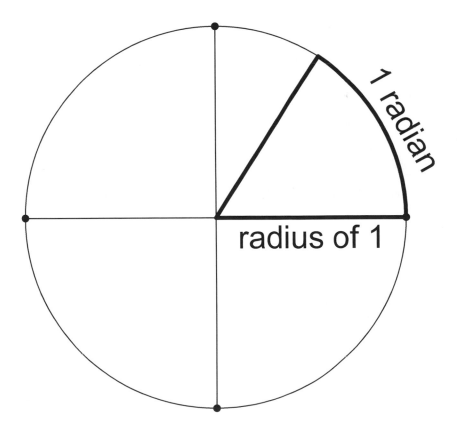

Figure I-3. *The radian in relation to the radius of a circle*

Because one radian is always related to the radius mapped on the circle's circumference, it is tightly related to the radius of the circle. To calculate the entire circumference of a circle, you would use the formula

$$c = 2 \cdot \pi \cdot r$$

Therefore, the total number of radians to describe 180° equals $2 \cdot \pi$ radians.

Derived from this statement, it is easy to convert degrees into radians by multiplying by π and dividing by 180:

$$180^\circ = \frac{180 \cdot \pi}{180} = \pi$$

To convert radians into degrees, you multiply by 180 and divide by π:

$$\pi = \frac{\pi \cdot 180}{\pi} = 180^\circ$$

EXERCISE I-2

Convert an angle of 60° to radians and convert an angle of 2π/3 to degrees.

Trigonometric Ratios

Trigonometric ratios describe the ratios between edges of a right-angled triangle. Figure I-4 illustrates a right-angled triangle where the edges are named a, b, and c and the vertices are named A, B, and C.

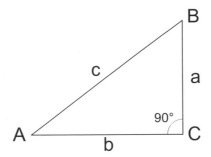

Figure I-4. *A right-angled triangle with edges a, b, and c and vertices A, B, and C*

Using Figure I-4, you can define a number of formulas to calculate the trigonometric ratios:

- The sine function on angle A is defined as the ratio of the opposite leg a and the hypotenuse c:

$$\sin A = \frac{opposite\ leg}{hypotenuse} = \frac{a}{c}$$

- The cosine function on the angle A is defined as the ratio of the adjacent leg b and the hypotenuse c:

$$\cos A = \frac{adjacent\ leg}{hypotenuse} = \frac{b}{c}$$

- The tangent function on the angle A is defined as the ratio of the opposite leg a and the adjacent leg b:

$$\tan A = \frac{opposite\ leg}{adjacent\ leg} = \frac{a}{b} = \frac{\sin A}{\cos A}$$

In quantum computing, thanks to these formulas, it becomes easier to convert between the angle of a superposition state vector on the Bloch sphere and the probabilities of collapsing to one of the computational basis states. This will become clearer to you in the next section that talks about "Unit Circles."

The Unit Circle

The "Unit Circle" is a circle with a radius of one, and it can help you to learn about length and angles. If you take a Cartesian coordinate system where the x-axis and y-axis cross at point $(0, 0)$ and you draw a circle with radius 1 that is centered at that $(0, 0)$ point, you are drawing a "Unit Circle."

Because the radius is equal to one, the trigonometric ratios are very easy to calculate. If you draw a vector that starts at the center location and ends somewhere on the circle, that vector always has length 1. To project the endpoint of that vector on the x-axis and y-axis, you can think of a right-angled triangle and use the trigonometric ratios to calculate the exact lengths of the projections.

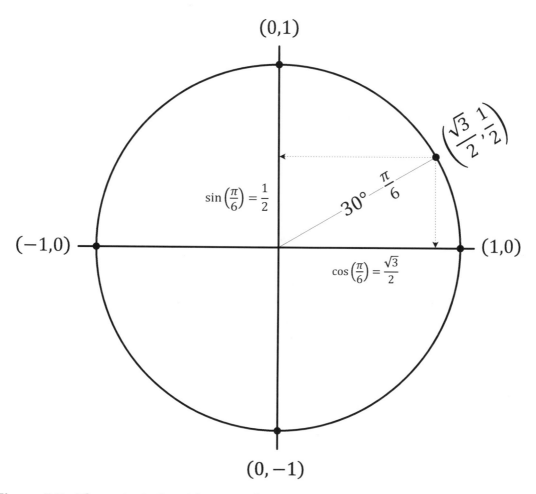

Figure I-5. *The unit circle with an angle at 30° and its projections on the x- and y-axes*

Figure I-5 shows you a vector of length 1 at angle 30° or $\pi/6$ radians. It also shows you the projections of the endpoint of that vector on the x-axis and the y-axis, calculated with the trigonometric ratios' formulas.

If you think about Figure I-5 as a simplified Bloch sphere, let us call it a Bloch circle, the vector represents the quantum superposition state vector of a single qubit. The point on the right side of the x-axis corresponds with the computational basis state $|0\rangle$, and the point on the top side of the y-axis corresponds with the computational basis state $|1\rangle$. If you now use the trigonometric ratios and project that vector onto the x-axis and y-axis, you are calculating the α and β values in the linear combination of basis states for a quantum state:

$$\alpha|0\rangle + \beta|1\rangle \rightarrow \cos\frac{\pi}{6}|0\rangle + \sin\frac{\pi}{6}|1\rangle \rightarrow \frac{\sqrt{3}}{2}|0\rangle + \frac{1}{2}|1\rangle$$

From this linear combination, you can calculate the probabilities because

$$|\alpha|^2 + |\beta|^2 = 1$$

A quantum superposition state vector similar to the vector visualized in Figure I-5 has a 75% chance of collapsing to $|0\rangle$ and a 25% chance of collapsing to $|1\rangle$:

$$\left|\frac{\sqrt{3}}{2}\right|^2 = \frac{3}{4} = 0.75$$

$$\left|\frac{1}{2}\right|^2 = \frac{1}{4} = 0.25$$

Table I-1. *Common trigonometric values from 0 to 5π/6*

	0	$\frac{\pi}{6}$	$\frac{\pi}{4}$	$\frac{\pi}{3}$	$\frac{\pi}{2}$	$\frac{2\pi}{3}$	$\frac{3\pi}{4}$	$\frac{5\pi}{6}$
sin	0	$\frac{1}{2}$	$\frac{\sqrt{2}}{2}$	$\frac{\sqrt{3}}{2}$	1	$\frac{\sqrt{3}}{2}$	$\frac{\sqrt{2}}{2}$	$\frac{1}{2}$
cos	1	$\frac{\sqrt{3}}{2}$	$\frac{\sqrt{2}}{2}$	$\frac{1}{2}$	0	$-\frac{1}{2}$	$-\frac{\sqrt{2}}{2}$	$-\frac{\sqrt{3}}{2}$

Table I-2. *Common trigonometric values from π to 11π/6*

	π	$\frac{7\pi}{6}$	$\frac{5\pi}{4}$	$\frac{4\pi}{3}$	$\frac{3\pi}{2}$	$\frac{5\pi}{3}$	$\frac{7\pi}{4}$	$\frac{11\pi}{6}$
sin	0	$-\frac{1}{2}$	$-\frac{\sqrt{2}}{2}$	$-\frac{\sqrt{3}}{2}$	-1	$\frac{1}{2}$	$\frac{\sqrt{2}}{2}$	$\frac{\sqrt{3}}{2}$
cos	-1	$-\frac{\sqrt{3}}{2}$	$-\frac{\sqrt{2}}{2}$	$-\frac{1}{2}$	0	$\frac{1}{2}$	$\frac{\sqrt{2}}{2}$	$\frac{\sqrt{3}}{2}$

Common Trigonometric Values

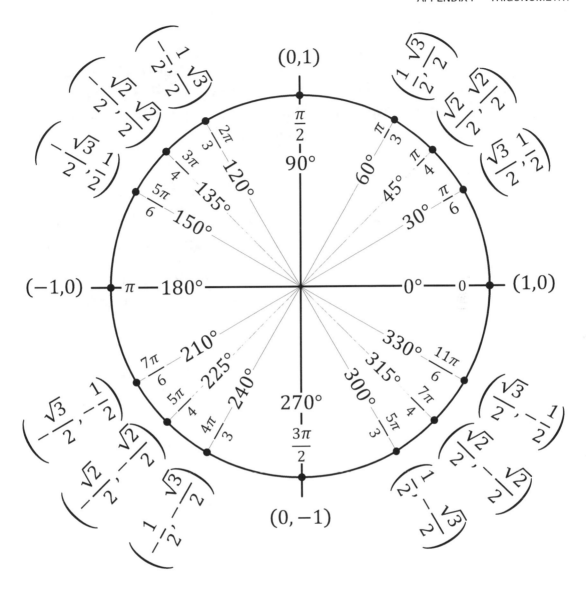

Figure I-6. *The unit circle with angles and common trigonometric values*

Based on the trigonometric ratios, there are several angles that result in easy-to-remember values. Tables I-1 and I-2 contain these values. You shouldn't learn them by heart, but it is easy to recognize them.

For your convenience and entertainment, Figure I-6 organizes these values on the unit circle.

The Last Word

Now that you have read this appendix and solved the exercises, you should have gathered some necessary knowledge about trigonometry that is needed to comprehend and work with the basics of quantum computing. You can continue with the next appendix to refresh your understanding of complex numbers.

Solutions to Exercises

EXERCISE I-1

Keeping Pythagoras' theorem in mind, find the lengths of the edges of a right-angled triangle that has a hypotenuse of length 10. Try to get whole-numbered lengths; there are multiple possibilities to choose from.

Solution

Keeping Pythagoras' theorem in mind, you know that the sum of the lengths of the edges squared should equal 100, because 100 equals 10 squared. The only thing you need to figure out is which two numbers added together make 100, and if you take the square root of those numbers individually, the result should be a whole number. You can start by squaring all the numbers from 1 to 9, and then try to add two of them that make 100:

- $1^2 = 1$

- $2^2 = 4$

- $3^2 = 9$

- $4^2 = 16$

- $5^2 = 25$

- $6^2 = 36$

- $7^2 = 49$

- $8^2 = 64$

- $9^2 = 81$

From this list, you can figure out that $36 + 64 = 100$ so that a right-angled triangle with sides of lengths 6 and 8 will have a hypotenuse of length 10.

It should be very clear that this solution is only one of an infinite number of possibilities.

EXERCISE I-2

Convert an angle of 60° to radians and convert an angle of $2\pi/3$ to degrees:

Solution

$$60^\circ = \frac{60 \cdot \pi}{180} = \frac{\pi}{3} = \pi / 3$$

$$2\pi / 3 = \frac{2\pi}{3} = \frac{180 \cdot 2\pi}{3 \cdot \pi} = \frac{360}{3} = 120^\circ$$

APPENDIX II

Complex Numbers

Mathematics lies at the core of quantum computing, and to have a basic understanding, you need to know a little bit about complex numbers. For most people, learning about complex numbers was part of their curriculum in school. As I experienced myself, a lot of information gets lost if you are not using the material you learned in school on a daily basis. This optional appendix will help you refresh the basics on complex numbers.

Complex Numbers

In mathematics, we use different number systems that group together numbers which share a property. The following list of number systems are commonly used and are represented by double-struck letters:

- Positive numbers $\mathbb{P} = \{1, 2, 3, 4, 5, 6, 7, 8, 9, \cdots\}$

- Natural numbers $\mathbb{N} = \{0, 1, 2, 3, 4, 5, 6, 7, 8, 9, \cdots\}$

- Whole numbers $\mathbb{Z} = \{\cdots, -5, -4, -3, -2, -1, 0, 1, 2, 3, 4, 5, \cdots\}$

- Rational numbers $\mathbb{Q} = \left\{ \frac{a}{b} \,|, a \in \mathbb{Z}|, b \in \mathbb{P} \right\}$

- Real numbers $\mathbb{R} = \mathbb{Q} \cup \left\{ \cdots, \sqrt{2}, \cdots, e, \cdots, \pi, \cdots \right\}$

The positive numbers $\mathbb{P}$ group all whole numbers ranging from one to positive infinity. The natural numbers $\mathbb{N}$ group all positive numbers and zero. The whole numbers $\mathbb{Z}$ group all integer numbers, including all negative whole numbers from -1 to negative infinity. The rational numbers $\mathbb{Q}$ group all numbers that can be formed as a fraction where the numerator is an integer number and the denominator is a positive

369

number. The real numbers $\mathbb{R}$ group all rational numbers and all numbers that cannot be expressed as fractions, also referred to as irrational numbers.

Each number system is a subset of another number system. Figure II-1 shows you that $\mathbb{P}$ is a subset of $\mathbb{N}$, which is a subset of $\mathbb{Z}$, which is a subset of $\mathbb{Q}$, which is a subset of $\mathbb{R}$.

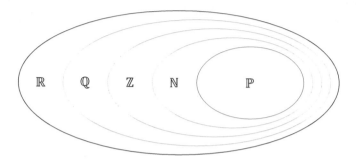

Figure II-1. *The different number systems, where one system is a subset of another*

Thanks to this collection of different number systems, mathematics can be used as a tool to describe and solve a lot of problems related to the world we live in. There are, however, still many problems that cannot have a solution because of the limitations there still are with these number systems. For example:

$$1 + x^2 = 0$$

This easy equation, also called a cubic equation, where one plus x squared should equal zero does not have a solution. Squaring a real number always results in a positive number, and adding two positive numbers together can never result in zero. To be able to solve these kinds of equations, mathematicians invented yet another number system that extends real numbers. This number system is called the group of complex numbers and is noted by the double-struck $\mathbb{C}$.

Complex numbers extend real numbers with an additional imaginary component. A complex number is, therefore, defined as an imaginary number added to a real number where the imaginary number is a real number combined with i and where $i^2 = -1$:

$$\mathbb{C} = a + bi \mid a \in \mathbb{R}, b \in \mathbb{R}, i^2 = -1$$

Complex numbers have a real part a and an imaginary part b. Both the real and imaginary parts are optional. If the real part is omitted, the complex number only has an imaginary part. If the imaginary part is omitted, you are just talking about a real number because there is no imaginary part.

Looking back at the equation from before, using complex numbers, it should be solved with ease. Just replace x with i, and you are done!

$$1 + x^2 = 0$$

$$x = i \rightarrow 1 + i^2 = 1 - 1 = 0$$

From the rule that $i^2 = -1$ also comes the reverse rule, which you can derive from moving the power of two to the other side of the equal sign:

$$\sqrt{-1} = i$$

EXERCISE II-1

Now that you know about complex numbers, try to solve the value for x in the following equation:

$$4 + x^2 = 0$$

Visualizing a Complex Number

To help yourself while working with complex numbers, you can visualize them using a two-dimensional complex plane. The real part of the complex number should be drawn on the horizontal axis, and the imaginary part of the complex number should be drawn on the vertical axis. The complex number, a combination of the real part and the imaginary part, will then be visualized as a vector.

Figure II-2 shows you the graphical representation of the complex number $4 + 3i$ where 4 is plotted on the horizontal, real axis and $3i$ is plotted on the vertical, imaginary axis.

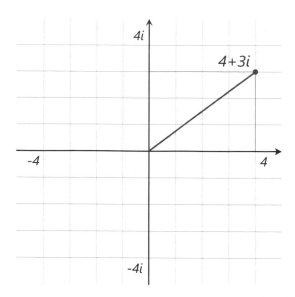

Figure II-2. *The 4 + 3i complex number, visualized on the two-dimensional complex plane*

Calculating with Complex Numbers

Because complex numbers have two parts, the real part and the complex part, some algebra rules are a bit different.

Starting with equality, complex numbers are very similar to real numbers. Two complex numbers are equal if their real and imaginary parts are both equal:

$$a + bi = c + di \qquad \text{if } a = c \text{ and } b = d$$

Adding Complex Numbers

Adding complex numbers is easy. A complex number has a real part and an imaginary part. If you want to add two complex numbers, you need to add the real numbers and the imaginary numbers separately:

$$(a + bi) + (c + di) = (a + c) + (b + d)i$$

Figure II-3 shows you the graphical representation for adding $-3 - i$ and $6 + 5i$, which results in $3 + 4i$.

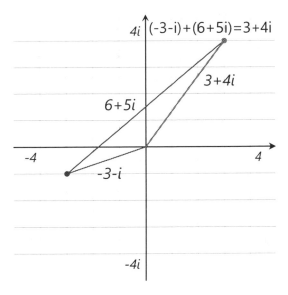

Figure II-3. *Adding* $-3 - i$ *and* $6 + 5i$

EXERCISE II-2

Solve the following expressions using your knowledge on adding complex numbers:
$$(-134 + 54i) + (241 - 13i)$$
$$(-31i) + (333)$$

Subtracting Complex Numbers

Subtracting complex numbers is very similar to adding complex numbers. If you want to subtract two complex numbers, you need to subtract the real numbers and the imaginary numbers separately:

$$(a + bi) - (c + di) = (a - c) + (b - d)i$$

EXERCISE II-3

Solve the following expressions using your knowledge on subtracting complex numbers:
$$(-134 + 54i) - (241 - 13i)$$
$$(-31i) - (333)$$

Multiplying Complex Numbers

Multiplying complex numbers is a bit more complicated. Each part of the first complex number gets multiplied with each part of the second complex number:

$$(a+bi)\cdot(c+di) = ac + adi + bci + bdi^2$$

or because $i^2 = -1$:

$$(a+bi)\cdot(c+di) = (ac - bd) + (ad + bc)i$$

For example:

$$(2+5i)\cdot(3+2i) = 6 + 4i + 15i + 10i^2 = 6 + 4i + 15i - 10 = -4 + 19i$$

or

$$(2+5i)\cdot(3+2i) = (6-10) + (4+15)i = -4 + 19i$$

EXERCISE II-4

Solve the following expressions using your knowledge on multiplying complex numbers:

$$(-7+8i)\cdot(2-11i)$$

$$(-3i)\cdot(12)$$

Complex Conjugates

Just like binomials, which are expressions with two terms like $3x^2 + 9$, complex numbers also know the concept of a conjugate, which is called a complex conjugate.

The complex conjugate of a complex number z is denoted by $\bar{z}$ and flips the sign of the imaginary part:

$$z = a + bi$$

$$\bar{z} = \overline{a + bi} = a - bi$$

Complex conjugates are very helpful when dividing complex numbers. Complex conjugates have the interesting property that multiplying a complex number with its complex conjugate results in a real number:

$$(a+bi)\cdot(a-bi)=a^2+b^2$$

Dividing Complex Numbers

Just like multiplication, division of complex numbers is much more complicated than what you are used to with real numbers.

To divide two complex numbers, you need to multiply both the numerator and denominator with the conjugate of the denominator. Multiplying a complex number with its complex conjugate results in a real number, and dividing by a real number is easier! For this, you need previous knowledge from multiplying complex numbers and complex conjugates:

$$\frac{(a+bi)}{(c+di)}=\frac{(a+bi)}{(c+di)}\cdot\frac{(c-di)}{(c-di)}=\frac{(ac+bd)+(ad-bc)i}{(cc+dd)+(-cd+dc)i}=\frac{(ac+bd)+(ad-bc)i}{c^2+d^2}$$

For the denominator in the previous formula, the terms $-cd$ and dc cancel each other out, which is why you are left with c^2+d^2. If you perform this with actual complex numbers, you will get something like

$$\frac{(6+5i)}{(-3-i)}=\frac{(6+5i)}{(-3-i)}\cdot\frac{(-3+i)}{(-3+i)}=\frac{(-18-5)+(6-15)i}{9+1}=\frac{(-23-9i)}{10}=-\frac{23}{10}-\frac{9}{10}i$$

Multiplying both the numerator and denominator with the complex conjugate of the denominator is a smart trick to eliminate the imaginary number from the denominator. This trick is used often in mathematics to simplify expressions, also outside of the realm of complex numbers, for example, to eliminate roots in denominators.

EXERCISE II-5

Solve the following expressions using your knowledge on dividing complex numbers:

$$\frac{(-7+8i)}{(2-11i)}$$

$$\frac{-3i}{12}$$

Absolute Value or Modulus for Complex Numbers

If you think about real numbers, calculating the absolute value of a real number is very easy. Just remove the sign to make it positive, and your calculation is done! For complex numbers, calculating the absolute value is slightly more complex, pun intended.

For real numbers, the absolute value is nothing more than the distance from zero. Figure II-4 Shows you the value −3 plotted on a horizontal line. The absolute value of −3 is the distance from −3 to 0 and thus equals 3.

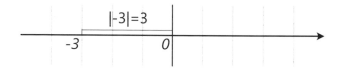

Figure II-4. *The asbolute value of −3, plotted on a horizontal line*

The absolute value of a complex number, also called the modulus, can be described as the distance from the number to zero on the complex plane, 0 + 0*i*. Remember that you can draw a complex number on a two-dimensional complex grid. Figure II-5 shows you the graphical representation for the absolute value of the complex number 4 + 3*i*.

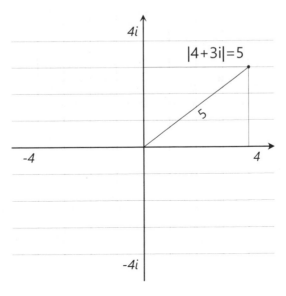

Figure II-5. *The absolute value of 4 + 3i, plotted on the complex plane*

Thanks to Pythagoras, if *a* + *bi* is your complex number, then $\sqrt{a^2 + b^2}$ is the absolute value of that complex number. Think about right-angled triangles and the hypotenuse from Appendix I.

$$|4 + 3i| = \sqrt{4^2 + 3^2} = \sqrt{25} = 5$$

EXERCISE II-6

Calculate the absolute value for the following complex numbers:

$$-20 + 21i$$

$$-31i$$

$$18$$

$$5 - 12i$$

The Last Word

Now that you have read this appendix and solved the exercises, you should have gathered all necessary information about complex numbers that is necessary to comprehend and work with quantum computing.

Solutions to Exercises

EXERCISE II-1

Now that you know about complex numbers, try to solve the value for x in the following equation:

$$4 + x^2 = 0$$

Solution

Just like the example $4 + x^2 = 0$, where $x = i$, you can try to think about it logically, or you can execute the following steps to derive your answer:

$$4 + x^2 = 0$$

Move the 4 to the other side of the equal sign:

$$x^2 = -4$$

Move the power of two to the other side of the equal sign to separate the x:

$$x = \sqrt{-4}$$

The square root of a negative number is only possible with complex numbers, so try to separate $\sqrt{-1}$ from the equation:

$$x = \sqrt{-1 \cdot 4} = 2\sqrt{-1} = 2i$$

The value for x is $2i$:

$$4 + x^2 = 4 + 2i^2 = 0$$

EXERCISE II-2

Solve the following expressions using your knowledge on adding complex numbers:

$$(-134 + 54i) + (241 - 13i)$$

$$(-31i) + (333)$$

Solution

$$(-134 + 54i) + (241 - 13i) = (-134 + 241) + (54 - 13)i = 107 + 41i$$
$$(-31i) + (333) = (0 + 333) + (-31 + 0)i = 333 - 31i$$

EXERCISE II-3

Solve the following expressions using your knowledge on subtracting complex numbers:

$$(-134 + 54i) - (241 - 13i)$$

$$(-31i) - (333)$$

Solution

$$(-134 + 54i) - (241 - 13i) = (-134 - 241) + (54 + 13)i = -375 + 67i$$
$$(-31i) - (333) = (0 - 333) + (-31 - 0)i = -333 - 31i$$

EXERCISE II-4

Solve the following expressions using your knowledge on multiplying complex numbers:

$$(-7+8i)\cdot(2-11i)$$

$$(-3i)\cdot(12)$$

Solution

$$(-7+8i)\cdot(2-11i)=(-14+88)+(77+16)i=74+93i$$

$$(-3i)\cdot(12)=(0-0)+(0-36)i=-36i$$

EXERCISE II-5

Solve the following expressions using your knowledge on dividing complex numbers:

$$\frac{(-7+8i)}{(2-11i)}$$

$$\frac{-3i}{12}$$

Solution

$$\frac{(-7+8i)}{(2-11i)}=\frac{(-7+8i)}{(2-11i)}\cdot\frac{(2+11i)}{(2+11i)}=\frac{(-14-88)+(-77+16)i}{4+121}=-\frac{102}{125}-\frac{61}{125}i$$

$$\frac{-3i}{12}=\frac{(0-3i)}{(12+0i)}\cdot\frac{(12-0i)}{(12-0i)}=\frac{(0+0)+(0-36)i}{144}=-\frac{36}{144}i=-\frac{1}{4}i$$

For this final exercise, multiplying with the complex conjugate is not necessary because there is no imaginary number in the denominator that needs to be eliminated. You can just write the complex number as a fraction and simplify it immediately:

$$\frac{-3i}{12}=-\frac{3}{12}i=-\frac{3\cdot1}{3\cdot4}=-\frac{1}{4}i$$

EXERCISE II-6

Calculate the absolute value for the following complex numbers:

$$-20 + 21i$$

$$-31i$$

$$18$$

$$5 - 12i$$

Solution

$$\left|-20 + 21i\right| = \sqrt{(-20)^2 + 21^2} = \sqrt{841} = 29$$

$$\left|-31i\right| = \left|0 - 31i\right| = \sqrt{0^2 + (-31)^2} = \sqrt{961} = 31$$

$$\left|18\right| = \left|18 + 0i\right| = \sqrt{18^2 + 0^2} = \sqrt{324} = 18$$

$$\left|5 - 12i\right| = \sqrt{5^2 + (-12)^2} = \sqrt{169} = 13$$

APPENDIX III

Linear Algebra

Linear algebra is a branch of mathematics that discusses linear equations using vector spaces. Linear algebra is used heavily in quantum computing and can be considered as the main language for quantum computing. Just like trigonometry and complex numbers, which were introduced to you in previous appendixes, linear algebra is equally as important and can be helpful to fully understand the world of quantum computing.

The goal of this appendix is to teach you the foundation of introductory linear algebra, which will aide you during your adventure into quantum computing.

Vectors and Vector Spaces

The vector is one of the most important mathematical concepts in quantum theory. A vector can intuitively be thought of as an arrow that points in a specific direction with a magnitude. A vector is always part of a set of vectors that together form a vector space. A vector v that is part of an abstract vector space V is often denoted as the ket $|v\rangle$ and can be visualized like the arrow in Figure III-1 if it has x and y components 4 and 7.

© Johnny Hooyberghs 2022
J. Hooyberghs, *Introducing Microsoft Quantum Computing for Developers*,
https://doi.org/10.1007/978-1-4842-7246-6_15

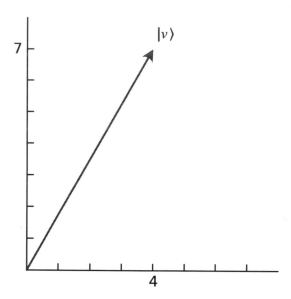

Figure III-1. *The visualization of a vector* $|v\rangle$

In quantum computing specifically, you talk about a special kind of vector: a state vector. A state vector describes a particular quantum state, which can be visualized within a state vector space, or state space in short. The Bloch sphere from Chapter 2 is a visualization of this state vector space. All possible state vectors within this state space originate from the sphere's origin and point toward the sphere's surface. In Figure III-2 you can see a visualization of this Bloch sphere with a single state vector $|\varphi\rangle$.

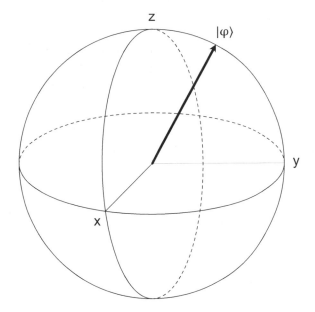

Figure III-2. *The state vector* $|\varphi\rangle$ *visualized in its state space represented by the Bloch sphere*

Matrices

Matrices can be used to describe vectors or objects that are used to transform vectors into other vectors. For quantum computing specifically, state vectors can be described with a single-column matrix that contain the components α and β from the linear combination $\alpha\,|\,0\rangle + \beta\,|\,1\rangle$. Operations, performed on quantum states, can also be represented by transformation matrices that transform state vectors into other state vectors.

In general, matrices are rectangular arrays of numbers built from columns and rows. The following example shows a 2 × 3 matrix or a two-row and three-column matrix:

$$\begin{pmatrix} 2 & -i & \dfrac{3}{4} \\[2mm] \dfrac{1}{2} & 1 & \sqrt{2} \end{pmatrix}$$

Matrix Operations

Because matrices are mathematical objects, you can use them for calculations like adding and multiplication.

Matrix Multiplication

Two matrices can be multiplied only when the number of columns in the matrix on the left-hand side of the expression is equal to the number of rows in the matrix on the right-hand side of the expression.

If A and B are two matrices that meet this demand, multiplying these matrices looks like

$$A = \begin{pmatrix} a_{11} & a_{12} \\ a_{21} & a_{22} \\ a_{31} & a_{32} \end{pmatrix}, B = \begin{pmatrix} b_{11} & b_{12} & b_{13} \\ b_{21} & b_{22} & b_{23} \end{pmatrix}$$

$$A \cdot B = \begin{pmatrix} a_{11} & a_{12} \\ a_{21} & a_{22} \\ a_{31} & a_{32} \end{pmatrix} \cdot \begin{pmatrix} b_{11} & b_{12} & b_{13} \\ b_{21} & b_{22} & b_{23} \end{pmatrix}$$

$$A \cdot B = \begin{pmatrix} a_{11}b_{11} + a_{12}b_{21} & a_{11}b_{12} + a_{12}b_{22} & a_{11}b_{13} + a_{12}b_{23} \\ a_{21}b_{11} + a_{22}b_{21} & a_{21}b_{12} + a_{22}b_{22} & a_{21}b_{13} + a_{22}b_{23} \\ a_{31}b_{11} + a_{32}b_{21} & a_{31}b_{12} + a_{32}b_{22} & a_{31}b_{13} + a_{32}b_{23} \end{pmatrix}$$

For example:

$$A = \begin{pmatrix} 1 & 2 \\ 3 & 4 \\ 5 & 6 \end{pmatrix}, B = \begin{pmatrix} 1 & 2 & 3 \\ 4 & 5 & 6 \end{pmatrix}$$

$$A \cdot B = \begin{pmatrix} 1 & 2 \\ 3 & 4 \\ 5 & 6 \end{pmatrix} \cdot \begin{pmatrix} 1 & 2 & 3 \\ 4 & 5 & 6 \end{pmatrix}$$

$$A \cdot B = \begin{pmatrix} 1 \cdot 1 + 2 \cdot 4 & 1 \cdot 2 + 2 \cdot 5 & 1 \cdot 3 + 2 \cdot 6 \\ 3 \cdot 1 + 4 \cdot 4 & 3 \cdot 2 + 4 \cdot 5 & 3 \cdot 3 + 4 \cdot 6 \\ 5 \cdot 1 + 6 \cdot 4 & 5 \cdot 2 + 6 \cdot 5 & 5 \cdot 3 + 6 \cdot 6 \end{pmatrix} = \begin{pmatrix} 9 & 12 & 15 \\ 19 & 26 & 33 \\ 29 & 40 & 51 \end{pmatrix}$$

Multiplying matrices is not commutative. When you take two matrices A and B, $A \cdot B$ is not equal to $B \cdot A$. Multiplying matrices is associative, which means that when multiplying three matrices A, B, and C, $(A \cdot B) \cdot C$ is equal to $A \cdot (B \cdot C)$.

EXERCISE III-1

You now know how to multiply two matrices. Solve the following three expressions to get some exercise:

1. $\begin{pmatrix} 1 & 3 & 5 & 7 \\ 6 & 4 & 2 & 0 \end{pmatrix} \cdot \begin{pmatrix} 2 \\ 1 \\ 4 \\ 2 \end{pmatrix}$

2. $\begin{pmatrix} 11 & 22 \\ 33 & 44 \end{pmatrix} \cdot \begin{pmatrix} 7 & 6 \\ 6 & 7 \end{pmatrix} \cdot \begin{pmatrix} 0 & 1 \\ 1 & 0 \end{pmatrix}$

3. $\begin{pmatrix} 2 & 1 \\ 1 & 2 \end{pmatrix} \cdot \begin{pmatrix} 1-3i \\ 3+i \end{pmatrix}$

Tensor Products

In quantum computing, a tensor product can be very helpful to multiply vector spaces together. The CNOT-gate, for example, works on two qubits and can only be calculated if the state for those two qubits is combined beforehand. If two state vectors $|a\rangle$ and $|b\rangle$ must be combined to form a combined state vector $|ab\rangle$, you need to use the tensor product on their state vectors $|a\rangle \otimes |b\rangle$.

Calculating the tensor product for two matrices A and B works like this:

$$A = \begin{pmatrix} a_{11} & a_{12} \\ a_{21} & a_{22} \end{pmatrix}, B = \begin{pmatrix} b_{11} & b_{12} \\ b_{21} & b_{22} \end{pmatrix}$$

$$A \otimes B = \begin{pmatrix} a_{11} & a_{12} \\ a_{21} & a_{22} \end{pmatrix} \otimes \begin{pmatrix} b_{11} & b_{12} \\ b_{21} & b_{22} \end{pmatrix}$$

$$A \otimes B = \begin{pmatrix} a_{11} \cdot \begin{pmatrix} b_{11} & b_{12} \\ b_{21} & b_{22} \end{pmatrix} & a_{12} \cdot \begin{pmatrix} b_{11} & b_{12} \\ b_{21} & b_{22} \end{pmatrix} \\ a_{21} \cdot \begin{pmatrix} b_{11} & b_{12} \\ b_{21} & b_{22} \end{pmatrix} & a_{22} \cdot \begin{pmatrix} b_{11} & b_{12} \\ b_{21} & b_{22} \end{pmatrix} \end{pmatrix}$$

$$A \otimes B = \begin{pmatrix} a_{11} \cdot b_{11} & a_{11} \cdot b_{12} & a_{12} \cdot b_{11} & a_{12} \cdot b_{12} \\ a_{11} \cdot b_{21} & a_{11} \cdot b_{22} & a_{12} \cdot b_{21} & a_{12} \cdot b_{22} \\ a_{21} \cdot b_{11} & a_{21} \cdot b_{12} & a_{22} \cdot b_{11} & a_{22} \cdot b_{12} \\ a_{21} \cdot b_{21} & a_{21} \cdot b_{22} & a_{22} \cdot b_{21} & a_{22} \cdot b_{22} \end{pmatrix}$$

For example:

$$A = \begin{pmatrix} 2 & 3 \\ 4 & 5 \end{pmatrix}, B = \begin{pmatrix} 6 & 7 \\ 8 & 9 \end{pmatrix}$$

$$A \otimes B = \begin{pmatrix} 2 & 3 \\ 4 & 5 \end{pmatrix} \otimes \begin{pmatrix} 6 & 7 \\ 8 & 9 \end{pmatrix}$$

$$A \otimes B = \begin{pmatrix} 2 \cdot \begin{pmatrix} 6 & 7 \\ 8 & 9 \end{pmatrix} & 3 \cdot \begin{pmatrix} 6 & 7 \\ 8 & 9 \end{pmatrix} \\ 4 \cdot \begin{pmatrix} 6 & 7 \\ 8 & 9 \end{pmatrix} & 5 \cdot \begin{pmatrix} 6 & 7 \\ 8 & 9 \end{pmatrix} \end{pmatrix}$$

$$A \otimes B = \begin{pmatrix} 2\cdot6 & 2\cdot7 & 3\cdot6 & 3\cdot7 \\ 2\cdot8 & 2\cdot9 & 3\cdot8 & 3\cdot9 \\ 4\cdot6 & 4\cdot7 & 5\cdot6 & 5\cdot7 \\ 4\cdot8 & 4\cdot9 & 5\cdot8 & 5\cdot9 \end{pmatrix} = \begin{pmatrix} 12 & 14 & 18 & 21 \\ 16 & 18 & 24 & 27 \\ 24 & 28 & 30 & 35 \\ 32 & 36 & 40 & 45 \end{pmatrix}$$

The tensor product is not commutative. When you have two matrices A and B, $A \otimes B$ is not equal to $B \otimes A$. But calculating the tensor product for matrices is associative, which means that when calculating it for three matrices A, B, and C, $(A \otimes B) \otimes C$ is equal to $A \otimes (B \otimes C)$.

EXERCISE III-2

You know how to perform a tensor product on two matrices. Solve the following expressions:

1. $\begin{pmatrix} 1 \\ 2 \\ 3 \end{pmatrix} \otimes \begin{pmatrix} 4 \\ 5 \end{pmatrix}$

2. $\begin{pmatrix} 11 & 22 \\ 33 & 44 \end{pmatrix} \otimes \begin{pmatrix} 7 & 6 \\ 6 & 7 \end{pmatrix} \otimes \begin{pmatrix} 0 & 1 \\ 1 & 0 \end{pmatrix}$

3. $\begin{pmatrix} 2 & 1 \\ 1 & 2 \end{pmatrix} \otimes \begin{pmatrix} 1-3i \\ 3+i \end{pmatrix}$

Transformation Matrix

A matrix can represent a linear transformation. Quantum gates, which transform a quantum state vector into another quantum state vector, can be described using such a matrix. The transformation matrix itself can be applied to a state matrix by multiplying both matrices.

The following matrix describes the transformation performed by the quantum X-gate. It is a 2 × 2 matrix that can be applied to a 2 × 1 state matrix:

$$\begin{pmatrix} 0 & 1 \\ 1 & 0 \end{pmatrix}$$

Other possible, frequently used, transformation matrices in quantum computing are the ones for the Y-gate, Z-gate, and H-gate:

$$\begin{pmatrix} 0 & -i \\ i & 0 \end{pmatrix}_Y, \begin{pmatrix} 1 & 0 \\ 0 & -1 \end{pmatrix}_Z, \begin{pmatrix} \dfrac{1}{\sqrt{2}} & \dfrac{1}{\sqrt{2}} \\ \dfrac{1}{\sqrt{2}} & -\dfrac{1}{\sqrt{2}} \end{pmatrix}_H$$

EXERCISE III-3

You know the transformation matrices for the quantum X-gate, H-gate, and Z-gate. Prove that the quantum X-gate can be recreated by combining the H-gate and Z-gate as follows:

$X = HZH$

The Last Word

You are now able to use basic linear algebra to calculate with quantum states. Use matrix multiplication to perform quantum operations on quantum state vectors, and use tensor products to combine quantum states.

Solutions to Exercises

EXERCISE III-1

You know how to multiply two matrices. Solve the following expressions:

1. $\begin{pmatrix} 1 & 3 & 5 & 7 \\ 6 & 4 & 2 & 0 \end{pmatrix} \cdot \begin{pmatrix} 2 \\ 1 \\ 4 \\ 2 \end{pmatrix}$

2. $\begin{pmatrix} 11 & 22 \\ 33 & 44 \end{pmatrix} \cdot \begin{pmatrix} 7 & 6 \\ 6 & 7 \end{pmatrix} \cdot \begin{pmatrix} 0 & 1 \\ 1 & 0 \end{pmatrix}$

3. $\begin{pmatrix} 2 & 1 \\ 1 & 2 \end{pmatrix} \cdot \begin{pmatrix} 1-3i \\ 3+i \end{pmatrix}$

Solution

1. $\begin{pmatrix} 1 & 3 & 5 & 7 \\ 6 & 4 & 2 & 0 \end{pmatrix} \cdot \begin{pmatrix} 2 \\ 1 \\ 4 \\ 2 \end{pmatrix} = \begin{pmatrix} 1 \cdot 2 + 3 \cdot 1 + 5 \cdot 4 + 7 \cdot 2 \\ 6 \cdot 2 + 4 \cdot 1 + 2 \cdot 4 + 0 \cdot 2 \end{pmatrix} = \begin{pmatrix} 39 \\ 24 \end{pmatrix}$

2.
$$\begin{pmatrix} 11 & 22 \\ 33 & 44 \end{pmatrix} \cdot \begin{pmatrix} 7 & 6 \\ 6 & 7 \end{pmatrix} \cdot \begin{pmatrix} 0 & 1 \\ 1 & 0 \end{pmatrix} = \begin{pmatrix} 11 \cdot 7 + 22 \cdot 6 & 11 \cdot 6 + 22 \cdot 7 \\ 33 \cdot 7 + 44 \cdot 6 & 33 \cdot 6 + 44 \cdot 7 \end{pmatrix} \cdot \begin{pmatrix} 0 & 1 \\ 1 & 0 \end{pmatrix}$$
$$= \begin{pmatrix} 209 & 220 \\ 495 & 506 \end{pmatrix} \cdot \begin{pmatrix} 0 & 1 \\ 1 & 0 \end{pmatrix} = \begin{pmatrix} 209 \cdot 0 + 220 \cdot 1 & 209 \cdot 1 + 220 \cdot 0 \\ 495 \cdot 0 + 506 \cdot 1 & 495 \cdot 1 + 506 \cdot 0 \end{pmatrix} = \begin{pmatrix} 220 & 209 \\ 506 & 495 \end{pmatrix}$$

3. $\begin{pmatrix} 2 & 1 \\ 1 & 2 \end{pmatrix} \cdot \begin{pmatrix} 1 - 3i \\ 3 + i \end{pmatrix} = \begin{pmatrix} 2 - 6i + 3 + i \\ 1 - 3i + 6 + 2i \end{pmatrix} = \begin{pmatrix} 5 - 5i \\ 7 - i \end{pmatrix}$

EXERCISE III-2

You know how to perform a tensor product on two matrices. Solve the following expressions:

1. $\begin{pmatrix} 1 \\ 2 \\ 3 \end{pmatrix} \otimes \begin{pmatrix} 4 \\ 5 \end{pmatrix} =$

2. $\begin{pmatrix} 11 & 22 \\ 33 & 44 \end{pmatrix} \otimes \begin{pmatrix} 7 & 6 \\ 6 & 7 \end{pmatrix} \otimes \begin{pmatrix} 0 & 1 \\ 1 & 0 \end{pmatrix}$

3. $\begin{pmatrix} 2 & 1 \\ 1 & 2 \end{pmatrix} \otimes \begin{pmatrix} 1 - 3i \\ 3 + i \end{pmatrix}$

Solution

1. $\begin{pmatrix} 1 \\ 2 \\ 3 \end{pmatrix} \otimes \begin{pmatrix} 4 \\ 5 \end{pmatrix} = \begin{pmatrix} 1 \cdot \begin{pmatrix} 4 \\ 5 \end{pmatrix} \\ 2 \cdot \begin{pmatrix} 4 \\ 5 \end{pmatrix} \\ 3 \cdot \begin{pmatrix} 4 \\ 5 \end{pmatrix} \end{pmatrix} = \begin{pmatrix} 1 \cdot 4 \\ 1 \cdot 5 \\ 2 \cdot 4 \\ 2 \cdot 5 \\ 3 \cdot 4 \\ 3 \cdot 5 \end{pmatrix} = \begin{pmatrix} 4 \\ 5 \\ 8 \\ 10 \\ 12 \\ 15 \end{pmatrix}$

2. $\begin{pmatrix} 11 & 22 \\ 33 & 44 \end{pmatrix} \otimes \begin{pmatrix} 7 & 6 \\ 6 & 7 \end{pmatrix} \otimes \begin{pmatrix} 0 & 1 \\ 1 & 0 \end{pmatrix} = \begin{pmatrix} 11 \cdot \begin{pmatrix} 7 & 6 \\ 6 & 7 \end{pmatrix} & 22 \cdot \begin{pmatrix} 7 & 6 \\ 6 & 7 \end{pmatrix} \\ 33 \cdot \begin{pmatrix} 7 & 6 \\ 6 & 7 \end{pmatrix} & 44 \cdot \begin{pmatrix} 7 & 6 \\ 6 & 7 \end{pmatrix} \end{pmatrix} \otimes \begin{pmatrix} 0 & 1 \\ 1 & 0 \end{pmatrix}$

$= \begin{pmatrix} 11 \cdot 7 & 11 \cdot 6 & 22 \cdot 7 & 22 \cdot 6 \\ 11 \cdot 6 & 11 \cdot 7 & 22 \cdot 6 & 22 \cdot 7 \\ 33 \cdot 7 & 33 \cdot 7 & 44 \cdot 7 & 44 \cdot 6 \\ 33 \cdot 6 & 33 \cdot 7 & 44 \cdot 6 & 44 \cdot 7 \end{pmatrix} \otimes \begin{pmatrix} 0 & 1 \\ 1 & 0 \end{pmatrix}$

$= \begin{pmatrix} 77 & 66 & 154 & 132 \\ 66 & 77 & 132 & 154 \\ 231 & 198 & 308 & 264 \\ 198 & 231 & 264 & 308 \end{pmatrix} \otimes \begin{pmatrix} 0 & 1 \\ 1 & 0 \end{pmatrix}$

$= \begin{pmatrix} 77 \cdot \begin{pmatrix} 0 & 1 \\ 1 & 0 \end{pmatrix} & 66 \cdot \begin{pmatrix} 0 & 1 \\ 1 & 0 \end{pmatrix} & 154 \cdot \begin{pmatrix} 0 & 1 \\ 1 & 0 \end{pmatrix} & 132 \cdot \begin{pmatrix} 0 & 1 \\ 1 & 0 \end{pmatrix} \\ 66 \cdot \begin{pmatrix} 0 & 1 \\ 1 & 0 \end{pmatrix} & 77 \cdot \begin{pmatrix} 0 & 1 \\ 1 & 0 \end{pmatrix} & 132 \cdot \begin{pmatrix} 0 & 1 \\ 1 & 0 \end{pmatrix} & 154 \cdot \begin{pmatrix} 0 & 1 \\ 1 & 0 \end{pmatrix} \\ 231 \cdot \begin{pmatrix} 0 & 1 \\ 1 & 0 \end{pmatrix} & 198 \cdot \begin{pmatrix} 0 & 1 \\ 1 & 0 \end{pmatrix} & 308 \cdot \begin{pmatrix} 0 & 1 \\ 1 & 0 \end{pmatrix} & 264 \cdot \begin{pmatrix} 0 & 1 \\ 1 & 0 \end{pmatrix} \\ 198 \cdot \begin{pmatrix} 0 & 1 \\ 1 & 0 \end{pmatrix} & 231 \cdot \begin{pmatrix} 0 & 1 \\ 1 & 0 \end{pmatrix} & 264 \cdot \begin{pmatrix} 0 & 1 \\ 1 & 0 \end{pmatrix} & 308 \cdot \begin{pmatrix} 0 & 1 \\ 1 & 0 \end{pmatrix} \end{pmatrix}$

$= \begin{pmatrix} 0 & 77 & 0 & 66 & 0 & 154 & 0 & 132 \\ 77 & 0 & 66 & 0 & 154 & 0 & 132 & 0 \\ 0 & 66 & 0 & 77 & 0 & 132 & 0 & 154 \\ 66 & 0 & 77 & 0 & 132 & 0 & 154 & 0 \\ 0 & 231 & 0 & 198 & 0 & 308 & 0 & 264 \\ 231 & 0 & 198 & 0 & 308 & 0 & 264 & 0 \\ 0 & 198 & 0 & 231 & 0 & 264 & 0 & 308 \\ 198 & 0 & 231 & 0 & 264 & 0 & 308 & 0 \end{pmatrix}$

3. $\begin{pmatrix} 2 & 1 \\ 1 & 2 \end{pmatrix} \otimes \begin{pmatrix} 1-3i \\ 3+i \end{pmatrix} = \begin{pmatrix} 2 \cdot \begin{pmatrix} 1-3i \\ 3+i \end{pmatrix} & 1 \cdot \begin{pmatrix} 1-3i \\ 3+i \end{pmatrix} \\ 1 \cdot \begin{pmatrix} 1-3i \\ 3+i \end{pmatrix} & 2 \cdot \begin{pmatrix} 1-3i \\ 3+i \end{pmatrix} \end{pmatrix} = \begin{pmatrix} 2 \cdot (1-3i) & 1-3i \\ 2 \cdot (3+i) & 3+i \\ 1-3i & 2 \cdot (1-3i) \\ 3+i & 2 \cdot (3+i) \end{pmatrix} = \begin{pmatrix} 2-6i & 1-3i \\ 6+2i & 3+i \\ 1-3i & 2-6i \\ 3+i & 6+2i \end{pmatrix}$

EXERCISE III-3

You know the transformation matrices for the quantum X-gate, H-gate, and Z-gate. Prove that the quantum X-gate can be recreated by combining the H-gate and Z-gate as follows:

$$X = HZH$$

Solution

First, replace the names of the quantum gates with their corresponding transformation matrices:

$$\begin{pmatrix} 0 & 1 \\ 1 & 0 \end{pmatrix}_X = \begin{pmatrix} \dfrac{1}{\sqrt{2}} & \dfrac{1}{\sqrt{2}} \\ \dfrac{1}{\sqrt{2}} & -\dfrac{1}{\sqrt{2}} \end{pmatrix}_H \begin{pmatrix} 1 & 0 \\ 0 & -1 \end{pmatrix}_Z \begin{pmatrix} \dfrac{1}{\sqrt{2}} & \dfrac{1}{\sqrt{2}} \\ \dfrac{1}{\sqrt{2}} & -\dfrac{1}{\sqrt{2}} \end{pmatrix}_H$$

Next, use matrix multiplication to solve the right-hand side of the expression:

$$\begin{pmatrix} 0 & 1 \\ 1 & 0 \end{pmatrix}_X = \begin{pmatrix} \left(\dfrac{1}{\sqrt{2}}\cdot 1 + \dfrac{1}{\sqrt{2}}\cdot 0\right) & \left(\dfrac{1}{\sqrt{2}}\cdot 0 - \dfrac{1}{\sqrt{2}}\cdot 1\right) \\ \left(\dfrac{1}{\sqrt{2}}\cdot 1 - \dfrac{1}{\sqrt{2}}\cdot 0\right) & \left(\dfrac{1}{\sqrt{2}}\cdot 0 + \dfrac{1}{\sqrt{2}}\cdot 1\right) \end{pmatrix}_{HZ} \begin{pmatrix} \dfrac{1}{\sqrt{2}} & \dfrac{1}{\sqrt{2}} \\ \dfrac{1}{\sqrt{2}} & -\dfrac{1}{\sqrt{2}} \end{pmatrix}_H$$

$$\begin{pmatrix} 0 & 1 \\ 1 & 0 \end{pmatrix}_X = \begin{pmatrix} \dfrac{1}{\sqrt{2}} & -\dfrac{1}{\sqrt{2}} \\ \dfrac{1}{\sqrt{2}} & \dfrac{1}{\sqrt{2}} \end{pmatrix}_{HZ} \begin{pmatrix} \dfrac{1}{\sqrt{2}} & \dfrac{1}{\sqrt{2}} \\ \dfrac{1}{\sqrt{2}} & -\dfrac{1}{\sqrt{2}} \end{pmatrix}_H$$

$$\begin{pmatrix} 0 & 1 \\ 1 & 0 \end{pmatrix}_X = \begin{pmatrix} \left(\dfrac{1}{\sqrt{2}}\cdot\dfrac{1}{\sqrt{2}} - \dfrac{1}{\sqrt{2}}\cdot\dfrac{1}{\sqrt{2}}\right) & \left(\dfrac{1}{\sqrt{2}}\cdot\dfrac{1}{\sqrt{2}} + \dfrac{1}{\sqrt{2}}\cdot\dfrac{1}{\sqrt{2}}\right) \\ \left(\dfrac{1}{\sqrt{2}}\cdot\dfrac{1}{\sqrt{2}} + \dfrac{1}{\sqrt{2}}\cdot\dfrac{1}{\sqrt{2}}\right) & \left(\dfrac{1}{\sqrt{2}}\cdot\dfrac{1}{\sqrt{2}} - \dfrac{1}{\sqrt{2}}\cdot\dfrac{1}{\sqrt{2}}\right) \end{pmatrix}_{HZH}$$

$$\begin{pmatrix} 0 & 1 \\ 1 & 0 \end{pmatrix}_X = \begin{pmatrix} 0 & 1 \\ 1 & 0 \end{pmatrix}_{HZH}$$

If you look at the left-hand side and the right-hand side of the final expression, you can see that both the X-operation and the combined HZH-operation correspond to the exact same transformation matrix.

Index

A

Adjoint functor, 153, 154, 156, 157, 159, 160
American Standard Code for Information Interchange (ASCII), 28
Azure CLI, 312, 324, 326
Azure Cloud account, 346
Azure Quantum, 307, 308, 310
  jobs, 317, 319, 320
    computing, 320, 322–325
    inspired optimization, 331–333
    optimization, 330, 334, 336
  providers, 312–315
  targets, 312–316
  workspace, 311, 312

B

Bitflip gate, 52
Bloch sphere, 32, 33, 35–37, 361, 364, 384
Bobs possession, 64
BoolAsResult function, 167
Boolean literals, 141

C

CalculateSum function, 163
Callables
  definition, 151
  functions, 152
  functors, 153, 155–157, 159, 160
  operations, 152
  operations/functions, 162–165
  return/terminator, 161, 162
  type parameterizations, 165–167
Cartesian coordinate system, 361
Central processing units (CPUs), 28
CHSH game
  definition, 276
  implementation, 279–283
  playing classic, 276, 277, 279
  Q# implementation, 295–297, 299, 301, 302
  quantum techniques, 284–286, 288–294
Classical bits, 49, 64
Classical computer, 7, 27
CNOT-gate, 59, 60, 300, 387
Complex conjugate, 374, 375
Complex numbers, 369–371
  add, 372, 373
  division, 375
  modulus, 376, 377
  multiply, 374
  subtract, 373
constant-1 binary function, 211, 212, 251
constant-1 function, 224, 235, 236, 250, 251, 266
ConstantOne operation, 230, 266
Controlled functor, 157, 158
Copenhagen interpretation, 18
Cubic equation, 370

395

© Johnny Hooyberghs 2022
J. Hooyberghs, *Introducing Microsoft Quantum Computing for Developers*,
https://doi.org/10.1007/978-1-4842-7246-6

D

DebugYourQuantumProgram
    operation, 184
Destructive interference, 12, 13
Deutsch-Jozsa algorithm
    back-box function, 247
    constant function, 233
    constant-0 function, 234
    constant-1 function, 235
    functions, 233
    generic circuit, 246
    modulo-2, 236, 237
    odd number of ones, 237, 238
    Q# implementation, 239, 240, 242–244
    quantum representation
        constant-0, 247, 248, 250
        constant-1, 250–252
        modulo 2, 253–257
        odd-number-of-ones, 258–263
        Q# implementation, 263,
            265–267, 269
DeutschJozsa function, 242, 243, 245
Deutsch's algorithm
    binary functions, 206
    circuit
        constant-0, 209–211
        constant-1, 211–213
        identity, 214–216
        negation, 217, 218, 220
    definition, 205
    functions, 205, 206
    oracle, 207
    Q#
        classical version, 220–224
        quantum version, 225, 226, 228, 230
    quantum operation, 207
Double slit experiment, 9, 14

DumpMachine function, 195
DumpRegister function, 196, 197, 199

E

Entanglement, 19, 20
ExecuteH operation, 191
ExecuteManyTimes operation, 163–165
ExecuteRy operation, 192
ExecuteX-operation, 189
External interference, 23

F

Full-state simulator, 169, 171, 172

G

GetRandomBit operation, 282, 299
Global Positioning System (GPS), 357

H

Hadamard gate, 50–52, 61, 67, 107, 247
HelloQ, 77, 78, 105

I

Identity operation, 182, 230
Integrated development environment
    (IDE), 78, 121
Interference pattern, 13–16
Intermediate representation, 342–344
IonQ provider, 313, 314, 323
IonQ simulator, 327

J

Just-in-time (JIT), 343

K

Knight's Tour problem, 6

L

Linear algebra, 30, 383, 390
Linear polarization, 45
Logical operators, 141
Logical qubits, 23, 24, 63

M

Matrices, 385
    multiply, 386, 387
    tensor products, 387, 388
    transformation, 389
MeasureForAlice operation, 301
Measurement gate, 58
Microsoft.Quantum.Intrinsics
        namespace, 131
Microsoft Visual Studio
    editor window, 95
    install, 88, 89
    install QDK, 89
    opening window, 89, 90
    Q# application template, 93, 94
    quantum console application, 95
    VSIX Installer, 91
    welcome window, 92
modulo-2 function, 236, 237
Moore's law, 7
MResetZ operation, 302
Multiple-qubit-gate, 59
    controlled X, 59, 60
    mathematical representation,
        39, 40, 43
Multiply function, 164

N

Negation function, 225
Negation operation, 231
.NET programming language, 108, 120
newtype keyword, 137
Nonuniversal quantum computers, 24

O

odd-number-of-ones function, 258
Operators
    arithmetic, 142
    comparative, 140
    concatenations, 143
    conditional expressions, 141
    copy-and-update
        expressions, 139
    logical, 141

P

Pauli X, 52–54
Pauli Y, 54, 55
Pauli Z, 56, 57
Physical quantum computer, 22, 307, 308,
        311, 329
PlayClassic function, 282, 283
PlayQuantum operation, 299
Polarization, 44, 45
Positive numbers, 369, 370
Pseudo-random numbers, 101–103, 172
Pythagoras' theorem, 358, 359, 366
Python web page
    command-line interface, 98
    install, 96, 97
    PATH environment, 97
    QDK, 98–100

Q

Q# application, 83
Q# development, 72, 346
Q# language
 arrays, 135, 136
 classical programming languages, 121
 comments, 123, 124
 definition, 121
 namespaces, 125–128
 operators, 139
 project file, 122
 quantum data types, 131
 ranges, 136
 scopes, 129–131
 types, 135
 user-defined types, 136–138
 variable declrations/assignments, 128
Q# quantum programs, 308
qsharp package, 99
Quantum algorithms, 108, 113, 133, 153, 352
Quantum circuits, 60
 entanglement, 61
 single-qubit, 62
 teleportation, 63, 64
 two-qubit, 62
Quantum computers, 22, 49, 153, 271, 308
Quantum computing, 3, 8, 21, 384
Quantum data types
 literals, 134
 memory management, 132, 133
 Pauli literals, 134
 qubit, 131
Quantum Development Kit (QDK)
 command-line, 76–78
 install, 72, 74
 .NET ecosystem, 72–74

.NET SDK, 75, 76
Quantum error correction, 342
Quantum gates, 49, 50
Quantum-inspired optimization, 348
Quantum Intermediate Representation (QIR), 343, 344
Quantum mechanics, 3, 8, 9, 16, 19–22, 50
Quantum physics, 8, 207
Quantum processing unit (QPU), 122, 307, 322
Quantum programming languages, 24, 101, 330, 343, 344
Quantum programs
 debugging
  actions, 187, 188
  breakpoints, 185, 186
  DumpMachine, 193, 195, 196
  DumpRegister, 196–198, 200–202
  variables, 189–191, 193
  Visual Studio code, 184, 185
 testing
  qubit |0⟩ state, 181
  qubit |1⟩ state, 182
  superposition state, 183
  unit, 178–180
Quantum superposition, 113, 172, 228, 363
Quantum supremacy, 24, 341, 342
Quantum teleportation, 60, 63, 64, 197
Quantum tunneling, 20
Qubit
 measuring
  CHSH game, 276
  computational basis, 271–273
  custom basis, 275, 276
  sign basis, 273, 275
 multiple, 39
 physical implementation, 44
 single, 29

R

Radian, 36, 37, 359, 360
Random number generator
    classical computer, 101
    mathematical function, 101
    Python host, 118, 119
    Q#, 114, 115
    quantum computers, 102
    qubits, 113
    Q#, with C# host, 116, 117
    random bit
        C# host, 108–111
        python host, 111, 113
        Q#, 104–107
        single qubit, 103
Real-life object, 29
repeat-statement, 147
Reset operation, 172, 173
Right-angled triangle, 357–362, 366
Right triangle, 357
Ry operation, 50, 63, 153, 303

S

set statement, 128
Simulator
    full-state, 169–172
    resource estimator, 172–175
    Toffoli simulator, 175–177
Single-qubit gates, 50
    Bloch sphere, 32–37
    H-gate, 50–52
    mathematical representation, 30, 31
    M-gate, 58
    X-gate, 52–54

    Y-gate, 54, 55
    Z-gate, 56, 57
Statements
    conditional, 143
    conditional loops, 145
    conjugations, 148–150
    iterations, 144
    repeat loops, 146
    while loops, 146
Superposition, 17, 18, 21

T

Three-qubit system, 39, 41, 43
Trigonometric ratios, 360, 365
Two-qubit state, 62, 210

U

Unit Circle, 271–275, 301, 302, 361
Unit literal, 161
Universal quantum computers, 24

V

Vector, 213, 383
Vertical polarization, 44, 45
Visual Studio Code, 78
    installation options, 80
    official website, 79
    QDK, 82, 83
    Q# project, 84
    quantum applications, 85, 87
    set up wizard, 81
    setup wizard, 79
    terminal window, 88

W

with keyword, 139

X, Y

x-mod-2 function, 236, 237, 253–255, 257, 263

Z

Zero and One literals, 134